D0994620

Visit *The Economic Environment of Business* Companion Website at **www.pearsoned.co.uk/sloman** to find valuable **student** learning material including:

- Learning objectives for each chapter
- Multiple choice questions to help test your learning
- Case study material
- Economic news articles and topical economic issues
- Hotlinks to relevant sites on the web
- Answers to odd-numbered end of chapter questions
- Answers to pause for thought questions

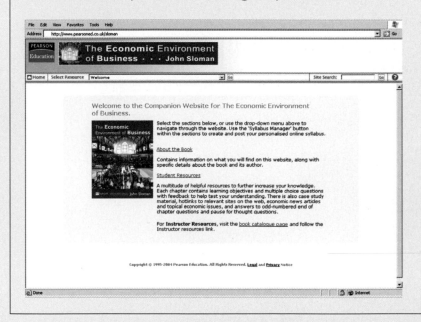

PEARSON
Education

We work with leading authors to develop the
strongest educational materials in economics,
bringing cutting-edge thinking and best
learning practice to a global market.

Under a range of well-known imprints, including
Financial Times Prentice Hall, we craft high
quality print and electronic publications which
help readers to understand and apply their content,
whether studying or at work.

To find out more about the complete range of our
publishing, please visit us on the World Wide Web at:
www.pearsoned.co.uk

The
Economic Environment
of Business

John Sloman

 Prentice Hall
FINANCIAL TIMES

An imprint of **Pearson Education**
Harlow, England • London • New York • Boston • San Francisco • Toronto
Sydney • Tokyo • Singapore • Hong Kong • Seoul • Taipei • New Delhi
Cape Town • Madrid • Mexico City • Amsterdam • Munich • Paris • Milan

Pearson Education Limited
Edinburgh Gate
Harlow
Essex CM20 2JE
England

and Associated Companies throughout the world

Visit us on the World Wide Web at:
www.pearsoned.co.uk

First published 2005

© Pearson Education Limited 2005

The right of John Sloman to be identified as author of this work has been asserted by him in accordance with the Copyright, Designs and Patents Act 1988.

All rights reserved. No part of this publication may be reproduced, stored in a retrieval system, or transmitted in any form or by any means, electronic, mechanical, photocopying, recording or otherwise, without either the prior written permission of the publisher or a licence permitting restricted copying in the United Kingdom issued by the Copyright Licensing Agency Ltd, 90 Tottenham Court Road, London W1T 4LP.

All trademarks used herein are the property of their respective owners. The use of any trademark in this text does not vest in the author or publisher any trademark ownership rights in such trademarks, nor does the use of such trademarks imply any affiliation with or endorsement of this book by such owners.

ISBN 0 273 68132 X

British Library Cataloguing-in-Publication Data
A catalogue record for this book is available from the British Library

Library of Congress Cataloging-in-Publication Data
A catalog record for this book is available from the Library of Congress

10 9 8 7 6 5 4 3 2 1
10 09 08 07 06 05

Typeset in 9/12 pt Stone Serif by 35
Printed by Ashford Colour Press Ltd., Gosport

The publisher's policy is use paper manufactured from sustainable forests.

Brief Contents

Contents

Part D   The macroeconomic environment of business   211

Supporting resources

Visit **www.pearsoned.co.uk/sloman** to find valuable online resources

Companion Website for students
- Learning objectives for each chapter
- Multiple choice questions to help test your learning
- Case study material
- Economic news articles and topical economic issues
- Hotlinks to relevant sites on the web
- Answers to odd-numbered end of chapter questions
- Answers to pause for thought questions

For instructors
- Complete, downloadable Instructor's Manual
- PowerPoint slides that can be downloaded and used as OHTs
- Lecture plans
- Teaching and learning case study material
- Answers to even-numbered end of chapter questions
- Answers to boxed questions
- Answers to web cases

Also: The regularly maintained Companion Website provides the following features:

- Search tool to help locate specific items of content
- E-mail results and profile tools to send results of quizzes to instructors
- Online help and support to assist with website usage and troubleshooting

For more information please contact your local Pearson Education sales representative or visit **www.pearsoned.co.uk/sloman**

OneKey: All you and your students need to succeed

OneKey is an exclusive new resource for instructors and students, giving you access to the best online teaching and learning tools 24 hours a day, 7 days a week.

OneKey is all you need

Convenience. Simplicity. Success.

OneKey means all your resources are in one place for maximum convenience, simplicity and success.

A OneKey product is available for *The Economic Environment of Business* for use with Blackboard™, WebCT and CourseCompass. It contains:

- An interactive Study Guide
- Introductory quizzes for each section
- Further assignments and further reading sections
- Quick tests throughout each topic

For more information about the OneKey product please contact your local Pearson Education sales representative or visit **www.pearsoned.co.uk/onekey**

Preface

Welcome to this introduction to economics and the business environment. If you are a student on a business or management degree or diploma and taking a module which includes economics, then this book is written for you. Such modules may go under the title of Business Environment or Business Context, or they may simply be called Introduction to Economics or Introduction to Business Economics. Alternatively, you may be studying on an MBA and need a grounding in basic economic concepts and how they apply to the business environment.

The book covers the core economics that you will need as a business student, but it also covers various business-related topics not typically covered in an introductory economics textbook. These topics include elements of business organisation and business strategy.

As well as making considerable use of business examples throughout the text, I have included many case studies in boxes (32 in all). These illustrate how economics can be used to understand particular business problems or aspects of the business environment. Many of these case studies cover issues that you are likely to read about in the newspapers. Some cover general business issues; others look at specific companies. There are also many additional case studies appearing on the book's website (www.pearsoned.co.uk/sloman). These, along with references to various useful websites, are listed at the end of each of the five Parts of the book.

I hope that, in using this book, you will share my fascination for economics. It is a subject that is highly relevant to the world in which we live. And it is a world where many of our needs are served by business – whether as employers or as producers of the goods and services we buy. After graduating, you will probably take up employment in business. A grounding in economic principles and how they relate to the world of business should prove invaluable in the business decisions you may well have to make.

The aim throughout the book is to make this intriguing subject clear for you to understand and as relevant as possible to you as a student of business.

The written style is direct and straightforward, with short paragraphs to aid rapid comprehension. Definitions of all key terms are given in the margin, with defined terms appearing in bold. I have highlighted 19 Key Ideas, which are fundamental to 'thinking like an economist'. I refer back to these every time they recur throughout the book. This helps you to see how the subject ties together, and also helps you to develop a toolkit of concepts that can be used in a whole host of different contexts.

Summaries are given at the end of each section of each chapter. These should help you in reviewing the material you have just covered and in revising for exams. Each chapter finishes with a series of questions. These can be used to check your understanding of the chapter and help you to see how its material can be applied to various business problems.

There are also questions interspersed throughout the text in 'Pause for Thought' panels. These encourage you to reflect on what you are learning and to see how the various ideas and theories relate to different issues. Answers to these questions are given on the book's website.

I hope you enjoy the book and come to appreciate the crucial role that economics plays in all our lives, and in particular in the practice of business.

Good luck and enjoy. Perhaps this will be just the beginning of a life-long interest in economic issues and how they apply to the world of business – and in your own personal life too!

To the tutor

The aim of this book is to provide a short course in economic principles as they apply to the business environment. It is designed to be used by first-year undergraduates on business studies degrees and diplomas where economics is taught from the business perspective, either as a separate one-semester module or as part of a business environment module. It is also suitable for students studying economics on MBA, CMS, DMS and various professional courses.

In addition to covering core economic principles, various specialist business topics are also covered that do not appear in conventional introductory economics textbooks. The following are some examples of these additional topics:

- Business organisations
- Industrial structure
- The multinational corporation
- Globalisation and business
- Marketing the product
- Strategic analysis and choice
- Porter's five forces model
- Growth strategy
- Alternative aims of firms
- Pricing in practice
- The product life cycle
- The small-firm sector
- Flexible labour markets and firms
- Business ethics and corporate social responsibility
- Government and the firm, including competition policy and regulation
- The macroeconomic environment of business, including the impact of macroeconomic policy on business
- Trading blocs
- Monetary union

The text is split into five Parts containing a total of 12 chapters. Each chapter could be covered in a week, giving enough material for a semester. Each chapter is divided into discrete sections, each with its own summary, providing an ideal coverage for a single study session for a student. Chapters finish with review questions, which can be used for seminars or discussion sessions.

The first eight chapters cover microeconomics and its relation to business. The final four cover the macroeconomic and international environment of business. This higher weighting for microeconomics reflects the structure of many economics for business or business environment modules.

Special features

The book contains the following special features:

- *A direct and straightforward written style,* with short paragraphs to aid rapid comprehension. The aim all the time is to provide maximum clarity.

- *Attractive full-colour design.* The careful and consistent use of colour and shading makes the text more attractive to students and easier to use by giving clear signals as to the book's structure.

- *Key Ideas* highlighted and explained where they first appear. There are 19 of these ideas, which are fundamental to the study of economics on business courses. Students can see them recurring throughout the book, and an icon appears in the margin to refer back to the page where the idea first appears. Showing how ideas can be used in a variety of contexts helps students to 'think like an economist' and to relate the different parts of the subject together. All 19 Key Ideas are defined in a special section at the very end of the book.

- *'Pause for thought'* questions integrated throughout the text. These encourage students to reflect on what they have just read and make the learning process a more active one. Answers to these questions appear in the student section of the book's website.

- *Special Part opening sections* for each of the five Parts of the book, setting the scene and introducing the material to be covered.

- *Chapter opening sections* that identify key business issues to be covered in that chapter.

- *All technical terms are highlighted and clearly defined in the margin* on the page they appear. This feature is especially useful for students when revising.

- *A comprehensive index,* including reference to all defined terms. This enables students to look up a definition as required and to see it used in context.

- *Many boxes with additional applied material.* All boxes include questions so as to relate the material back to the chapter in which the box is located. The extensive use of applied material makes learning much more interesting for students and helps to bring the subject alive. This is particularly important for business students who need to relate economic theory to their other subjects and to the world of business generally.

- *Additional case studies appearing on the book's website* are referred to at the end of each Part.

■ *Detailed summaries appear at the end of each section.* These allow students not only to check their comprehension of section's contents, but also to get a clear overview of the material they have been studying.

■ *Review questions at the end of each chapter.* These are designed to test students' understanding of the chapter's salient points. These questions can be used for seminars or as set work to be completed in the students' own time.

■ *A list of relevant websites given at the end of each Part.* Details of these websites can be found in the Web Appendix at the end of the book. You can easily access any of these sites from the book's own website

(at http://www.pearsoned.co.uk/sloman). When you enter the site, click on Hotlinks. You will find all the sites from the Web Appendix listed. Click on the one you want and the 'hot link' will take you straight to it.

Supplements

Web site

Visit the book's website at http://www.pearsoned.co.uk/sloman
This has an extensive range of materials for students and tutors.

For students

■ *Study material* designed to help you improve your results.

■ *Economics news articles,* updated monthly: some 15 to 20 news items per month, with links to one or more newspaper articles per item. There are questions on each item and references to the relevant chapter(s) of the book.

■ *Topical economic issues,* with analysis and links to key concepts and pages in the book.

■ *Hotlinks* to over 200 useful websites listed in the book's Web Appendix and referenced at the end of each Part of the text.

■ *Case studies* (87 in total) with questions for self study. These are the case studies referred to at the end of each Part of the text.

■ *Answers to all Pause for Thought and odd-numbered end-of-chapter questions* to allow you to check your understanding as you progress.

■ Self-test questions, organised chapter by chapter. You get a computer-generated answer to any test you take.

For tutors

■ A range of *teaching and learning case studies,* with the focus on improving student learning outcomes.

■ All *figures and tables* from the book in PowerPoint®, in two versions, each animated and in full colour.

■ Full colour OHTs of all figures and tables (on a clear background). Also suitable for black-and-white printing. Can be used for handouts.

- Customisable full-colour *lecture plans* in PowerPoint, with integrated animated diagrams and tables. Can also be used for handouts.

- *Answers* to all even-numbered end-of-chapter questions, boxes and Web case studies in a secure password protected area of the site.

Acknowledgements

Many thanks to all the reviewers of the text, who have given me valuable advice for improvements. Thanks also to the team at Pearson, and especially Sadie McClelland, Justinia Seaman, Paula Parish, Karen McLaren and Kevin Ancient.

A special thank-you to Mark Sutcliffe, my co-author on *Economics for Business* (now in its third edition). Many ideas for this text were drawn from that larger book.

Finally, thanks to all my family and especially to my wife Alison. Without her love and support, the project would not have been possible.

Publisher's acknowledgements

We are grateful to the following for permission to reproduce copyright material:

The European Communities for Box 4.1 table (b) from Economies of scale, *The Single Market Review, Sub Series V, Volume 4* (1997), European Commission/ Economics Advisory Group Ltd.; Freefoto.com for the photograph on page 103 of a modern day office with TFT monitors, reference 04-04-26, © Ian Britton; The Free Press for Figure 6.1 from *Competitive Strategy: Techniques for Analyzing Industries and Competitors* (Porter, M. E. 1998), copyright © 1980, 1998 by The Free Press, reprinted with the permission of The Free Press, a Division of Simon & Schuster Adult Publishing Group, all rights reserved; Palgrave Macmillan for Figure 6.3 from *Non-Price Decisions* (Koutsoyiannis, A. 1982); The Bank of England for Table 11.3 from the *Bank of England Interactive Database*.

We are grateful to the following for permission to reproduce copyright material:

News International Syndication Limited for permission to reproduce text extracted and amended from 'Deflation Danger, Running Out of Steam' by Dominic Rushe originally published in *The Sunday Times*, 11 May 2003; and McGraw-Hill Companies for extracts from 'Samsung's 'Sashmi Theory' of Success' reprinted from 11 June 2003 issue of *Business Week* and 'The Samsung Way' reprinted from 16 June 2003 issue of *Business Week* by permission, © 2003 McGraw-Hill Companies.

We are grateful to the Financial Times Limited for permission to reprint the following material:

Box 7.2 National News: How a mouse can make short work of finding a job, © *Financial Times*, 22 February 2000; Box 8.1 Body Shop's 'Green Queen' steps aside, FT.com, © *Financial Times*, 18 September 2000; Box 10.3 Inflation targets lose their glamour, FT.com, © *Financial Times*, 15 January 2004.

Guided tour

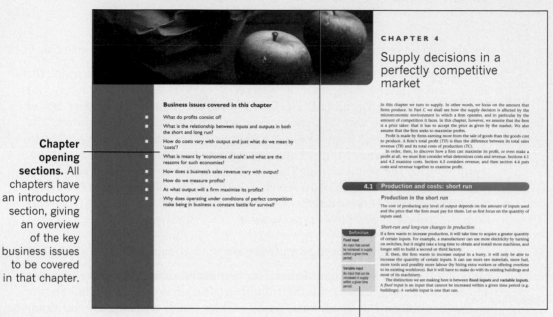

Chapter opening sections. All chapters have an introductory section, giving an overview of the key business issues to be covered in that chapter.

Definitions. All key terms are highlighted in the text where they first appear and are defined in the margin. This is very useful for revision and allows you to see the terms used in context.

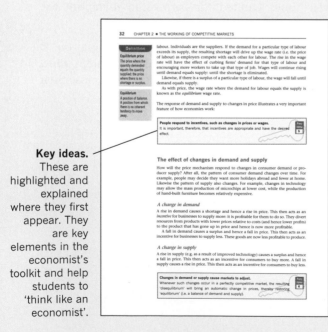

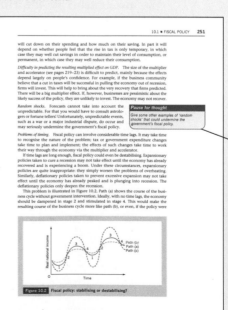

Key ideas. These are highlighted and explained where they first appear. They are key elements in the economist's toolkit and help students to 'think like an economist'.

Pause for thought questions. These help you reflect on what you have just read and to check on your understanding.

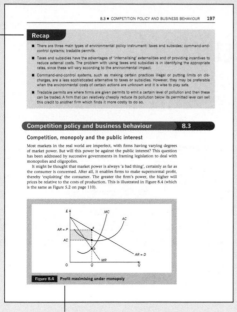

Recap sections. Summaries at the end of each section allow you to check up on your understanding at frequent intervals and provide an important revision tool.

Full colour design. A consistent use of colour is made in the diagrams which allows you to see at a glance how the diagram is constructed and the 'before' and 'after' positions when the diagram is used to illustrate the effects of a change in circumstances.

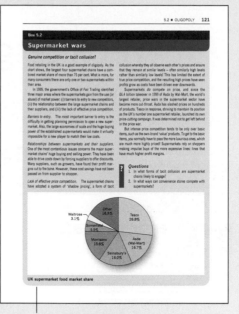

Boxes. These provide case studies to show how economics can be used to understand particular business problems or aspects of the business environment. Each box also has questions to relate the material back to the chapter.

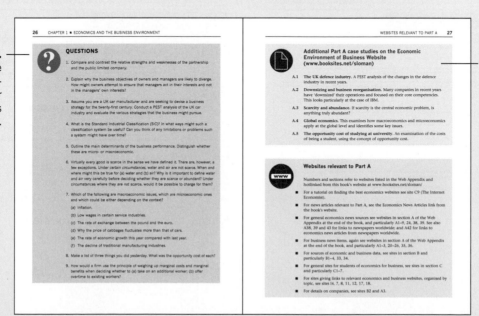

Questions. These can be used for self-testing, or for class exercises or debate.

Web material. At the end of each Part there are lists of additional case studies appearing on the book's Website and references to various other useful Websites.

Website guided tour

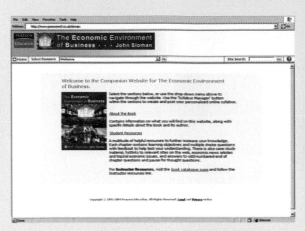

The Companion Website

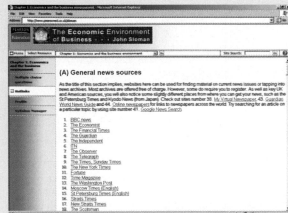

Hotlinks

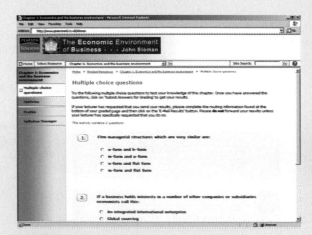

Multiple choice questions

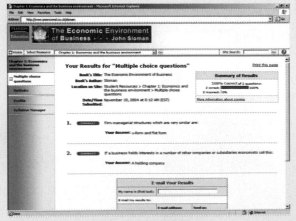

Results for multiple choice questions

PART A

Introduction

In this book we will be looking at the economic environment in which firms operate and at how economics can help in the process of business decision taking. In doing so, you will gain an insight into how economists think and the sorts of concepts they use to analyse business problems.

But what particular aspects of business does the economist study? Firms are essentially concerned with using inputs to make output. Inputs cost money and output earns money. The difference between the revenue earned and the costs incurred constitutes the firm's profit. Firms will normally want to make as much profit as possible, or at the very least to avoid a decline in profits.

In order to meet these and other objectives, managers will need to make choices: choices of what types of output to produce, how much to produce and at what price; choices of what techniques of production to use, what types of workers to employ and how many, what suppliers to use for raw materials, equipment, etc. In each case, when weighing up alternatives, managers will want to make the best choices. Business economists study these choices. They study economic decision making by firms.

Business issues covered in this chapter

- What things influence a firm's behaviour and performance?

- How are businesses organised and structured?

- What are the various legal categories of business and how do different legal forms suit different types of business?

- What are the aims of business?

- Will owners, managers and other employees necessarily have the same aims? How can those working in the firm be persuaded to achieve the objectives of their employers?

- How are businesses influenced by their national and global market environment?

- How are different types of industry classified in the official statistics?

- How do economists set about analysing business decision taking?

- What are the core economic concepts that are necessary to understand the economic choices that businesses have to make, such as what to produce, what inputs and what technology to use, where to locate their production and how best to compete with other firms?

CHAPTER 1

Economics and the business environment

The world economy has undergone many changes in recent times, and these changes have had profound effects on business. For a start, most countries have increasingly embraced the 'market' as the means of boosting prosperity. You can see this in the abandonment of state planning in former communist countries, the privatisation of state industries around the world, the dismantling of barriers to international trade, the development of global financial markets, the use of government policies to promote competition and reductions in government regulation of business in order to attract inward investment. A consequence has been the growth of multinational businesses seeking the best market opportunities and the cheapest sources of supply.

Other important influences on businesses around the world have included the development of computers and IT, improvements in transport and communications and, more recently, a rapid growth in the use of the Internet. These technological advances have allowed businesses to take advantage of growing market opportunities.

Today, for many firms the world is their market. Their business environment is global. This is obviously the case with large multinational companies, such as McDonald's, Sony, VW, HSBC, Nestlé and Shell. But many small and medium-sized enterprises (SMEs) also have global reach, selling their products in various countries and buying their supplies from wherever in the world they get the best deal.

For other firms, however, their market is much more local. Take a restaurant or firm of heating engineers – in fact, look in the Yellow Pages and you will see a host of companies serving a market whose radius is no more than a few miles. But these firms too often face competition from global companies. A local shop is likely to face competition from a supermarket, such as Tesco or Wal-Mart, both of which have shops around the world and source their supplies from across the globe.

In this chapter, we take an overview of the types of environment in which firms operate and of the role of the economist in business decision taking.

We start by looking at the internal environment of the firm – the organisation and aims of the business. We then look at the external environment in which the firm operates – the nature of competition it faces, the type of industry in which it operates, the prices of its inputs, the general state of the economy (e.g. whether growing or in recession), the actions of the government and other authorities that might affect the firm (e.g. changes in taxes or interest rates or changes in competition legislation) and the global environment (e.g. the extent to which the company operates internationally and how it is influenced by global market opportunities and the state of the world economy).

Finally we look at the approach of the economist to analysing the business environment and business decision taking.

Box 1.1 introduces many of the topics that you will be covering in this book by taking the case of Gap and seeing how it is affected by its environment.

QUESTIONS

1. Compare and contrast the relative strengths and weaknesses of the partnership and the public limited company.

2. Explain why the business objectives of owners and managers are likely to diverge. How might owners attempt to ensure that managers act in their interests and not in the managers' own interests?

3. Assume you are a UK car manufacturer and are seeking to devise a business strategy for the twenty-first century. Conduct a PEST analysis of the UK car industry and evaluate the various strategies that the business might pursue.

4. What is the Standard Industrial Classification (SIC)? In what ways might such a classification system be useful? Can you think of any limitations or problems such a system might have over time?

5. Outline the main determinants of the business performance. Distinguish whether these are micro- or macroeconomic.

6. Virtually every good is scarce in the sense we have defined it. There are, however, a few exceptions. Under *certain circumstances*, water and air are not scarce. When and where might this be true for (a) water and (b) air? Why is it important to define water and air very carefully before deciding whether they are scarce or abundant? Under circumstances where they are *not* scarce, would it be possible to charge for them?

7. Which of the following are macroeconomic issues, which are microeconomic ones and which could be either depending on the context?

    (a) Inflation.

    (b) Low wages in certain service industries.

    (c) The rate of exchange between the pound and the euro.

    (d) Why the price of cabbages fluctuates more than that of cars.

    (e) The rate of economic growth this year compared with last year.

    (f) The decline of traditional manufacturing industries.

8. Make a list of three things you did yesterday. What was the opportunity cost of each?

9. How would a firm use the principle of weighing up marginal costs and marginal benefits when deciding whether to (a) take on an additional worker; (b) offer overtime to existing workers?

Additional Part A case studies on the Economic Environment of Business Website (www.booksites.net/sloman)

A.1 **The UK defence industry.** A PEST analysis of the changes in the defence industry in recent years.

A.2 **Downsizing and business reorganisation.** Many companies in recent years have 'downsized' their operations and focused on their core competencies. This looks particularly at the case of IBM.

A.3 **Scarcity and abundance.** If scarcity is the central economic problem, is anything truly abundant?

A.4 **Global economics.** This examines how macroeconomics and microeconomics apply at the global level and identifies some key issues.

A.5 **The opportunity cost of studying at university**. An examination of the costs of being a student, using the concept of opportunity cost.

Websites relevant to Part A

Numbers and sections refer to websites listed in the Web Appendix and hotlinked from this book's website at www.booksites.net/sloman/

- For a tutorial on finding the best economics websites see site C9 (The Internet Economist).

- For news articles relevant to Part A, see the Economics News Articles link from the book's website.

- For general economics news sources see websites in section A of the Web Appendix at the end of the book, and particularly A1–9, 24, 38, 39. See also A38, 39 and 43 for links to newspapers worldwide; and A42 for links to economics news articles from newspapers worldwide.

- For business news items, again see websites in section A of the Web Appendix at the end of the book, and particularly A1–3, 20–26, 35, 36.

- For sources of economic and business data, see sites in section B and particularly B1–4, 33, 34.

- For general sites for students of economics for business, see sites in section C and particularly C1–7.

- For sites giving links to relevant economics and business websites, organised by topic, see sites I4, 7, 8, 11, 12, 17, 18.

- For details on companies, see sites B2 and A3.

PART B

Markets, demand and supply

One of the key determinants of a business's profitability is the price of its product. In most cases, firms have the option of changing their prices in order to increase their profits. Sometimes, a cut in price might be in order, if the firm anticipates that this will generate a lot more sales. At other times, a firm may prefer to raise its prices, believing there will be little effect on sales – perhaps it believes that its competitors will follow suit; or, perhaps, there are no close competitors, making it easy for the firm to get away with raising prices.

For some firms, however, the prices of the products they sell are determined not by them, but by the **market**. The 'market' is what we call the coming together of buyers and sellers: whether it be a street market, a shop, an auction, a mail-order system, the Internet or whatever. Thus we talk about the market for apples, the market for oil, for cars, for houses, for televisions and so on. As we shall see, market prices are determined by the interaction of demand (buyers) and supply (sellers).

> **Definition**
>
> **Market**
> The interaction between buyers and sellers.

When the price is determined by the market, the firm is called a *price taker*. It has to accept the market price as given. If the firm attempts to raise the price above the market price, it will simply be unable to sell its product: it will lose all its sales to its competitors. Take the case of farmers selling wheat. They have to accept the price as dictated by the market. If individually they try to sell above the market price, no one will buy.

So how does a competitive market work? How are prices determined in such markets? We examine this question in Chapter 2.

In Chapter 3 we look more closely at demand and at firms' attempt to understand demand and the behaviour of consumers. Then in Chapter 4 we look at supply and ask how much will a profit maximising firm produce at the market price.

Business issues covered in this chapter

- How do markets operate?

- How are market prices determined and when are they likely to rise or fall?

- Under what circumstances do firms have to accept a price given by the market rather than being able to set the price themselves?

- What are the influences on consumer demand?

- How responsive is consumer demand to changes in the market price? How responsive is it to changes in consumer incomes and to the prices of competitor products?

- How is a firm's sales revenue affected by a change in price?

- What factors determine the amount of supply coming onto the market?

- How responsive is business output to changes in price?

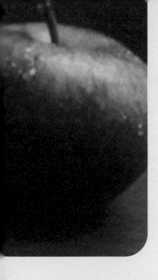

CHAPTER 2

The working of competitive markets

The price mechanism under perfect competition

Free market
One in which there is an absence of government intervention. Individual producers and consumers are free to make their own economic decisions.

Perfectly competitive market (preliminary definition)
A market in which all producers and consumers of the product are price takers. (There are other features of a perfectly competitive market; these are examined in Chapter 4.)

Price taker
A person or firm with no power to be able to influence the market price.

The price mechanism
The system in a market economy whereby changes in price in response to changes in demand and supply have the effect of making demand equal to supply.

In a **free market** individuals are free to make their own economic decisions. Consumers are free to decide what to buy with their incomes: free to make demand decisions. Firms are free to choose what to sell and what production methods to use: free to make supply decisions.

For simplicity we will examine the case of a **perfectly competitive market**. This is where both producers and consumers are too numerous to have any control over prices whatsoever: a situation where everyone is a **price taker**. In such markets, the demand and supply decisions of consumers and firms are transmitted to each other through their effect on *prices*: through the **price mechanism**. The prices that result are the prices that firms have to accept.

The working of the price mechanism

The price mechanism works as follows. Prices respond to *shortages* and *surpluses*. Shortages result in prices rising. Surpluses result in prices falling. Let us take each of these in turn.

If consumers decide they want more of a good (or if producers decide to cut back supply), demand will exceed supply. The resulting *shortage* will encourage sellers to *raise* the price of the good. This will act as an incentive to producers to supply more, since production will now be more profitable. On the other hand, it will discourage consumers from buying so much. *The price will continue rising until the shortage has thereby been eliminated.*

If, on the other hand, consumers decide they want less of a good (or if producers decide to produce more), supply will exceed demand. The resulting *surplus* will cause sellers to *reduce* the price of the good. This will act as a disincentive to producers, who will supply less, since production will now be less profitable. It will encourage consumers to buy more. *The price will continue falling until the surplus has thereby been eliminated.*

This price, where demand equals supply, is called the **equilibrium price**. By **equilibrium** we mean a point of balance or a point of rest: i.e. a point towards which there is a tendency to move.

The same analysis can be applied to labour (and other input) markets, except that here the demand and supply roles are reversed. Firms are the demanders of

Definition

Equilibrium price
The price where the quantity demanded equals the quantity supplied: the price where there is no shortage or surplus.

Equilibrium
A position of balance. A position from which there is no inherent tendency to move away.

labour. Individuals are the suppliers. If the demand for a particular type of labour exceeds its supply, the resulting shortage will drive up the wage rate (i.e. the price of labour) as employers compete with each other for labour. The rise in the wage rate will have the effect of curbing firms' demand for that type of labour and encouraging more workers to take up that type of job. Wages will continue rising until demand equals supply: until the shortage is eliminated.

Likewise, if there is a surplus of a particular type of labour, the wage will fall until demand equals supply.

As with price, the wage rate where the demand for labour equals the supply is known as the *equilibrium* wage rate.

The response of demand and supply to changes in price illustrates a very important feature of how economies work:

> **People respond to incentives, such as changes in prices or wages.**
> It is important, therefore, that incentives are appropriate and have the desired effect.

Key Idea 5

The effect of changes in demand and supply

How will the price mechanism respond to changes in consumer demand or producer supply? After all, the pattern of consumer demand changes over time. For example, people may decide they want more holidays abroad and fewer at home. Likewise the pattern of supply also changes. For example, changes in technology may allow the mass production of microchips at lower cost, while the production of hand-built furniture becomes relatively expensive.

A change in demand

A rise in demand causes a shortage and hence a rise in price. This then acts as an *incentive* for businesses to supply more: it is profitable for them to do so. They divert resources from products with lower prices relative to costs (and hence lower profits) to the product that has gone up in price and hence is now more profitable.

A fall in demand causes a surplus and hence a fall in price. This then acts as an incentive for businesses to supply less. These goods are now less profitable to produce.

A change in supply

A rise in supply (e.g. as a result of improved technology) causes a surplus and hence a fall in price. This then acts as an incentive for consumers to buy more. A fall in supply causes a rise in price. This then acts as an incentive for consumers to buy less.

> **Changes in demand or supply cause markets to adjust.**
> Whenever such changes occur in a perfectly competitive market, the resulting 'disequilibrium' will bring an automatic change in prices, thereby restoring 'equilibrium' (i.e. a balance of demand and supply).

Key Idea 6

Let us now turn to examine each side of the market – demand and supply – in more detail.

Recap

- A firm is greatly affected by its market environment. The more competitive the market, the less discretion the firm has in determining its price. In the extreme case of a perfect market, the price is entirely outside the firm's control. The price is determined by demand and supply in the market, and the firm has to accept this price: the firm is a price taker.

- In a perfect market, price changes act as the mechanism whereby demand and supply are balanced.

- If there is a shortage, price will rise until the shortage is eliminated. If there is a surplus, price will fall until that is eliminated.

Demand   2.2

The relationship between demand and price

The headlines announce, 'Major crop failures in Brazil and East Africa: coffee prices soar.' Shortly afterwards you find that coffee prices have doubled in the shops. What do you do? Presumably you will cut back on the amount of coffee you drink. Perhaps you will reduce it from, say, six cups per day to two. Perhaps you will give up drinking coffee altogether.

This is simply an illustration of the general relationship between price and consumption: *when the price of a good rises, the quantity demanded will fall*. This relationship is known as the **law of demand**. There are two reasons for this law:

- People will feel poorer. They will not be able to afford to buy so much of the good with their money. The purchasing power of their income (their *real income*) has fallen. This is called the **income effect** of a price rise.

- The good will now be dearer relative to other goods. People will thus switch to alternative or 'substitute' goods. This is called the **substitution effect** of a price rise.

Similarly, when the price of a good falls, the quantity demanded will rise. People can afford to buy more (the income effect), and they will switch away from consuming alternative goods (the substitution effect).

Therefore, returning to our example of the increase in the price of coffee, we will not be able to afford to buy as much as before, and we will probably drink more tea, cocoa, fruit juices or even water instead.

A word of warning: be careful about the meaning of the words **quantity demanded**. They refer to the amount consumers are willing and able to purchase at a given price over a given time period (e.g. a week, or a month, or a year). They do *not* refer to what people would simply *like* to consume. You might like to own a luxury yacht, but your demand for luxury yachts will almost certainly be zero at current prices.

Definition

The law of demand
The quantity of a good demanded per period of time will fall as the price rises and rise as the price falls, other things being equal (*ceteris paribus*).

Income effect
The effect of a change in price on quantity demanded arising from the consumer becoming better or worse off as a result of the price change.

Substitution effect
The effect of a change in price on quantity demanded arising from the consumer switching to or from alternative (substitute) products.

Quantity demanded
The amount of a good that a consumer is willing and able to buy at a given price over a given period of time.

The demand curve

Definition

Demand schedule for an individual

A table showing the different quantities of a good that a person is willing and able to buy at various prices over a given period of time.

Market demand schedule

A table showing the different total quantities of a good that consumers are willing and able to buy at various prices over a given period of time.

Demand curve

A graph showing the relationship between the price of a good and the quantity of the good demanded over a given time period. Price is measured on the vertical axis; quantity demanded is measured on the horizontal axis. A demand curve can be for an individual consumer or a group of consumers, or more usually for the whole market.

Consider the hypothetical data in Table 2.1. The table shows how many kilos of potatoes per month would be purchased at various prices.

Columns (2) and (3) show the **demand schedules** for two individuals, Tracey and Darren. Column (4), by contrast, shows the total **market demand schedule**. This is the total demand by all consumers. To obtain the market demand schedule for potatoes, we simply add up the quantities demanded at each price by *all* consumers: i.e. Tracey, Darren and everyone else who demands potatoes. Notice that we are talking about demand *over a period of time* (not at a *point* in time). Thus we would talk about daily demand or weekly demand or annual demand or whatever.

The demand schedule can be represented graphically as a **demand curve**. Figure 2.1 shows the market demand curve for potatoes corresponding to the schedule in Table 2.1. The price of potatoes is plotted on the vertical axis. The quantity demanded is plotted on the horizontal axis.

Point *E* shows that at a price of 100p per kilo, 100 000 tonnes of potatoes are demanded each month. When the price falls to 80p we move down the curve to point *D*. This shows that the quantity demanded has now risen to 200 000 tonnes per month. Similarly, if price falls to 60p, we move down the curve again to point *C*: 350 000 tonnes are now demanded. The five points on the graph (*A–E*) correspond to the figures in columns (1) and (4) of Table 2.1. The graph also enables us to read off the likely quantities demanded at prices other than those in the table.

A demand curve could also be drawn for an individual consumer. Like market demand curves, individuals' demand curves generally slope downward from left to right: the lower the price of the product, the more is a person likely to buy.

Two points should be noted at this stage:

■ In textbooks, demand curves (and other curves too) are only occasionally used to plot specific data. More frequently they are used to illustrate general theoretical arguments. In such cases the axes will simply be price and quantity, with the units unspecified.

■ The term 'curve' is used even when the graph is a straight line! In fact, when using demand curves to illustrate arguments we frequently draw them as straight lines – it's easier.

Table 2.1 The demand for potatoes (monthly)

	Price (pence per kg) (1)	Tracey's demand (kg) (2)	Darren's demand (kg) (3)	Total market demand (tonnes: 000s) (4)
A	20	28	16	700
B	40	15	11	500
C	60	5	9	350
D	80	1	7	200
E	100	0	6	100

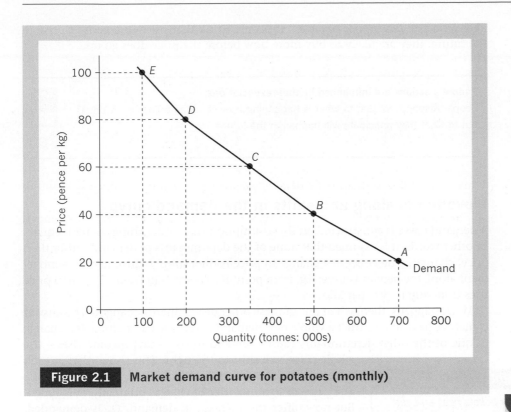

Figure 2.1 **Market demand curve for potatoes (monthly)**

Other determinants of demand

Price is not the only factor that determines how much of a good people will buy. Demand is also affected by the following.

Tastes. The more desirable people find the good, the more they will demand. Tastes are affected by advertising, by fashion, by observing other consumers, by considerations of health and by the experiences from consuming the good on previous occasions.

The number and price of substitute goods (i.e. competitive goods). The higher the price of **substitute goods**, the higher will be the demand for this good as people switch from the substitutes. For example, the demand for coffee will depend on the price of tea. If tea goes up in price, the demand for coffee will rise.

The number and price of complementary goods. **Complementary goods** are those that are consumed together: coffee and milk, cars and petrol, shoes and polish. The higher the price of complementary goods, the fewer of them will be bought and hence the less the demand for this good. For example, the demand for electricity depends on the price of electrical goods. If the price of electrical goods goes up, so that fewer are bought, the demand for electricity will fall.

Income. As people's incomes rise, their demand for most goods will rise. Such goods are called **normal goods**. There are exceptions to this general rule, however. As people get richer, they spend less on **inferior goods**, such as cheap margarine, and switch to better quality goods.

Definition

Substitute goods
A pair of goods which are considered by consumers to be alternatives to each other. As the price of one goes up, the demand for the other rises.

Complementary goods
A pair of goods consumed together. As the price of one goes up, the demand for both goods will fall.

Normal goods
Goods whose demand rises as people's incomes rise.

Inferior goods
Goods whose demand falls as people's incomes rise.

Expectations of future price changes. If people think that prices are going to rise in the future, they are likely to buy more now before the price does go up.

> **People's actions are influenced by their expectations.**
> People respond not just to what is happening now (such as a change in price), but to what they anticipate will happen in the future.
>
> **Key Idea 7**

Movements along and shifts in the demand curve

A demand curve is constructed on the assumption that 'other things remain equal'. In other words, it is assumed that none of the determinants of demand, other than price, changes. The effect of a change in price is then simply illustrated by a movement along the demand curve: e.g. from point *B* to point *D* in Figure 2.1 when price rises from 40p to 80p per kilo.

What happens, then, when one of these other determinants changes? The answer is that we have to construct a whole new demand curve: the curve shifts. If a change in one of the other determinants causes demand to rise – say, income rises – the whole curve will shift to the right. This shows that at each price more will be demanded than before. Thus in Figure 2.2 at a price of P, a quantity of Q_0 was originally demanded. But now, after the increase in demand, Q_1 is demanded. (Note that D_1 is not necessarily parallel to D_0.)

If a change in a determinant other than price causes demand to fall, the whole curve will shift to the left.

> **Pause for thought**
>
> *The price of cinema tickets rises and yet it is observed that cinema attendance increases. Does this means that the demand for cinema tickets is upward sloping?*

Definition

Change in demand
The term used for a shift in the demand curve. It occurs when a determinant of demand *other* than price changes.

Change in the quantity demanded
The term used for a movement along the demand curve to a new point. It occurs when there is a change in price.

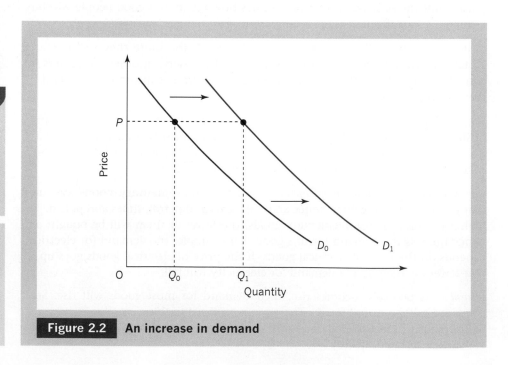

Figure 2.2   An increase in demand

To distinguish between shifts in and movements along demand curves, it is usual to distinguish between a change in *demand* and a change in the *quantity demanded*. A shift in demand is referred to as a **change in demand**, whereas a movement along the demand curve as a result of a change in price is referred to as a **change in the quantity demanded**.

Recap

■ When the price of a good rises, the quantity demanded per period of time will fall. This is known as the 'law of demand'. It applies both to individuals' demand and to the whole market demand.

■ The law of demand is explained by the income and substitution effects of a price change.

■ The relationship between price and quantity demanded per period of time can be shown in a table (or 'schedule') or as a graph. On the graph, price is plotted on the vertical axis and quantity demanded per period of time on the horizontal axis. The resulting demand curve is downward sloping (negatively sloped).

■ Other determinants of demand include tastes, the number and price of substitute goods, the number and price of complementary goods, income and expectations of future price changes.

■ If price changes, the effect is shown by a movement along the demand curve. We call this effect 'a change in the quantity demanded'.

■ If any other determinant of demand changes, the whole curve will shift. We call this effect 'a change in demand'. A rightward shift represents an increase in demand; a leftward shift represents a decrease in demand.

Supply   2.3

Supply and price

Imagine you are a farmer deciding what to do with your land. Part of your land is in a fertile valley. Part is on a hillside where the soil is poor. Perhaps, then, you will consider growing vegetables in the valley and keeping sheep on the hillside.

Your decision will depend to a large extent on the price that various vegetables will fetch in the market, and likewise the price you can expect to get from sheep and wool. As far as the valley is concerned, you will plant the vegetables that give the best return. If, for example, the price of potatoes is high, you will probably use a lot of the valley for growing potatoes. If the price gets higher, you may well use the whole of the valley, perhaps being prepared to run the risk of potato disease. If the price is very high indeed, you may even consider growing potatoes on the hillside, even though the yield per hectare is much lower there. In other words, the higher the price of a particular crop, the more you are likely to grow in preference to other crops.

This illustrates the general relationship between supply and price: *when the price of a good rises, the quantity supplied will also rise*. There are three reasons for this:

■ As firms supply more, they are likely to find that, beyond a certain level of output, costs rise more and more rapidly. Only if price rises will it be worth producing more and incurring these higher costs.

In the case of the farm we have just considered, once potatoes have to be grown on the hillside, the costs of producing them will increase. Also if the land has to be used more intensively, say by the use of more and more fertilisers, again the cost of producing extra potatoes is likely to rise quite rapidly. It is the same for manufacturers. Beyond a certain level of output, costs are likely to rise rapidly as workers have to be paid overtime and as machines approach their full capacity. If higher output involves higher costs of production, producers will need to get a higher price if they are to be persuaded to produce extra output.

■ The higher the price of the good, the more profitable it becomes to produce. Firms will thus be encouraged to produce more of it by switching from producing less profitable goods.

■ Given time, if the price of a good remains high, new producers will be encouraged to set up in production. Total market supply thus rises.

The first two determinants affect supply in the short run. The third affects supply in the long run. We distinguish between short-run and long-run supply later (see page 54).

The supply curve

The amount that producers would like to supply at various prices can be shown in a **supply schedule**. Table 2.2 shows a monthly supply schedule for potatoes, both for an individual farmer (farmer X) and for all farmers together (the whole market).

The supply schedule can be represented graphically as a **supply curve**. A supply curve may be an individual firm's supply curve or a market supply curve (i.e. that of the whole industry).

Figure 2.3 shows the *market* supply curve of potatoes. As with demand curves, price is plotted on the vertical axis and quantity on the horizontal axis. Each of the points *a–e* corresponds to a figure in Table 2.2. Thus for example, a price rise from 60p per kilogram to 80p per kilogram causes a movement along the supply curve from point *c* to point *d*: total market supply rises from 350 000 tonnes per month to 530 000 tonnes per month.

Not all supply curves are upward sloping (positively sloped). Sometimes they are vertical, or horizontal, or even downward sloping. This depends largely on the time period over which the response of firms to price changes is considered. (This question is examined on pages 53–4.)

Other determinants of supply

Like demand, supply is not determined simply by price. The other determinants of supply are as follows.

The costs of production. The higher the costs of production, the less profit will be made at any price. As costs rise, firms will cut back on production, probably switching to alternative products whose costs have not risen so much. Costs could change as a result of changing input prices, changes in technology, organisational changes within the firm, changes in taxation, etc.

Definition

Supply schedule
A table showing the different quantities of a good that producers are willing and able to supply at various prices over a given time period. A supply schedule can be for an individual producer or group of producers, or for all producers (the market supply schedule).

Supply curve
A graph showing the relationship between the price of a good and the quantity of the good supplied over a given period of time.

Pause for thought

1. How much would be supplied at a price of 70p per kilo?
2. Draw a supply curve for farmer X. Are the axes drawn to the same scale as in Figure 2.3?

Table 2.2 The supply of potatoes (monthly)

	Price of potatoes (pence per kg)	Farmer X's supply (tonnes)	Total market supply (tonnes: 000s)
a	20	50	100
b	40	70	200
c	60	100	350
d	80	120	530
e	100	130	700

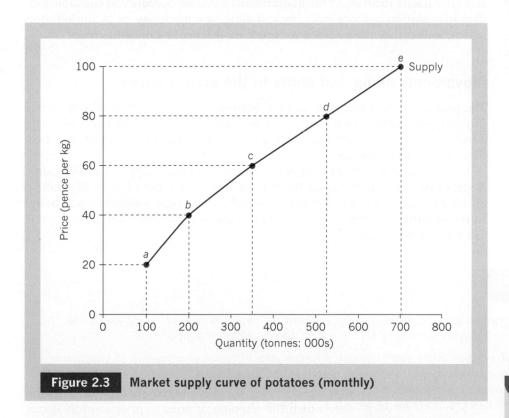

Figure 2.3   Market supply curve of potatoes (monthly)

The profitability of alternative products (substitutes in supply). If some alternative product (**a substitute in supply**) becomes more profitable to supply than before, producers are likely to switch from the first good to this alternative. Supply of the first good falls. Substitutes in supply are likely to become more profitable if their price rises or their cost of production falls. For example, if the price of carrots goes up, or the cost of producing carrots comes down, farmers may decide to cut down potato production in order to produce more carrots. The supply of potatoes is therefore likely to fall.

The profitability of goods in joint supply. Sometimes when one good is produced, another good is also produced at the same time. These are said to be **goods in joint supply**. An example is the refining of crude oil to produce petrol. Other grade fuels

Definition

Substitutes in supply
These are two goods where an increased production of one means diverting resources away from producing the other.

Goods in joint supply
These are two goods where the production of more of one leads to the production of more of the other.

will be produced as well, such as diesel and paraffin. If more petrol is produced, due to a rise in demand, then the supply of these other fuels will rise too.

Nature, 'random shocks' and other unpredictable events. In this category we would include the weather and diseases affecting farm output, wars affecting the supply of imported raw materials, the breakdown of machinery, industrial disputes, earthquakes, floods and fire, and so on.

The aims of producers. A profit-maximising firm will supply a different quantity from a firm that has a different aim, such as maximising sales.

Expectations of future price changes. If price is expected to rise, producers may temporarily reduce the amount they sell. Instead they are likely to build up their stocks and only release them on to the market when the price does rise. At the same time they may plan to produce more, by installing new machines, or taking on more labour, so that they can be ready to supply more when the price has risen.

Movements along and shifts in the supply curve

The principle here is the same as with demand curves. The effect of a change in price is illustrated by a movement along the supply curve: e.g. from point *d* to point *e* in Figure 2.3 when price rises from 80p to 100p. Quantity supplied rises from 530 000 to 700 000 tonnes.

If any other determinant of supply changes, the whole supply curve will shift. A rightward shift illustrates an increase in supply. A leftward shift illustrates a decrease in supply. A movement along a supply curve is often referred to as a **change in the quantity supplied**, whereas a shift in the supply curve is simply referred to as a **change in supply**.

Definition

Change in the quantity supplied
The term used for a movement along the supply curve to a new point. It occurs when there is a change in price.

Change in supply
The term used for a shift in the supply curve. It occurs when a determinant other than price changes.

Recap

- When the price of a good rises, the quantity supplied per period of time will usually also rise. This applies both to individual producers' supply and to the whole market supply.

- There are two reasons in the short run why a higher price encourages producers to supply more: (a) they are now willing to incur the higher costs per unit associated with producing more; (b) they will switch to producing this product and away from now less profitable ones. In the long run there is a third reason: new producers will be attracted into the market.

- The relationship between price and quantity supplied per period of time can be shown in a table (or schedule) or as a graph. As with a demand curve, price is plotted on the vertical axis and quantity per period of time on the horizontal axis. The resulting supply curve is upward sloping (positively sloped).

- Other determinants of supply include the costs of production, the profitability of alternative products, the profitability of goods in joint supply, random shocks and expectations of future price changes.

- If price changes, the effect is shown by a movement along the supply curve. We call this effect 'a change in the quantity supplied'.

- If any determinant *other* than price changes, the effect is shown by a shift in the whole supply curve. We call this effect 'a change in supply'. A rightward shift represents an increase in supply; a leftward shift represents a decrease in supply.

Price and output determination   2.4

Equilibrium price and output

We can now combine our analysis of demand and supply. This will show how the actual price of a product and the actual quantity bought and sold are determined in a free and competitive market.

Let us return to the example of the market demand and market supply of potatoes, and use the data from Tables 2.1 and 2.2. These figures are given again in Table 2.3.

What will be the price and output that actually prevail? If the price started at 20p per kilogram, demand would exceed supply by 600 000 tonnes ($A - a$). Consumers would be unable to obtain all they wanted and would thus be willing to pay a higher price. Producers, unable or unwilling to supply enough to meet the demand, will be only too happy to accept a higher price. The effect of the shortage, then, will be to drive up the price. The same would happen at a price of 40p per kilogram. There would still be a shortage; price would still rise. But as the price rises, the quantity demanded falls and the quantity supplied rises. The shortage is progressively eliminated.

What would happen if the price started at a much higher level: say at 100p per kilogram? In this case supply would exceed demand by 600 000 tonnes ($e - E$). The effect of this surplus would be to drive the price down as farmers competed against each other to sell their excess supplies. The same would happen at a price of 80p per kilogram. There would still be a surplus; price would still fall.

In fact, only one price is sustainable. This is the price where demand equals supply: namely 60p per kilogram, where both demand and supply are 350 000 tonnes. When supply matches demand the market is said to **clear**. There is no shortage and no surplus.

As we have already seen, the price where demand equals supply is called the *equilibrium price*. In Table 2.3, if the price starts at other than 60p per kilogram, there will be a tendency for it to move towards 60p. The equilibrium price is the only price at which producers' and consumers' wishes are mutually reconciled: where the producers' plans to supply exactly match the consumers' plans to buy.

Definition

Market clearing
A market clears when supply matches demand, leaving no shortage or surplus.

Equilibrium is the point where conflicting interests are balanced.
Only at this point is the amount that demanders are willing to purchase the same as the amount that suppliers are willing to supply. It is a point which will be automatically reached in a free market through the operation of the price mechanism.

Key Idea 8

Table 2.3   **The market demand and supply of potatoes (monthly)**

Price of potatoes (pence per kg)	Total market demand (tonnes: 000s)	Total market supply (tonnes: 000s)
20	700 (A)	100 (a)
40	500 (B)	200 (b)
60	350 (C)	350 (c)
80	200 (D)	530 (d)
100	100 (E)	700 (e)

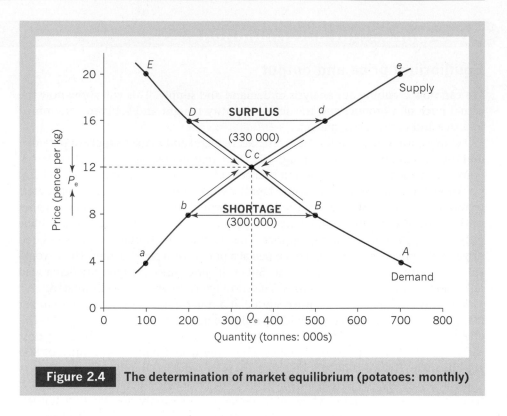

Figure 2.4 **The determination of market equilibrium (potatoes: monthly)**

Demand and supply curves

The determination of equilibrium price and output can be shown using demand and supply curves. Equilibrium is where the two curves intersect.

Figure 2.4 shows the demand and supply curves of potatoes corresponding to the data in Table 2.3. Equilibrium price is P_e (60p) and equilibrium quantity is Q_e (350 000 tonnes).

At any price above 60p, there would be a surplus. Thus at 80p there is a surplus of 330 000 tonnes ($d - D$). More is supplied than consumers are willing and able to purchase at that price. Thus a price of 80p fails to clear the market. Price will fall to the equilibrium price of 60p. As it does so, there will be a movement along the demand curve from point D to point C, and a movement along the supply curve from point d to point c.

At any price below 60p, there would be a shortage. Thus at 40p there is a shortage of 300 000 tonnes ($B - b$). Price will rise to 60p. This will cause a movement along the supply curve from point b to point c and along the demand curve from point B to point C.

Point Cc is the equilibrium: where demand equals supply.

Movement to a new equilibrium

The equilibrium price will remain unchanged only so long as the demand and supply curves remain unchanged. If either of the curves shifts, a new equilibrium will be formed.

A change in demand

If one of the determinants of demand changes (other than price), the whole demand curve will shift. This will lead to a movement *along* the *supply* curve to the new intersection point.

For example, in Figure 2.5(a), if a rise in consumer incomes led to the demand curve shifting to D_2, there would be a shortage of $h - g$ at the original price P_{e_1}. This would cause price to rise to the new equilibrium P_{e_2}. As it did so there would be a movement along the supply curve from point g to point i, and along the new demand curve (D_2) from point h to point i. Equilibrium quantity would rise from Q_{e_1} to Q_{e_2}.

The effect of the shift in demand, therefore, has been a movement *along* the supply curve from the old equilibrium to the new: from point g to point i.

> **Pause for thought**
>
> *What would happen to price and quantity if the demand curve shifted to the left? Draw a diagram to illustrate your answer.*

A change in supply

Likewise, if one of the determinants of supply changes (other than price), the whole supply curve will shift. This will lead to a movement *along* the *demand* curve to the new intersection point.

For example, in Figure 2.5(b), if costs of production rose, the supply curve would shift to the left: to S_2. There would be a shortage of $g - j$ at the old price of P_{e_1}. Price would rise from P_{e_1} to P_{e_3}. Quantity would fall from Q_{e_1} to Q_{e_3}. In other words, there would be a movement along the demand curve from point g to point k, and along the new supply curve (S_2) from point j to point k.

To summarise: a shift in one curve leads to a movement along the other curve to the new intersection point.

Sometimes a number of determinants might change. This may lead to a shift in *both* curves. When this happens, equilibrium simply moves from the point where the old curves intersected to the point where the new ones intersect.

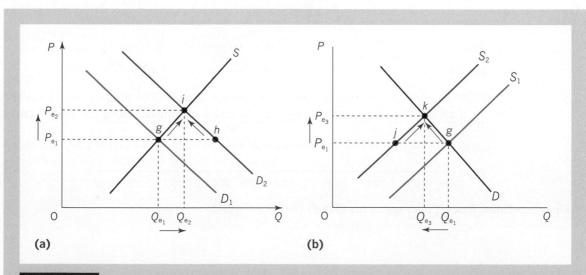

(a) **(b)**

Figure 2.5   **The effect of a shift in the demand or supply curve: (a) effect of a shift in the demand curve; (b) effect of a shift in the supply curve**

Box 2.1

Stock market prices

Demand and supply in action

As we saw in section 1.1, public limited companies can raise money by issuing shares. These are sold on the 'primary stock market'. People who own the shares receive a 'dividend' on them, normally paid six-monthly. This varies with the profitability of the company.

People or institutions that buy these shares, however, may not wish to hold on to them for ever. This is where the 'secondary stock market' comes in. It is where existing shares are bought and sold. There are stock markets, primary and secondary, in all the major countries of the world.

There are more than 2700 companies whose shares are listed on the London Stock Exchange and shares are traded each Monday to Friday (excluding Bank Holidays). The prices of shares depend on demand and supply. For example, if the demand for Tesco shares at any one time exceeds the supply on offer, the price will rise until demand and supply are equal. Share prices fluctuate throughout the trading day and sometimes price changes can be substantial.

To give an overall impression of share price movements, stock exchanges publish share price indices. The best known one in the UK is the FTSE 100, which stands for the 'Financial Times Stock Exchange' index of the 100 largest companies' shares. The index represents an average price of these 100 shares. The chart shows movements in the FTSE 100 from 1995 to 2004. The index was first calculated on 3 January 1984 with a base level of 1000 points. It reached a peak of 6930 points on 30 December 1999 and fell to 3287 on 12 March 2003.

But what causes share prices to change? Why were they so high in 1999, but only just over half that value just three years later? The answer lies in the determinants of the demand and supply of shares.

Financial Times Stock Exchange Index (FTSE) (3/1/84 = 1000)

Demand

There are four main factors that affect the demand for shares.

The price of and/or return on substitutes. The main substitutes for shares in specific companies are other shares. Thus if, in comparison with other shares, Tesco shares are expected to pay high dividends relative to the share price, people will buy Tesco shares. As far as shares in general are concerned, the main substitutes are other forms of saving. Thus if the interest rate on savings accounts in banks and building societies fell, people with such accounts would be tempted to take their money out and buy shares instead.

Incomes. If the economy is growing rapidly and people's incomes are thus rising rapidly, they are likely to buy more shares. Thus in the mid- to late 1990s, when UK incomes were rising at an average annual rate of over 3 per cent, share prices rose rapidly (see chart). As growth rates fell in the early 2000s, so share prices fell.

Wealth. 'Wealth' is people's accumulated savings and property. Wealth rose in the 1990s and many people used their increased wealth to buy shares.

Expectations. In the mid- to late 1990s, people expected share prices to go on rising. They were optimistic about continued growth in the economy and that certain sectors, such as leisure and high-tech industries, would grow particularly strongly. But as people bought shares, this pushed their prices up even more, thereby fuelling further speculation that they would go on rising and encouraging further share buying. In the early 2000s, by contrast, confidence was shaken. Most countries experienced a slowing down in economic growth, or even a recession (as fall in national output). This combined with other negative factors, such as the 11 September 2001 attack on the World Trade Center and various corporate scandals, such as the accounting fraud concerning the giant US company Enron, caused share prices to plummet. As people anticipated further price falls, so they held back from buying, thereby pushing prices even lower.

Supply

The factors affecting supply are largely the same as those affecting demand, but in the opposite direction.

If the return on alternative forms of saving falls, people with shares are likely to hold on to them, as they represent a better form of saving. The supply of shares to the market will fall. If incomes or wealth rises, people again are likely to want to hold on to their shares. As far as expectations are concerned, if people believe that share prices will rise, they will hold on to the shares they have. Supply to the market will fall, thereby pushing up prices. If, however, they believe that prices will fall, they will sell their shares now before prices do fall. Supply will increase, driving down the price.

Share prices and business

Companies are crucially affected by their share price. If a company's share price falls, this is taken as a sign that 'the market' is losing confidence in the company. This will make it more difficult to raise finance, not only by issuing additional shares in the primary market, but also from banks. It will also make the company more vulnerable to a takeover bid. This is where one company seeks to buy out another by offering to buy all its shares. A takeover will succeed if the owners of more than half of the company's shares vote to accept the offered price. Shareholders are more likely to agree to the takeover if the company's shares have not being doing very well recently.

Question

If the rate of economic growth in the economy is 3 per cent in a particular year, why are share prices likely to rise by more than 3 per cent that year?

Recap

- If the demand for a good exceeds the supply, there will be a shortage. This will result in a rise in the price of the good.

- If the supply of a good exceeds the demand, there will be a surplus. This will result in a fall in the price.

- Price will settle at the equilibrium. The equilibrium price is the one that clears the market: the price where demand equals supply. This is shown in a demand and supply diagram by the point where the two curves intersect.

- If the demand or supply curves shift, this will lead either to a shortage or to a surplus. Price will therefore either rise or fall until a new equilibrium is reached at the position where the supply and demand curves *now* intersect.

2.5 Elasticity of demand and supply

Price elasticity of demand

When the price of a good rises, the quantity demanded will fall. That much is fairly obvious. But in most cases we will want to know more than this. We will want to know just *how much* the quantity demanded will fall. In other words, we will want to know how *responsive* demand is to a rise in price.

Take the case of two products: oil and cauliflowers. In the case of oil, a rise in price is likely to result in only a slight fall in the quantity demanded. If people want to continue driving, they have to pay the higher prices for fuel. A few may turn to riding bicycles, and some people may try to make fewer journeys, but for most people, a rise in the price of petrol and diesel will make little difference to how much they use their cars.

In the case of cauliflowers, however, a rise in price may lead to a substantial fall in the quantity demanded. The reason is that there are alternative vegetables that people can buy. Many people, when buying vegetables, are very conscious of their prices and will buy whatever is reasonably priced.

We call the responsiveness of demand to a change in price the **price elasticity of demand**. If we know the price elasticity of demand for a product, we can predict the effect on price and quantity of a shift in the *supply* curve for that product.

Definition

Price elasticity of demand
A measure of the responsiveness of quantity demanded to a change in price.

> **Elasticity.**
> The responsiveness of one variable (e.g. demand) to a change in another (e.g. price). This concept is fundamental to understanding how markets work. The more elastic variables are, the more responsive is the market to changing circumstances.
>
> Key Idea 9

Figure 2.6 shows the effect of a shift in supply with two quite different demand curves (D and D′). Curve D′ is more elastic than curve D over any given price range. In other words, for any given change in price, there will be a larger change in quantity demanded along curve D′ than along curve D.

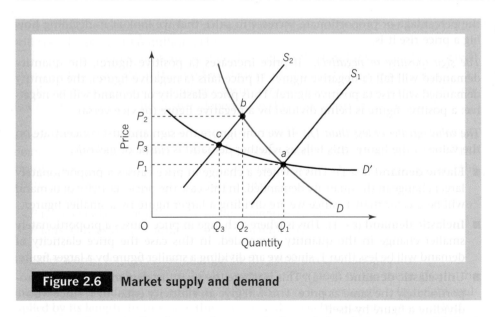

Figure 2.6 **Market supply and demand**

Assume that initially the supply curve is S_1, and that it intersects with both demand curves at point a, at a price of P_1 and a quantity of Q_1. Now supply shifts to S_2. What will happen to price and quantity? In the case of the less elastic demand curve D, there is a relatively large rise in price (to P_2) and a relatively small fall in quantity (to Q_2): equilibrium is at point b. In the case of the more elastic demand curve D', however, there is only a relatively small rise in price (to P_3) but a relatively large fall in quantity (to Q_3): equilibrium is at point c.

Defining price elasticity of demand

What we want to compare is the size of the change in quantity demanded of a given product with the size of the change in price. Price elasticity of demand does just this. It is defined as follows:

$$P\varepsilon_D = \frac{\text{Proportionate (or percentage) change in quantity demanded}}{\text{Proportionate (or percentage) change in price}}$$

If, for example, a 20 per cent rise in the price of a product causes a 10 per cent fall in the quantity demanded, the price elasticity of demand will be:

$$-10\%/20\% = -0.5$$

Three things should be noted about the figure that is calculated for elasticity.

The use of proportionate or percentage measures. Elasticity is measured in proportionate or percentage terms because this allows comparison of changes in two qualitatively different things, which are thus measured in two different types of unit: i.e. it allows comparison of quantity changes (quantity demanded) with monetary changes (price).

It is also the only sensible way of deciding *how big* a change in price or quantity is. Take a simple example. An item goes up in price by £1. Is this a big increase or a small increase? We can answer this only if we know what the original price was. If a can of beans goes up in price by £1, that is a huge price increase. If, however, the price of a house goes up by £1, that is a tiny price increase. In other words, it is

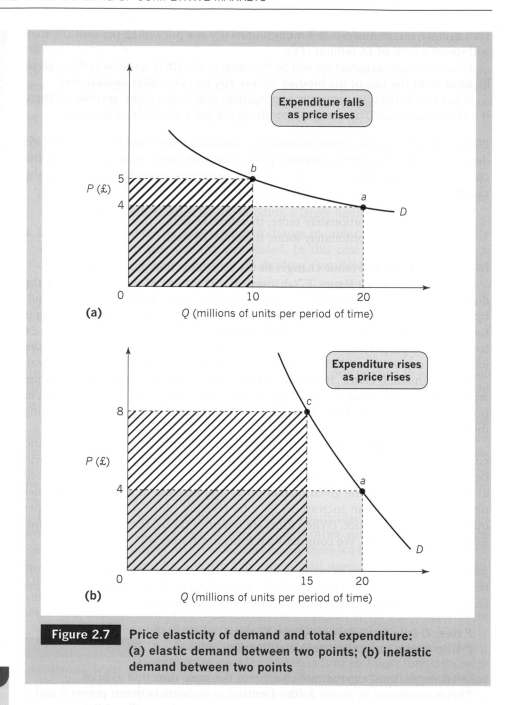

Figure 2.7 Price elasticity of demand and total expenditure: (a) elastic demand between two points; (b) inelastic demand between two points

Definition

Income elasticity of demand

The responsiveness of demand to a change in consumer incomes: the proportionate change in demand divided by the proportionate change in income.

Other elasticities

Firms are interested to know the responsiveness of demand not just to a change in price: they will also want to know the responsiveness of demand to changes in other determinants, such as consumers' incomes and the prices of substitute or complementary goods to theirs. They will want to know the **income elasticity of demand** – the responsiveness of demand to a change in consumers' incomes (Y);

Box 2.2

Shall we put up our price?

Competition, price and revenue

When you buy a can of drink on a train, or an ice-cream in the cinema, or a bottle of wine in a restaurant, you may well be horrified by its price. How can they get away with it?

The answer is that these firms are *not* price takers. They can choose what price to charge. We will be examining the behaviour of such firms in Chapter 4, but here it is useful to see how price elasticity of demand can help to explain their behaviour.

Take the case of the can of drink on the train. If you are thirsty, and if you haven't brought a drink with you, then you will have to get one from the train's bar, or go without. There is no substitute. What we are saying here is that the demand for drink on the train is inelastic at the normal shop price. This means that the train operator can put up the price of its drinks, and food too, and earn *more* revenue.

Generally, the less the competition a firm faces, the lower will be the elasticity of demand for its products, since there will be fewer substitutes (competitors) to which consumers can turn. The lower the price elasticity of demand, the higher is likely to be the price that the firm charges.

When there is plenty of competition, it is quite a different story. Petrol stations in the same area may compete fiercely in terms of price. One station may hope that by reducing its price by 1p or even 0.1p per litre below that of its competitors, it can attract customers away from them. With a highly elastic demand, a small reduction in price may lead to a substantial increase in their revenue. The problem is, of course, that when they *all* reduce prices, no firm wins. No one attracts customers away from the others! In this case it is the customer who wins.

? Questions

1. Why might a restaurant charge very high prices for wine and bottled water and yet quite reasonable prices for food?
2. Why are clothes with designer labels so much more expensive than similar 'own brand' clothes from a chain store, even though they may cost a similar amount to produce?

and the **cross-price elasticity of demand** – the responsiveness of demand for their good to a change in the price of another (whether a substitute or a complement).

Income elasticity of demand ($Y\varepsilon_D$)

We define the income elasticity of demand for a good as follows:

$$Y\varepsilon_D = \frac{\text{Proportionate (or percentage) change in quantity demanded}}{\text{Proportionate (or percentage) change in income}}$$

For example, if a 2 per cent rise in consumer incomes causes an 8 per cent rise in a product's demand, then its income elasticity of demand will be:

$$8\%/2\% = 4$$

Note that in the case of a normal good, the figure for income elasticity will be positive: a *rise* in income leads to a *rise* in demand (a positive figure divided by a positive figure gives a positive answer).

The major determinant of income elasticity of demand is the degree of 'necessity' of the good. Typically, the demand for luxury goods expands rapidly as people's incomes rise, whereas the demand for more basic goods, such as bread, rises only a little. Thus items such as cars and foreign holidays have a high income elasticity of demand, whereas items such as potatoes and bus journeys have a low income elasticity of demand.

Definition

Cross-price elasticity of demand
The responsiveness of demand for one good to a change in the price of another: the proportionate change in demand for one good divided by the proportionate change in price of the other.

- Short run. If a slightly longer time period is allowed to elapse, some inputs can be increased (e.g. raw materials), while others will remain fixed (e.g. heavy machinery). Supply can increase somewhat.

- Long run. In the long run, there will be sufficient time for all inputs to be increased and for new firms to enter the industry. Supply, therefore, is likely to be highly elastic. In some circumstances the supply curve may even slope downward. (See the section on economies of scale in Chapter 4.)

Box 2.3

Speculation

Taking a gamble on the future

In a world of shifting demand and supply curves, prices do not stay the same. Sometimes they go up; sometimes they come down.

If prices are likely to change in the foreseeable future, this will affect the behaviour of buyers and sellers *now*. If, for example, it is now December and you are thinking of buying a new winter coat, you might decide to wait until the January sales, and in the meantime make do with your old coat. If, on the other hand, when January comes you see a new summer dress in the sales, you might well buy it now and not wait until the summer for fear that the price will have gone up by then. Thus a belief that prices will go up will cause people to buy now; a belief that prices will come down will cause them to wait.

The reverse applies to sellers. If you are thinking of selling your house and prices are falling, you will want to sell it as quickly as possible. If, on the other hand, prices are rising sharply, you will wait as long as possible so as to get the highest price. Thus a belief that prices will come down will cause people to sell now; a belief that prices will go up will cause them to wait.

This behaviour of looking into the future and making buying and selling decisions based on your predictions is called **speculation**. Speculation is often based on current trends in price behaviour. If prices are currently rising, people may try

to decide whether they are about to peak and go back down again, or whether they are likely to go on rising. Having made their prediction, they will then act on it. This speculation will thus affect demand and supply, which in turn will affect price. Speculation is commonplace in many markets: the stock exchange (see Box 2.1), the foreign exchange market and the housing market are three examples. Large firms often employ specialist buyers who choose the right time to buy inputs, depending on what they anticipate will happen to their price.

Speculation tends to be **self-fulfilling**. In other words, the actions of speculators tend to bring about the very effect on prices that speculators had anticipated. For example, if speculators believe that the price of BP shares is about to rise, they will buy more of them. The demand curve for BP shares shifts to the right. Those owning BP shares and thinking of selling will wait until the price has risen. In the meantime, the supply curve shifts to the left. The result of these two shifts is that the share price rises. In other words, the prophecy has become self-fulfilling.

 Question
Under what circumstances are people engaging in speculation likely to (a) gain, (b) lose from doing so?

Definition

Speculation
This is where people make buying or selling decisions based on their anticipations of future prices.

Self-fulfilling speculation
The actions of speculators tend to cause the very effect that they had anticipated.

Recap

■ Price elasticity of demand measures the responsiveness of the quantity demanded to a change in price. It is defined as the proportionate (or percentage) change in quantity demanded divided by the proportionate (or percentage) change in price.

■ Given that demand curves are downward sloping, price elasticity of demand will have a negative value.

■ If quantity demanded changes proportionately more than price, the figure for elasticity will be greater than 1 (ignoring the sign): it is elastic. If the quantity demanded changes proportionately less than price, the figure for elasticity will be less than 1: it is inelastic. If they change by the same proportion, the elasticity has a value of 1: it is unit elastic.

■ Demand will be more elastic the greater the number and closeness of substitute goods and the longer the time period that elapses after the change in price.

■ When the demand for a firm's product is price elastic, a rise in price will lead to a reduction in consumer expenditure on the good and hence to a reduction in the total revenue of producers.

■ When demand is price inelastic, however, a rise in price will lead to an increase in total expenditure and revenue.

■ Income elasticity of demand measures the responsiveness of demand to a change in income. For normal goods it has a positive value. Demand will be more income elastic the more luxurious the good.

■ Cross-price elasticity of demand measures the responsiveness of demand for one good to a change in the price of another. For substitute goods the value will be positive; for complements it will be negative. The cross-price elasticity will be greater the closer the two goods are as substitutes or complements.

■ Price elasticity of supply measures the responsiveness of supply to a change in price. It has a positive value. Supply will be more elastic the less costs per unit rise as output rises and the longer the time period.

QUESTIONS

1. Referring to Table 2.1, assume that there are 200 consumers in the market. Of these, 100 have schedules like Tracey's and 100 have schedules like Darren's. What would be the total market demand schedule for potatoes now?

2. Refer to the list of determinants of demand (see pages 35–6). For what reasons might the demand for butter fall?

3. Refer to the list of determinants of supply (see pages 38–40). For what reasons might (a) the supply of potatoes fall; (b) the supply of leather rise?

4. This question is concerned with the supply of oil for central heating. In each case consider whether there is a movement along the supply curve (and in which

direction) or a shift in it (and whether left or right): (a) new oil fields start up in production; (b) the demand for central heating rises; (c) the price of gas falls; (d) oil companies anticipate an upsurge in the demand for central-heating oil; (e) the demand for petrol rises; (f) new technology decreases the costs of oil refining; (g) all oil products become more expensive.

5. The price of cod is much higher today than it was 20 years ago. Using demand and supply diagrams, explain why this should be so.

6. What will happen to the equilibrium price and quantity of butter in each of the following cases? You should state whether demand or supply or both have shifted and in which direction: (a) a rise in the price of margarine; (b) a rise in the demand for yoghurt; (c) a rise in the price of bread; (d) a rise in the demand for bread; (e) an expected increase in the price of butter in the near future; (f) a tax on butter production; (g) the invention of a new, but expensive, process of removing all cholesterol from butter, plus the passing of a law which states that butter producers must use this process. In each case assume that other things remain the same.

7. Why does price elasticity of demand have a negative value, whereas price elasticity of supply has a positive value?

8. Rank the following in ascending order of elasticity: jeans, black Levi jeans, black jeans, black Levi 501 jeans, trousers, outer garments, clothes.

9. Will a general item of expenditure like food or clothing have a price elastic or inelastic demand? Explain.

10. Explain which of these two pairs are likely to have the highest cross-price elasticity of demand: two brands of coffee, or coffee and tea?

11. Why are both the price elasticity of demand and the price elasticity of supply likely to be greater in the long run?

Business issues covered in this chapter

■ What determines the amount of a product that consumers wish to buy at each price?

■ Why are purchasing decisions sometimes risky for consumers and how can insurance help to reduce or remove the level of risk?

■ How do businesses set about gathering information on consumer attitudes and behaviour, and what methods can they use to forecast the demand for their products?

■ In what ways can firms differentiate their products from those of their rivals?

■ What strategies can firms adopt for gaining market share, developing their products and marketing them?

■ What are the effects of advertising and what makes a successful advertising campaign?

CHAPTER 3

Demand and the consumer

If a business is to be successful, it must be able to predict the strength of demand for its products and be able to respond to any changes in consumer tastes. It will also want to know how its customers are likely to react to changes in its price or its competitors' prices, or to changes in income. In other words, it will want to know the price, cross-price and income elasticities of demand for its product. The better the firm's knowledge of its market, the better will it be able to plan its output to meet demand, and the more able will it be to choose its optimum price, product design, marketing campaigns, etc.

3.1 Demand and the firm

In Chapter 2 we examined how prices are determined in perfectly competitive markets: by the interaction of market demand and market supply. In such markets, although the *market* demand curve is downward sloping, the demand curve faced by the individual firm will be horizontal. This is illustrated in Figure 3.1.

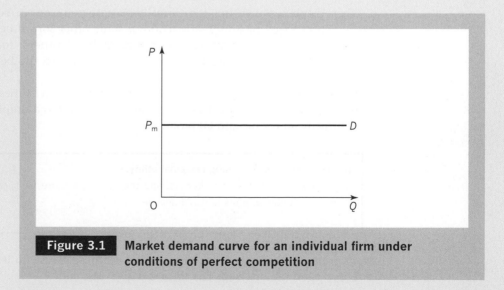

Figure 3.1 **Market demand curve for an individual firm under conditions of perfect competition**

The market price is P_m. The individual firm can sell as much as it likes at this market price: it is too small to have any influence on the market – it is a price taker. It will not force the price down by producing more because, in terms of the total market, this extra would be an infinitesimally small amount. If a farmer doubled the output of wheat sent to the market, it would be too small an increase to affect the world price of wheat!

In practice, however, most firms are not price takers; they have some discretion in choosing their price. Such firms face a downward-sloping demand curve. If they raise their price, they will sell less; if they lower their price, they will sell more. But firms will want to know more than this. They will want to know just *how much* the quantity demanded will change. In other words, they will want to know the price elasticity of demand for their product.

In general, the less price elastic the demand, the better it will be for firms, because this will give them more power over prices. In fact, where the price elasticity of demand for the firm's product is less than one, a rise in price will lead to an *increase* in the firm's revenue (see Figure 2.7(b) on page 50) despite the fall in sales.

It is clearly in firms' interests to try to make the demand for their product less elastic. Firms will generally try to do this by attempting to discriminate their product from those of their rivals. If they can produce a product that consumers feel does not have a close substitute, then demand will be relatively inelastic. Success here will depend partly on designing and producing a product that is clearly different, and partly on achieving an effective marketing and advertising programme.

3.2 Understanding consumer behaviour

In this section we examine the nature of consumer behaviour and in particular relate consumer demand to the amount of satisfaction that consumers get from products.

Marginal utility

When you buy something, it's normally because you want it. You want it because you expect to get pleasure, satisfaction or some other sort of benefit from it. This applies to everything from chocolate bars, to bus journeys, to CDs, to jeans, to insurance. Economists use the term 'utility' to refer to the benefit we get from consumption.

Clearly, the nature and amount of utility that people get varies from one product to another, and from one person to another. But there is a simple rule that applies to virtually all people and all products:

The principle of diminishing marginal utility.

As you consume more of a product, and thus become more satisfied, so your desire for additional units of it will decline.

Key Idea 10

For example, the second cup of tea in the morning gives you less additional satisfaction than the first cup. The third cup gives less still.

We call the additional utility you get from consuming an extra unit of a product the **marginal utility** (*MU*). So what the rule is stating is that the marginal utility will fall as we consume more of a product over a given period of time.

There is a problem, however, with the concept of marginal utility. How can it be measured? After all, we cannot get inside each other's heads to find out just how much pleasure we are getting from consuming a product!

One way round the problem is to measure marginal utility in money terms: i.e. the amount that a person would be prepared to pay for one more unit of a product. Thus if you were prepared to pay 30p for an extra packet of crisps per week, then we would say that your marginal utility from consuming it is 30p. As long as you are prepared to pay more or the same as the actual price, you will buy an extra packet. If you are not prepared to pay that price, you will not.

Pause for thought

Are there any goods or services where consumers do not experience diminishing marginal utility? If so, give some examples. If not, then explain why.

Definition

Marginal utility (*MU*)
The extra satisfaction gained from consuming one extra unit of a good within a given time period.

Marginal utility and the demand curve for a good

We can now see how marginal utility relates to a downward sloping demand curve. As the price of a good falls, it will be worth buying extra units. You will buy more because the price will now be below the amount you are prepared to pay: i.e. price is less than your marginal utility. But as you buy more, your marginal utility from consuming each extra unit will get less and less. How many extra units do you buy? You will stop when the marginal utility has fallen to the new lower price of the good: when $MU = P$.

An individual's demand curve

Individual people's demand curves for any good will be the same as their marginal utility curve for that good, measured in money.

This is demonstrated in Figure 3.2 (overleaf), which shows the marginal utility curve for a particular person and a particular good. If the price of the good were P_1, the person would consume Q_1: where $MU = P$. Thus point *a* would be one point on that person's demand curve. If the price fell to P_2, consumption would rise to Q_2, since this is where $MU = P_2$. Thus point *b* is a second point on the demand curve. Likewise if price fell to P_3, Q_3 would be consumed. Point *c* is a third point on the demand curve.

Thus as long as individuals consume where $P = MU$, their demand curve will be along the same line as their marginal utility curve.

The firm's demand curve

The firm's demand curve will simply be the (horizontal) sum of all individuals' demand curves for the product.

The shape of the demand curve. The price elasticity of demand will reflect the rate at which *MU* diminishes. If there are close substitutes for a good, it is likely to have an elastic demand, and its *MU* will diminish slowly as consumption increases. The reason is that increased consumption of this product will be accompanied by *decreased* consumption of the alternative product(s). Since total consumption of this product *plus* the alternatives has increased only slightly (if at all), the marginal utility will fall only slowly.

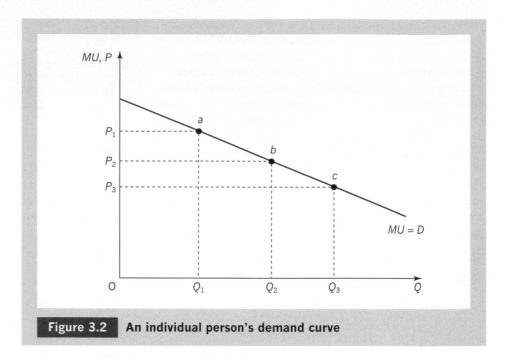

Figure 3.2   **An individual person's demand curve**

For example, the demand for a given brand of petrol is likely to have a fairly high price elasticity, since other brands are substitutes. If there is a cut in the price of Esso petrol (assuming the prices of other brands stay constant), consumption of Esso will increase a lot. The *MU* of Esso petrol will fall slowly, since people consume less of other brands. Petrol consumption *in total* may be only slightly greater and hence the *MU* of petrol only slightly lower.

Shifts in the demand curve.   How do *shifts* in demand relate to marginal utility? For example, how would the marginal utility of (and hence demand for) margarine be affected by a rise in the price of butter? The higher price of butter would cause less butter to be consumed. This would increase the marginal utility of margarine, since if people are using less butter, their desire for margarine is higher. The *MU* curve (and hence the demand curve) for margarine thus shifts to the right.

The problem of imperfect information

So far we have assumed that when people buy goods and services, they know exactly what price they will pay and how much utility they will gain. In many cases this is a reasonable assumption. When you buy a bar of chocolate, you clearly do know how much you are paying for it and have a very good idea how much you will like it. But what about a video recorder, or a car, or a washing machine, or any other **consumer durable**? In each of these cases you are buying something that will last you a long time, and the further into the future you look, the less certain you will be of its costs and benefits to you.

Take the case of a washing machine costing you £400. If you pay cash, your immediate outlay involves no uncertainty: it is £400. But washing machines can break down. In two years' time you could find yourself with a repair bill of £100.

Definition

Consumer durable
A consumer good that lasts a period of time, during which the consumer can continue gaining utility from it.

This cannot be predicted and yet it is a price you will have to pay, just like the original £400. In other words, when you buy the washing machine, you are uncertain as to the full 'price' it will entail over its lifetime.

If the costs of the washing machine are uncertain, so too are the benefits. You might have been attracted to buy it in the first place by the manufacturer's glossy brochure, or by the look of it, or by adverts on TV, in magazines, etc. When you have used it for a while, however, you will probably discover things you had not anticipated. The spin dryer does not get your clothes as dry as you had hoped; it is noisy; it leaks; the door sticks; and so on.

Buying consumer durables thus involves uncertainty. So too does the purchase of assets, whether a physical asset such as a house or financial assets such as shares. In the case of assets, the uncertainty is over their future *price*. If you buy shares in a recently privatised industry, what will happen to their price? Will they shoot up in price, thus enabling you to sell them at a large profit, or will they fall? You cannot know for certain.

At this point it is useful to distinguish between uncertainty and risk. **Risk** is where an outcome may or may not occur, but where the *probability* of its occurring is known. **Uncertainty** is where the probability is not known.

Insurance: a way of removing risks

Insurance is a means of eliminating, or at least reducing, uncertainty for people. If, for example, you could lose your job if you are injured, you can remove the risk of loss of income by taking out an appropriate insurance policy.

But why is it that the insurance companies are prepared to shoulder the risks that their customers were not? The answer is that the insurance company is able to **spread its risks**.

The spreading of risks

If there is a one in a thousand chance of your house burning down each year, although it is only a small chance it would be so disastrous that you are simply not prepared to take the risk. You thus take out house insurance and are prepared to pay a premium of *more than* 0.1 per cent (one in a thousand).

The insurance company, however, is not just insuring you. It is insuring many others at the same time. If your house burns down, there will be approximately 999 others that do not. The premiums the insurance company has collected will be more than enough to cover its payments. The more houses it insures, the smaller will be the variation in the proportion that actually burn down each year.

This is an application of the **law of large numbers**. What is unpredictable for an individual becomes highly predictable in the mass. The more people the insurance company insures, the more predictable is the total outcome.

What is more, the insurance company will be in a position to estimate just what the risks are. It can thus work out what premiums it must charge in order to make a profit. With individuals, however, the precise risk is rarely known. Do you know your chances of living to 70? Almost certainly you do not. But a life assurance company will know precisely the chances of a person of your age, sex and occupation living to 70! It will have the statistical data to show this. In other words, an insurance company will be able to convert your *uncertainty* into their *risk*.

Definition

Risk
This is when an outcome may or may not occur, but where the probability of its occurring is known.

Uncertainty
This is when an outcome may or may not occur and where its probability of occurring is not known.

Spreading risks (for an insurance company)
The more policies an insurance company issues and the more independent the risks of claims from these policies are, the more predictable will be the number of claims.

Law of large numbers
The larger the number of events of a particular type, the more predictable will be their average outcome.

Definition

Independent risks
Where two risky events are unconnected. The occurrence of one will not affect the likelihood of the occurrence of the other.

Diversification
Where a firm expands into new types of business.

The spreading of risks does not just require that there should be a large number of policies. It also requires that the risks should be **independent**. If any insurance company insured 1000 houses *all in the same neighbourhood*, and then there was a major fire in the area, the claims would be enormous. The risks of fire were not independent. The company would, in fact, have been taking a gamble on a single event. If, however, it provides fire insurance for houses scattered all over the country, the risks *are* independent.

Another way in which insurance companies can spread their risks is by **diversification**. The more types of insurance a company offers (car, house, life, health, etc.), the greater is likely to be the independence of the risks.

Box 3.1

Problems for unwary insurance companies

'Adverse selection' and 'moral hazard'

Adverse selection

This is where the people taking out insurance are those who have the highest risk.

For example, suppose that a company offers medical insurance. It surveys the population and works out that the average person requires £200 of treatment per year. The company thus sets the premium at £250 (the extra £50 to cover its costs and provide a profit). But it is likely that the people most likely to take out the insurance are those most likely to fall sick: those who have been ill before, those whose families have a history of illness, those in jobs that are hazardous to health, etc. These people on average may require £500 of treatment per year. The insurance company would soon make a loss.

But cannot the company then simply raise premiums to £550 or £600? It can, but the problem is that it will thereby be depriving the person of *average* health of reasonably priced insurance.

The answer is for the company to discriminate more carefully between people. You may have to fill out a questionnaire so that the company can assess your own particular risk and set an appropriate premium. There may need to be legal penalties for people caught lying!

? Question
What details does an insurance company require to know before it will insure a person to drive a car?

Moral hazard

This is where having insurance makes you less careful and thus increases your risk to the company. For example, if your bicycle is insured against theft, you may be less concerned to go through the hassle of chaining it up each time you leave it.

Again, if insurance companies work out risks by looking at the *total* number of bicycle thefts, these figures will understate the risks to the company because they will include thefts from *uninsured* people who are likely to be more careful.

? Question
How will the following reduce moral hazard?
(a) A no-claims bonus.
(b) Your having to pay the first so much of any claim.
(c) Offering lower premiums to those less likely to claim (e.g. lower house contents premiums for those with burglar alarms).

The problem of moral hazard occurs in many other walks of life. A good example is that of debt. If someone else is willing to pay your debts (e.g. your parents) it is likely to make you less careful in your spending! This argument has been used by some rich countries for not cancelling the debts of poor countries.

Recap

- Economists call consumer satisfaction 'utility'. Marginal utility diminishes as consumption increases.

- People will consume more of a good as long as its marginal utility to them (measured in terms of the price they are prepared to pay for it) exceeds its price. They will stop buying additional amounts once *MU* has fallen to equal the price.

- An individual's demand curve lies along the same line as the individual's marginal utility curve. The market demand curve is the sum of all individuals' marginal utility curves.

- When people buy consumer durables they may be uncertain of their benefits and any additional repair and maintenance costs. When they buy financial assets they may be uncertain of what will happen to their price in the future. Buying under these conditions of imperfect knowledge is therefore a form of gambling. When we take such gambles, if we know the odds we are said to be operating under conditions of *risk*. If we do not know the odds we are said to be operating under conditions of *uncertainty*.

- Insurance is a way of eliminating risks for policy holders. In order to avoid risks, people are prepared to pay premiums in order to obtain insurance. Insurance companies, on the other hand, are prepared to take on these risks because they can spread them over a large number of policies. According to the law of large numbers, what is unpredictable for a single policy holder becomes highly predictable for a large number of them provided that their risks are independent of each other.

Estimating and predicting demand   3.3

How might a business set about discovering the wants of consumers and hence the intensity of demand? The more effectively a business can identify such wants, the more likely it is to increase its sales and be successful. The clearer idea it can gain of the rate at which the typical consumer's utility will decline as consumption increases, the better estimate it can make of the product's price elasticity. Also the more it can assess the relative utility to the consumer of its product compared with those of its rivals, the more effectively will it be able to compete by differentiating its product from theirs.

In this section we first examine methods for gathering data on consumer behaviour and then see how firms set about forecasting changes in demand over time.

Methods of collecting data on consumer behaviour

There are three general approaches to gathering information about consumers. These are: **observations of market behaviour**, **market surveys** and **market experiments**.

Market observations

The firm can gather data on how demand for its product has changed over time. Virtually all firms will have detailed information on their sales broken down by week, and/or month, and/or year. They will probably also have information on how sales have varied from one part of the market to another.

In addition, the firm will need to obtain data on how the various determinants of demand (such as price, advertising and the price of competitors' products) have

Definition

Observations of market behaviour
Information gathered about consumers from the day-to-day activities of the business within the market.

Market surveys
Information gathered about consumers, usually via a questionnaire, that attempts to enhance the business's understanding of consumer behaviour.

Market experiments
Information gathered about consumers under artificial or simulated conditions. A method used widely in assessing the effects of advertising on consumers.

themselves changed over time. Firms are likely to have much of this information already: e.g. the amount spent on advertising and the prices of competitors' products. Other information might be relatively easy to obtain by paying an agency to do the research.

Having obtained this information, the firm can then use it to estimate how changes in the various determinants have affected demand in the past, and hence what effect they will be likely to have in the future.

Even the most sophisticated analysis based on market observations, however, will suffer from one major drawback. Relationships that held in the past will not necessarily hold in the future. Consumers are human, and humans change their minds. Their perceptions of products change (something that the advertising industry relies on!) and tastes change. It is for this reason that many firms turn to market surveys or market experiments to gain more information about the future.

Market surveys

It is not uncommon to be stopped in a city centre, or to have a knock at the door, and be asked whether you would kindly answer the questions of some market researcher. If the research interviewer misses you, then a postal questionnaire may well seek out the same type of information. A vast quantity of information can be collected in this way. It is a relatively quick and cheap method of data collection. Questions concerning all aspects of consumer behaviour might be asked, such as those relating to present and future patterns of expenditure, or how people might respond to changing product specifications or price, both of the firm in question and of its rivals.

A key feature of the market survey is that it can be targeted at distinct consumer groups, thereby reflecting the specific information requirements of a business. For example, businesses selling luxury goods will be interested only in consumers falling within higher income brackets. Other samples might be drawn from a particular age group or gender, or from those with a particular lifestyle, such as eating habits.

The major drawback with this technique concerns the accuracy of the information acquired. Accurate information requires various conditions to be met.

A random sample. If the sample is not randomly selected, it may fail to represent a cross-section of the population being surveyed.

Clarity of the questions. It is important for the questions to be phrased in an unambiguous way, so as not to mislead the respondent.

Avoidance of leading questions. It is very easy for the respondent to be led into giving the answer the firm wants to hear. For example, when asking whether the person would buy a new product that the firm is thinking of launching, the questionnaire might make the product sound really desirable. The respondents might, as a result, say that they would buy the product, but later, when they see the product in the shops, decide they do not want it.

Truthful response. It is very tempting for respondents who are 'keen to please' to give the answer that they think the questioner wants, or for other somewhat reluctant respondents to give 'mischievous' answers. In other words, people may lie!

Stability of demand. By the time the product is launched, or the changes to an existing product are made, time will have elapsed. The information may then be out of date. Consumer demand may have changed, as tastes and fashions have shifted, or as a result of the actions of competitors.

Market experiments

Rather than asking consumers questions and getting them to *imagine* how they *would* behave, the market experiment involves observing consumer *behaviour* under simulated conditions. It can be used to observe consumer reactions to a new product or to changes in an existing product.

A simple experiment might involve consumers being asked to conduct a blind taste test for a new brand of toothpaste. The experimenter will ensure that the same amount of paste is applied to the brush, and that the subjects swill their mouths prior to tasting a further brand. Once the experiment is over, the 'consumers' are quizzed about their perceptions of the product.

More sophisticated experiments could be conducted. For example, a *laboratory shop* might be set up to simulate a real shopping experience. People could be given a certain amount of money to spend in the 'shop' and their reactions to changes in prices, packaging, display, etc. could be monitored.

The major drawback with such 'laboratories' is that consumers might behave differently because they are being observed. For example, they might spend more time comparing prices than they would otherwise, simply because they think that this is what a *good*, rational consumer should do. With real shopping, however, it might simply be habit, or something 'irrational' such as the colour of the packaging, that determines which product they select.

> **Pause for thought**
>
> *Identify some other drawbacks in using market experiments to gather data on consumer behaviour.*

Another type of market experiment involves confining a marketing campaign to a particular town or region. The campaign could involve advertising, or giving out free samples, or discounting the price, or introducing an improved version of the product, but each confined to that particular locality. Sales in that area are then compared with sales in other areas in order to assess the effectiveness of the various campaigns.

Forecasting demand

Businesses are interested not just in knowing the current strength of demand for their products and how demand is likely to be affected by changes in factors such as product specifications and the price of competitors' products. They are also interested in trying to predict *future* demand. After all, if demand is going to increase, they may well want to invest *now* so that they have the extra capacity to meet the extra demand. But it will be a costly mistake to invest in extra capacity if demand is not going to increase.

We now, therefore, turn to examine some of the forecasting techniques used by business.

Simple time-series analysis

Simple time-series analysis involves directly projecting from past sales data into the future. Thus if it is observed that sales of a firm's product have been growing steadily by 3 per cent per annum for the past few years, the firm can use this to predict that sales will continue to grow at approximately the same rate in the future. Similarly, if it is observed that there are clear seasonal fluctuations in demand, as in the case of the demand for holidays, ice cream or winter coats, then again it can be assumed that fluctuations of a similar magnitude will continue into the future.

Using simple time-series analysis assumes that demand in the future will continue to behave in the same way as in the past. The problem is that it may not. Just because demand has followed a clear pattern in the past, it does not inexorably follow that it will continue to exhibit the same pattern in the future. After all, the determinants of demand may well have changed. Successful forecasting, therefore, will usually involve a more sophisticated analysis of trends.

The decomposition of time paths

One way in which the analysis of past data can be made more sophisticated is to identify different elements in the time path of sales. Figure 3.3 illustrates one such time path: the (imaginary) sales of woollen jumpers by firm X. It is shown by the continuous green line, labelled 'Actual sales'.

Four different sets of factors normally determine the shape of a time path like this.

Trends. These are increases or decreases in demand over a number of years. In our example, there is a long-term decrease in demand for this firm's woollen jumpers up to year 7 and then a recovery in demand thereafter.

Trends may reflect factors such as changes in population structure, or technological innovation or longer-term changes in fashion. Thus if wool were to become more expensive over time compared with other fibres, or if there were a gradual shift in tastes away from woollen jumpers and towards acrylic or cotton jumpers, or towards sweatshirts, this could explain the long-term decline in demand for the first few years. A gradual shift in tastes back towards natural fibres, and to wool in particular, or a gradual reduction in the price of wool, could then explain the subsequent recovery in demand.

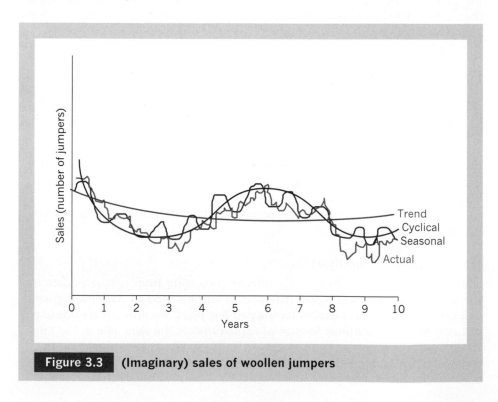

Figure 3.3 (Imaginary) sales of woollen jumpers

Alternatively, trends may reflect changes over time in the structure of an industry. For example, an industry might become more and more competitive, with new firms joining. This would tend to reduce sales for existing firms (unless the market were expanding very rapidly).

Cyclical fluctuations.   In practice, the level of actual sales will not follow the trend line precisely. One reason for this is the cyclical upswings and downswings in business activity in the economy as a whole. In some years incomes are rising rapidly and thus demand is buoyant. In other years, the economy will be in recession, with incomes falling. In these years, demand may well also fall. In our example, in boom years people may spend much more on clothes (including woollen jumpers), whereas in a recession, people may make do with their old clothes. The cyclical variations line is thus above the trend line in boom years and below the trend line during a recession.

Seasonal fluctuations.   The demand for many products also depends on the time of year. In the case of woollen jumpers, the peak demand is likely to be as winter approaches or just before Christmas. Thus the seasonal variations line is above the cyclical variations line in winter and below it in summer.

Short-term shifts in demand or supply.   Finally, the actual sales line will also reflect various short-term shifts in demand or supply, causing it to diverge from the smooth seasonal variations line.

There are many reasons why the demand curve might shift. A competitor might increase its price, or there may be a sudden change in fashion, caused, say, by a pop group deciding to wear woollen jumpers for their new video: what was once seen as unfashionable by many people now suddenly becomes fashionable! Alternatively, there may be an unusually cold or hot, or wet or dry spell of weather.

Likewise there are various reasons for sudden shifts in supply conditions. For example, there may be a sheep disease which ruins the wool of infected sheep. As a result, the price of wool goes up, and sales of woollen jumpers fall.

These sudden shifts in demand or supply conditions are often referred to as 'random shocks' because they are usually unpredictable and temporarily move sales away from the trend. (Note that *long-term* shifts in demand and supply will be shown by a change in the trend line itself.)

Even with sophisticated time-series analysis, which breaks time paths into their constituent elements, there is still one major weakness: time-series analysis is merely a projection of the *past*. Most businesses will want to anticipate *changes* to sales trends – to forecast any deviations from the current time path. One method for doing this is *barometric forecasting*.

Barometric forecasting

Assume that you are a manager of a furniture business and are wondering whether to invest in new capital equipment. You would only want to do this if the demand for your product was likely to rise. You will probably, therefore, look for some indication of this. A good barometer of future demand for furniture would be the number of new houses being built. People will tend to buy new furniture some months after the building of their new house has commenced.

Definition

Barometric forecasting
A technique used to predict future economic trends based upon analysing patterns of time-series data.

Leading indicators
Indicators that help predict future trends in the economy.

Barometric forecasting involves the use of **leading indicators**, such as housing starts, when attempting to predict the future. In fact some leading indicators, such as increased activity in the construction industry, rises in Stock Exchange prices, a rise in the rate of exchange and a rise in industrial confidence, are good indicators of a general upturn in the economy. In other words, firms use these indicators to predict what is likely to happen to their own demand.

Barometric forecasting suffers from two major weaknesses. The first is that it only allows forecasting a few months ahead – as far ahead as is the time lag between the change in the leading indicator and the variable being forecasted. The second is that it can only give a general indication of changes in demand. It is simply another form of time-series analysis. Just because a relationship existed in the past between a leading indicator and the variable being forecasted, it cannot be assumed that exactly the same relationship will exist in the future.

Recap

- Businesses seek information on consumer behaviour so as to predict market trends and improve strategic decision making.

- One source of data is the firm's own information on how its sales have varied in the past with changes in the various determinants of demand, such as consumer incomes and the prices of competitors' products.

- Another source of data is market surveys. These can generate a large quantity of cheap information. Care should be taken, however, to ensure that the sample of consumers investigated reflects the target consumer group.

- Market experiments involve investigating consumer behaviour within a controlled environment. This method is particularly useful when considering new products where information is scarce.

- It is not enough to know what will happen to demand if a determinant changes. Businesses will want to forecast what will actually happen to demand.

- Time-series analysis bases future trends on past events. Time-series data can be decomposed into different elements: trends, seasonal fluctuations, cyclical fluctuations and random shocks.

- Barometric forecasting involves making predictions based upon changes in key leading indicators.

3.4 Stimulating demand

For most firms, selling their product is not simply a question of estimating demand and then choosing an appropriate price and level of production. In other words, they do not simply take their market as given. Instead they will seek to *increase* demand. They will do this by developing their product and differentiating it from those of their rivals, and then marketing it by advertising and other forms of product promotion.

What firms are engaging in here is **non-price competition**. In such situations the job of the manager can be quite complex, involving strategic decisions about product design and quality, product promotion and the provision of various forms of after-sales service.

Definition

Non-price competition
Competition in terms of product promotion (advertising, packaging, etc.) or product development.

Product differentiation

Central to non-price competition is **product differentiation**. Most firms' products differ in various ways from those of their rivals. Take the case of washing machines. Although all washing machines wash clothes, and as such are close substitutes for each other, there are many differences between brands. They differ not only in price, but also in their capacity, their styling, their range of programmes, their economy in the use of electricity, hot water and detergent, their reliability, their noise, their after-sales service, etc. Firms will attempt to design their product so that they can stress its advantages (real or imaginary) over the competitor brands. Just think of the specific features of particular models of car, hi-fi equipment or brands of cosmetic, and then consider the ways in which these features are stressed by advertisements. In fact, think of virtually any advertisement and consider how it stresses the features of that particular brand.

A product has many dimensions, and a strategy to differentiate a product may focus on one or more of these. Dimensions include:

- *Technical standards*. These relate to the product's level of technical sophistication: how advanced it is in relation to the current state of technology. This would be a very important product dimension if, for example, you were purchasing a PC.

- *Quality standards*. These relate to aspects such as the quality of the materials used in the product's construction and the care taken in assembly. These will affect the product's durability and reliability. The purchase of consumer durables, such as televisions, furniture and toys, will be strongly influenced by quality standards.

- *Design characteristics*. These relate to the product's direct appeal to the consumer in terms of appearance or operating features. Examples of design characteristics are colour, style and even packaging. The demand for fashion products such as clothing will be strongly influenced by design characteristics.

- *Service characteristics*. This aspect is not directly concerned with the product itself, but with the support and back-up given to the customer after the product has been sold. Servicing, product maintenance and guarantees would be included under this heading. When purchasing a new car, the quality of after-sales service might strongly influence the choice you make.

Market segmentation

Different features of a product will appeal to different consumers. Where features are quite distinct, and where particular features or groups of features can be seen to appeal to a particular category of consumers, it might be useful for producers to divide the market into segments. Taking the example of cars again, the market could be divided into luxury cars, large, medium and small family cars, sports cars, multi-terrain vehicles, seven-seater people carriers, etc. Each type of car occupies a distinct market segment.

When consumer tastes change over time, or where existing models do not cater for every taste, a firm may be able to identify a new segment of the market – a **market niche**. Having identified the appropriate market niche for its product, the marketing division within the firm will then set about targeting the relevant consumer group(s) and developing an appropriate strategy for promoting the product.

Definition

Product differentiation
Where a firm's product is in some way distinct from its rivals' products.

Market niche
A part of a market (or new market) that has not been filled by an existing brand or business.

Box 3.2

Brands and own-brands

What's in a name?

The rise of supermarket own-brands since the early 1990s has been phenomenal. Their market penetration in the UK has been so great that, by 1995, 54.5 per cent of all sales in the major supermarket chains were of own-branded products. In 1992, just three years earlier, the figure had been a mere 27 per cent. What makes this rise even more striking is that it followed a period when branded products dominated the market and seemed to be growing in strength. During the 1980s, the profits of companies such as Kellogg's and Heinz were increasing by as much as 15 per cent a year.

As Alan Mitchell argued in *Marketing Week* (6 December 1996), the brand system seemed to be unassailable.

Brand manufacturers commanded economies of scale in both sourcing and production which enabled them to offer superior value to consumers. Mass advertising helped to drive the demand that, in turn, promoted mass production by keeping brands top of consumer awareness. National distribution created mass presence and availability, driving sales and reinforcing brands' share of mind.

And the healthy margins generated by the synergy between mass production, advertising and distribution, allowed manufacturers to invest in research and development and offer genuinely improved products. This in turn, created new reassurance of value for money and extra sales, thereby adding impetus to the virtuous circle.

However, towards the end of the 1980s, things started to go horribly wrong for branded products:

■ The economic boom came to an end, and the UK, along with many other countries, went into recession, with the result that consumers became more price conscious.

■ Supermarkets began to develop a more extensive range of own-label products.

As Alan Mitchell points out:

New technologies [were] allowing own-label manufacturers to produce smaller batch runs at lower costs: so the benefits of economies of scale [declined].

Own-label products also lay claim to cost advantages, both on marketing and distribution – a few dedicated trucks from factory to retailer regional distribution centre are nothing compared with the cost of a fleet serving every retailer, wholesaler, and convenience shop.

This means all the paraphernalia of advertising, distribution, and new product development that made the brand manufacturing model so powerful decades ago is unravelling, and becoming an enormous cost burden instead – a burden that adds up to 50 per cent on to the final consumer price and allows retailers to undercut brands while creaming off higher margins. The virtuous cycle goes into reverse, and becomes a vicious circle.

Marketing the product

Marketing covers the following activities: establishing the strength of consumer demand in existing parts of the market, and potential demand in new niches; developing an attractive and distinct image for the product; informing potential consumers of various features of the product; fostering a desire by consumers for the product; and, in the light of all these, persuading consumers to buy the product.

Product/market strategy

Once the nature and strength of consumer demand (both current and potential) have been identified, the business will set about meeting and influencing this demand. In most cases it will be hoping to achieve a growth in sales. To do this, one of the first things the firm must decide is its *product/market strategy*. This will involve addressing two major questions:

Such were the cost advantages of the own-label alternative that, for many products, the price discrepancy between brands and own-brands had become staggering, forcing brand manufacturers to make substantial price cuts. For example, the dairy producer Kraft was forced to slash prices on many of its cheese products, which in several cases were some 45 per cent more expensive than own-label alternatives.

The position of branded products has been further undermined. Technology has not only pushed down costs, but also raised the *quality* of products, making it easier for own-label producers to copy established brands, and in many cases to innovate themselves. Many own-brand retailers are now looking to move up market and compete with premium branded products.

> Supermarket ranges such as 'Be Good to Yourself' or 'Taste the Difference' are as recognised by consumers as any branded lines. The quality is as good if not better, and with dedicated marketing support from the likes of Jamie Oliver there is strong brand loyalty.[1]

What are brand manufacturers to do? One alternative adopted by many such firms is for themselves to make own-label products for the supermarkets. Such actions might be self-defeating, however, since they have reinforced the change in consumer perceptions of own-brands. Consumer surveys increasingly show that very little difference is perceived between branded products and own-brands. As a result, a product's price becomes far more significant in determining purchase. Established brand manufacturers are thus forced to cut costs in order to maintain profit margins on existing products.

There is another strategy, however, that they can pursue. This is to extend a brand to new products and use the brand image to promote them. Not only will this help raise revenue but it will also reduce the producer's reliance on a single product. Take the case of Virgin. The brand no longer applies just to record stores. It now embraces airlines, trains, finance, soft drinks, mobile phones, holidays, bridal wear, cinemas, radio, virtual car showrooms, online books, an online wine store, an Internet service provider, cosmetics, health clubs, balloon rides and gift 'experiences'. With the launching of Virgin Galactic in 2004 and orders for five 'spaceliners', it now even includes space tourism!

? *Questions*

1. How has the improvement in the quality of own-brands affected the price elasticity of demand for branded products? What implications does this have for the pricing strategy of brand manufacturers?
2. Do the brand manufacturers have any actual or potential cost advantages over own-brand manufacturers?

[1] *Marketing Week*, 17 April 2003

■ Should it focus on promoting its existing product, or should it develop new products?

■ Should it focus on gaining a bigger share of its existing market, or should it seek to break into new markets?

These choices can be shown in a **growth vector matrix**. This is illustrated in Figure 3.4 (overleaf).

The four boxes show the possible combinations of answers to the above questions: Box A – *market penetration* (existing product, existing market); Box B – *product development* (new product, existing market); Box C – *market development* (existing product, new market); Box D – *diversification* (new product, new market).

Market penetration.   In the market penetration strategy, the business will seek not only to retain current customers, but to expand its customer base with existing products in existing markets. Of the four strategies, this is generally the least risky: the business will be able to play to its product strengths and draw on its knowledge

Definition

Growth vector matrix
A means by which a business might assess its product/market strategy.

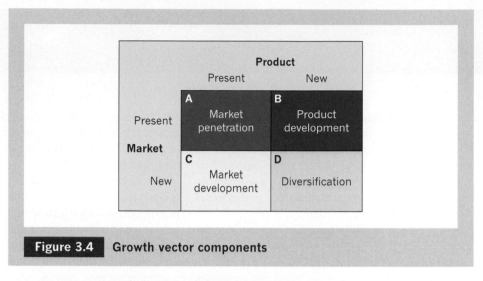

Figure 3.4   **Growth vector components**

of the market. The business's marketing strategy will tend to focus upon aggressive product promotion and distribution. Such a strategy, however, is likely to lead to fierce competition from existing business rivals, especially if the overall market is not expanding and if the firm can therefore gain an increase in sales only by taking market share from its rivals.

Product development.   Product development strategies will involve introducing new models and designs in existing markets.

Market development.   With a market development strategy the business will seek increased sales of current products by expanding into new markets. These may be in a different geographical location (e.g. overseas), or new market segments. Altern- atively, the strategy may involve finding new uses and applications for the product.

Pause for thought

What unknown factors is the business likely to face following a diversification strategy?

Diversification.   A diversification strategy will involve the business expanding into new markets with new products. Of all the strategies, this is the most risky given the unknown factors that the business is likely to face.

Once the product/market strategy has been decided upon, the business will then attempt to devise a suitable *marketing strategy*. This will involve looking at the marketing mix.

The marketing mix

In order to differentiate the firm's product from those of its rivals, there are four variables that can be adjusted. These are as follows:

Definition

Marketing mix
The mix of product, price, place (distribution) and promotion that will determine a business's marketing strategy.

■ product;

■ price;

■ place (distribution);

■ promotion.

The particular combination of these variables, known as 'the four Ps', represents the business's **marketing mix**, and it is around a manipulation of them that the business will devise its marketing strategy.

Product considerations.   These involve issues such as quality and reliability, as well as branding, packaging and after-sales service.

Pricing considerations.   These involve not only the product's basic price in relation to those of competitors' products, but also opportunities for practising price discrimination (the practice of charging different prices in different parts of the market: see section 5.5), offering discounts to particular customers, and adjusting the terms of payment for the product.

Place considerations.   These focus on the product's distribution network, and involve issues such as where the business's retail outlets should be located, what warehouse facilities the business might require, and how the product should be transported to the market.

Promotion considerations.   These focus primarily upon the amount and type of advertising the business should use. In addition, promotion issues might also include selling techniques, special offers, trial discounts and various other public relations 'gimmicks'.

Every product is likely to have a distinct marketing *mix* of these four variables. Thus we cannot talk about an ideal value for one (e.g. the best price), without considering the other three. What is more, the most appropriate mix will vary from product to product and from market to market.

What the firm must seek to do is to estimate how sensitive demand is to the various aspects of marketing. The greater the sensitivity (elasticity) in each case, the more the firms should focus on that particular aspect.

Advertising

One of the most important aspects of marketing is advertising. The major aim of advertising is to sell more products, and business spends a vast quantity of money on advertising to achieve this goal.

In fact, there is a bit more to it than this. Advertisers are trying to do two things:

■ Shift the product's demand curve to the right.
■ Make it less price elastic.

This is illustrated in Figure 3.5 (overleaf). D_1 shows the original demand curve with price at P_1 and sales at Q_1. D_2 shows the curve after an advertising campaign. The rightward shift allows an increased quantity (Q_2) to be sold at the original price. If, at the same time, the demand is made less elastic, the firm can also raise its price and still experience an increase in sales. Thus in the diagram, price can be raised to P_2 and sales will be Q_3 – still substantially above Q_1. The total gain in revenue is shown by the shaded area.

How can advertising bring about this new demand curve?

Shifting the demand curve to the right.   This will occur if the advertising brings the product to more people's attention and if it increases people's desire for the product.

Making the demand curve less elastic.   This will occur if the advertising creates greater brand loyalty. People must be led to believe (rightly or wrongly) that competitors' brands are inferior. This will allow the firm to raise its price above that of its rivals with no significant fall in sales. There will be only a small substitution effect of this price rise because consumers have been led to believe that there are no close substitutes.

Business issues covered in this chapter

- What do profits consist of?

- What is the relationship between inputs and outputs in both the short and long run?

- How do costs vary with output and just what do we mean by 'costs'?

- What is meant by 'economies of scale' and what are the reasons for such economies?

- How does a business's sales revenue vary with output?

- How do we measure profits?

- At what output will a firm maximise its profits?

- Why does operating under conditions of perfect competition make being in business a constant battle for survival?

CHAPTER 4

Supply decisions in a perfectly competitive market

In this chapter we turn to supply. In other words, we focus on the amount that firms produce. In Part C we shall see how the supply decision is affected by the microeconomic environment in which a firm operates, and in particular by the amount of competition it faces. In this chapter, however, we assume that the firm is a price taker: that it has to accept the price as given by the market. We also assume that the firm seeks to maximise profits.

Profit is made by firms earning more from the sale of goods than the goods cost to produce. A firm's total profit (*TΠ*) is thus the difference between its total sales revenue (*TR*) and its total costs of production (*TC*).

In order, then, to discover how a firm can maximise its profit, or even make a profit at all, we must first consider what determines costs and revenue. Sections 4.1 and 4.2 examine costs. Section 4.3 considers revenue, and then section 4.4 puts costs and revenue together to examine profit.

4.1 Production and costs: short run

Production in the short run

The cost of producing any level of output depends on the amount of inputs used and the price that the firm must pay for them. Let us first focus on the quantity of inputs used.

Short-run and long-run changes in production

If a firm wants to increase production, it will take time to acquire a greater quantity of certain inputs. For example, a manufacturer can use more electricity by turning on switches, but it might take a long time to obtain and install more machines, and longer still to build a second or third factory.

If, then, the firm wants to increase output in a hurry, it will only be able to increase the quantity of certain inputs. It can use more raw materials, more fuel, more tools and possibly more labour (by hiring extra workers or offering overtime to its existing workforce). But it will have to make do with its existing buildings and most of its machinery.

The distinction we are making here is between **fixed inputs** and **variable inputs**. A *fixed* input is an input that cannot be increased within a given time period (e.g. buildings). A *variable* input is one that can.

Definition

Fixed input
An input that cannot be increased in supply within a given time period.

Variable input
An input that *can* be increased in supply within a given time period.

The distinction between fixed and variable inputs allows us to distinguish between the short run and the long run.

The short run.   The **short run** is a time period during which at least one input is fixed. In the short run, then, output can be increased only by using more variable inputs. For example, if a shipping line wanted to carry more passengers in response to a rise in demand, it could accommodate more passengers on existing sailings if there was space. It could increase the number of sailings with its existing fleet, by hiring more crew and using more fuel. But in the short run it could not buy more ships: there would not be time for them to be built.

The long run.   The **long run** is a time period long enough for all inputs to be varied. Given long enough, the shipping company can have a new ship built.

The actual length of the short run will differ from firm to firm. It is not a fixed period of time. Thus if it takes a farmer a year to obtain new land, buildings and equipment, the short run is any time period up to a year and the long run is any time period longer than a year. But if it takes a shipping company three years to obtain an extra ship, the short run is any period up to three years and the long run is any period longer than three years.

For this section we will concentrate on *short-run* production and costs. We will look at the long run in section 4.2.

> **Pause for thought**
>
> *How will the length of the short run for the shipping company depend on the state of the shipbuilding industry?*

Production in the short run: the law of diminishing returns

> **Definition**
>
> **Short run**
> The period of time over which at least one input is fixed.
>
> **Long run**
> The period of time long enough for *all* inputs to be varied.
>
> **Law of diminishing (marginal) returns**
> When one or more inputs are held fixed, there will come a point beyond which the extra output from additional units of the variable input will diminish.

Production in the short run is subject to *diminishing returns*. You may well have heard of 'the law of diminishing returns': it is one of the most famous of all 'laws' of economics. To illustrate how this law underlies short-run production, let us take the simplest possible case where there are just two inputs: one fixed and one variable.

Take the case of a farm. Assume the fixed input is land and the variable input is labour. Since the land is fixed in supply, output per period of time can be increased only by increasing the number of workers employed. But imagine what would happen as more and more workers crowded on to a fixed area of land. The land cannot go on yielding more and more output indefinitely. After a point the additions to output from each extra worker will begin to diminish.

We can now state the **law of diminishing (marginal) returns**.

> **The law of diminishing marginal returns.**
> When increasing amounts of a variable input are used with a given amount of a fixed input, there will come a point when each extra unit of the variable input will produce less extra output than the previous unit.
>
> Key Idea 12

A good example of the law of diminishing returns is given in Case B.8 on the book's website. The case looks at diminishing returns to the application of nitrogen fertiliser on farmland.

Opportunity cost

When measuring costs, economists always use the concept of **opportunity cost**. As we saw in section 1.3, opportunity cost is the cost of any activity measured in terms of the sacrifice made in doing it: i.e. the cost measured in terms of the opportunities forgone. If a car manufacturer can produce 10 small saloon cars with the same amount of inputs as it takes to produce 6 large saloon cars, then the opportunity cost of producing 1 small car is 0.6 of a large car. If a taxi and car hire firm uses its cars as taxis, then the opportunity cost includes not only the cost of employing taxi drivers and buying fuel, but also the sacrifice of rental income from hiring its vehicles out.

Measuring a firm's opportunity costs

Just how do we measure a firm's opportunity cost? First we must discover what inputs it has used. Then we must measure the sacrifice involved in using them. To do this it is necessary to put inputs into two categories.

Inputs not owned by the firm: explicit costs.   The opportunity cost of those inputs not already owned by the firm is simply the price that the firm has to pay for them. Thus if the firm uses £100 worth of electricity, the opportunity cost is £100. The firm has sacrificed £100 which could have been spent on something else.

These costs are called **explicit costs** because they involve direct payment of money by firms.

Inputs already owned by the firm: implicit costs.   When the firm already owns inputs (e.g. machinery) it does not as a rule have to pay out money to use them. Their opportunity costs are thus **implicit costs**. They are equal to what the inputs could earn for the firm in some alternative use, either within the firm or hired out to some other firm.

Here are some examples of implicit costs:

■ A firm owns some buildings. The opportunity cost of using them is the rent it could have received by letting them out to another firm.

■ A firm draws £100 000 from the bank out of its savings in order to invest in new plant and equipment. The opportunity cost of this investment is not just the £100 000 (an explicit cost), but also the interest it thereby forgoes (an implicit cost).

■ The owner of the firm could have earned £15 000 per annum by working for someone else. This £15 000 is the opportunity cost of the owner's time.

If there is no alternative use for an input, as in the case of a machine designed to produce a specific product, and if it has no scrap value, the opportunity cost of using it is *zero*. In such a case, if the output from the machine is worth more than the cost of all the *other* inputs involved, the firm might as well use the machine rather than let it stand idle.

What the firm paid for the machine – its **historic cost** – is irrelevant. Not using the machine will not bring that money back. It has been spent. These are sometimes referred to as 'sunk costs'.

Likewise, the **replacement cost** is irrelevant. That should be taken into account only when the firm is considering replacing the machine.

Definition

Opportunity cost
Cost measured in terms of the next best alternative forgone.

Explicit costs
The payments to outside suppliers of inputs.

Implicit costs
Costs which do not involve a direct payment of money to a third party, but which nevertheless involve a sacrifice of some alternative.

Historic costs
The original amount the firm paid for inputs it now owns.

Replacement costs
What the firm would have to pay to replace inputs it currently owns.

Pause for thought

Assume that a farmer decides to grow wheat on land that could be used for growing barley. Barley sells for £100 per tonne. Wheat sells for £150 per tonne. Seed, fertiliser, labour and other costs of growing crops are £80 per tonne for both wheat and barley. What are the farmer's costs and profit per tonne of growing wheat?

Costs and inputs

A firm's costs of production will depend on the inputs it uses. The more inputs it uses, the greater will its costs be. More precisely, this relationship depends on two elements.

■ The productivity of the inputs. The greater their physical productivity, the smaller will be the quantity of them that is needed to produce a given level of output, and hence the lower will be the cost of that output.

■ The price of the inputs. The higher their price, the higher will be the costs of production.

In the short run, some inputs are fixed in supply. Their total costs (*TC*), therefore, are fixed, in the sense that they do not vary with output. Rent on land is a **fixed cost**. It is the same whether the firm produces a lot or a little.

The cost of variable inputs, however, does vary with output. The cost of raw materials is a **variable cost**. The more that is produced, the more raw materials are used and therefore the higher is their total cost.

Total cost is thus total fixed cost (*TFC*) plus total variable cost (*TVC*).

Average and marginal cost

In addition to the total cost of production (fixed and variable) there are two other measures of cost which are particularly important for our analysis of profits. These are average and marginal cost.

Average cost (*AC*) is cost per unit of production.

$$AC = TC/Q$$

Thus if it costs a firm £2000 to produce 100 units of a product, the average cost would be £20 for each unit (£2000/100).

Like total cost, average cost can be divided into the two components, fixed and variable. In other words, average cost equals **average fixed cost** (*AFC* = *TFC/Q*) plus **average variable cost** (*AVC* = *TVC/Q*).

$$AC = AFC + AVC$$

Marginal cost (*MC*) is the *extra* cost of producing *one more unit*: that is, the rise in total cost per one unit rise in output.

$$MC = \frac{\Delta TC}{\Delta Q}$$

where Δ means 'a change in'.

For example, assume that a firm is currently producing 1 000 000 boxes of matches a month. It now increases output by 1000 boxes (another batch): $\Delta Q = 1000$. As a result its total costs rise by £30: $\Delta TC = £30$. What is the cost of producing *one* more box of matches? It is:

$$MC = \frac{\Delta TC}{\Delta Q} = \frac{£30}{1000} = 3\text{p}$$

Definition

Fixed costs
Total costs that do not vary with the amount of output produced.

Variable costs
Total costs that do vary with the amount of output produced.

Total cost (*TC*)
The sum of total fixed costs (*TFC*) and total variable costs (*TVC*): *TC* = *TFC* + *TVC*.

Average (total) cost (*AC*)
Total cost (fixed plus variable) per unit of output: *AC* = *TC/Q* = *AFC* + *AVC*.

Average fixed cost (*AFC*)
Total fixed cost per unit of output: *AFC* = *TFC/Q*.

Average variable cost (*AVC*)
Total variable cost per unit of output: *AVC* = *TVC/Q*.

Marginal cost (*MC*)
The cost of producing one more unit of output: *MC* = *ΔTC/ΔQ*.

Table 4.1 Costs for firm X

Output (Q) (1)	TFC (£000) (2)	TVC (£000) (3)	TC (TFC + TVC) (£000) (4)	AFC (TFC/Q) (£000) (5)	AVC (TVC/Q) (£000) (6)	AC (TC/Q) (£000) (7)	MC (ΔTC/ΔQ) (£000) (8)
0	12	0	12	–	–	–	
							10
1	12	10	22	12.6	10	22	
							6
2	12	16	28	6	8	14	
							5
3	12	21	33	4	7	11	
							7
4	12	28	40	3	7	10	
							12
5	12	40	52	2.4	8	10.4	
							20
6	12	60	72	2	10	12	
							31
7	12	91	103	1.7	13	14.7	

(Note that all marginal costs are variable, since, by definition, there can be no extra fixed costs as output rises.)

Table 4.1 shows costs for an imaginary firm, firm X, over a given period of time (e.g. a week). The table shows how average and marginal costs can be derived from total costs. It is assumed that total fixed costs are £12 000 (column 2) and that total variable costs are as shown in column 3.

The figures for *TVC* have been chosen to illustrate the law of diminishing returns. Initially, *before* diminishing returns set in, *TVC* rises less and less rapidly as more variable factors are added. For example, in the case of a factory with a fixed supply of machinery, initially as more workers are taken on the workers can do increasingly specialist tasks and make a fuller use of the capital equipment. Above a certain output (3 units in Table 4.1), diminishing returns set in. Given that extra workers (the extra variable factors) are producing less and less extra output, the extra units of output they do produce will be costing more and more in terms of wage costs. Thus *TVC* rises more and more rapidly. You can see this by examining column 3.

The figures in the remaining columns in Table 4.1 are derived from columns 1 to 3. Look at the figures in each of the columns and check how the figures are derived. Note the figures for marginal cost are plotted between the lines to illustrate that marginal cost represents the increase in costs as output increases from one unit to the next.

We can use the figures in Table 4.1 to draw *MC*, *AFC*, *AVC* and *AC* curves.

Pause for thought

Use the figures in the first three columns of Table 4.1 to plot TFC, TVC and TC curves (where costs are plotted on the vertical axis and quantity on the horizontal axis). Mark the point on each of the TVC and TC curves where diminishing returns set in. What do you notice about the slope of the two curves at this output?

Marginal cost (MC). The shape of the *MC* curve follows directly from the law of diminishing returns. Initially, in Figure 4.1, as more of the variable input is used, extra units of output cost less than previous units. *MC* falls.

Pause for thought

Before you read on, can you explain why the marginal cost curve will always cut the average cost curve at its lowest point?

Beyond a certain level of output, however, diminishing returns set in. This is shown as point *x*. Thereafter *MC* rises. Additional units of output cost more and more to produce, since they require ever-increasing amounts of the variable input.

Average fixed cost (AFC). This falls continuously as output rises, since total fixed costs are being spread over a greater and greater output.

Average (total) cost (AC). The shape of the *AC* curve depends on the shape of the *MC* curve. As long as new units of output cost less than the average, their production must pull the average cost down. That is, if *MC* is less than *AC*, *AC* must be falling. Likewise, if new units cost more than the average, their production must drive the average up. That is, if *MC* is greater than *AC*, *AC* must be rising. Therefore, the *MC* curve crosses the *AC* curve at its minimum point (point *z* in Figure 4.1).

Average variable cost (AVC). Since $AVC = AC - AFC$, the *AVC* curve is simply the vertical difference between the *AC* and the *AFC* curves. Note that as *AFC* gets less, the gap between *AVC* and *AC* narrows. Since all marginal costs are variable (by definition, there are no marginal fixed costs), the same relationship holds between *MC* and *AVC* as it did between *MC* and *AC*. That is, if *MC* is less than *AVC*, *AVC* must be falling, and if *MC* is greater than *AVC*, *AVC* must be rising. Therefore, as with the *AC* curve, the *MC* curve crosses the *AVC* curve at its minimum point (point *y* in Figure 4.1).

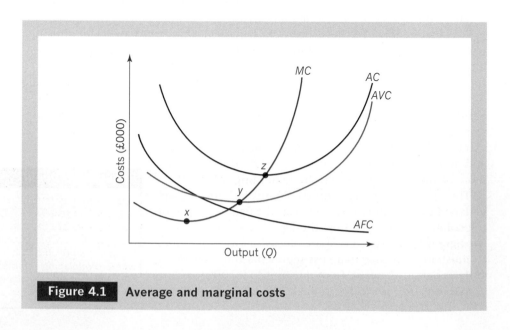

Figure 4.1 **Average and marginal costs**

Recap

■ Production in the short run is subject to diminishing returns. As greater quantities of the variable input(s) are used, so each additional unit of the variable input will add less to output than previous units: i.e. output will rise less and less rapidly.

■ When measuring costs of production, we should be careful to use the concept of opportunity cost. In the case of inputs not owned by the firm, the opportunity cost is simply the explicit cost of purchasing or hiring them. It is the price paid for them. In the case of inputs already owned by the firm, it is the implicit cost of what the factor could have earned for the firm in its best alternative use.

■ As some factors are fixed in supply in the short run, their total costs are fixed with respect to output. In the case of variable factors, their total cost increases as more output is produced and hence as more of them are used. Total cost can be divided into total fixed and total variable cost.

■ Marginal cost is the cost of producing one more unit of output. It will probably fall at first but will start to rise as soon as diminishing returns set in.

■ Average cost, like total cost, can be divided into fixed and variable costs. Average fixed cost will decline as more output is produced. The reason is that the total fixed cost is being spread over a greater and greater number of units of output. Average variable cost will tend to decline at first, but once the marginal cost has risen above it, it must then rise. The same applies to average cost.

Production and costs: long run   4.2

In the long run *all* inputs are variable. There is time for the firm to build a new factory (maybe in a different part of the country), to install new machines, to use different techniques of production, and in general to combine its inputs in whatever proportion and in whatever quantities it chooses.

In the long run, then, a firm will have to make a number of decisions: about the scale of its operations and the techniques of production it will use. These decisions will affect the costs of production. It is important, therefore, to get them right.

The scale of production

If a firm were to double all of its inputs – something it could do in the long run – would it double its output? Or would output more than double or less than double? We can distinguish three possible situations.

Constant returns to scale.   This is where a given percentage increase in inputs will lead to the same percentage increase in output.

Increasing returns to scale.   This is where a given percentage increase in inputs will lead to a larger percentage increase in output.

Decreasing returns to scale.   This is where a given percentage increase in inputs will lead to a smaller percentage increase in output.

Notice the terminology here. The words 'to scale' mean that *all* inputs increase by the same proportion. Decreasing returns to *scale* are therefore quite different from *diminishing* marginal returns (where only the *variable* input increases). The differences between marginal returns to a variable input and returns to scale are illustrated in Table 4.2 (overleaf).

Table 4.2   Short-run and long-run increases in output

Short run			Long run		
Input 1	Input 2	Output	Input 1	Input 2	Output
3	1	25	1	1	15
3	2	45	2	2	35
3	3	60	3	3	60
3	4	70	4	4	90
3	5	75	5	5	125

In the short run, input 1 is assumed to be fixed in supply (at 3 units). Output can be increased only by using more of the variable input (input 2). In the long run, however, both input 1 and input 2 are variable.

In the short-run situation, diminishing returns can be seen from the fact that output increases at a decreasing rate (25 to 45 to 60 to 70 to 75) as input 2 is increased. In the long-run situation, the table illustrates increasing returns to scale. Output increases at an *increasing* rate (15 to 35 to 60 to 90 to 125) as both inputs are increased.

Economies of scale

Definition

Economies of scale
When increasing the scale of production leads to a lower cost per unit of output.

Specialisation and division of labour
Where production is broken down into a number of simpler, more specialised tasks, thus allowing workers to acquire a high degree of efficiency.

Indivisibilities
The impossibility of dividing an input into smaller units.

The concept of increasing returns to scale is closely linked to that of **economies of scale**. A firm experiences economies of scale if costs per unit of output fall as the scale of production increases. Clearly, if a firm is getting increasing returns to scale from its inputs, then as it produces more, it will be using smaller and smaller amounts of inputs per unit of output. Other things being equal, this means that it will be producing at a lower unit cost.

There are a number of reasons why firms are likely to experience economies of scale. Some are due to increasing returns to scale; some are not.

Specialisation and division of labour.   In large-scale plants, workers can do more simple repetitive jobs. With this **specialisation and division of labour**, less training is needed; workers can become highly efficient in their particular job, especially with long production runs; there is less time lost in workers switching from one operation to another; supervision is easier. Workers and managers who have specific skills in specific areas can be employed.

Indivisibilities.   Some inputs are of a minimum size. They are indivisible. The most obvious example is machinery. Take the case of a combine harvester. A small-scale farmer could not make full use of one. They only become economical to use, therefore, on farms above a certain size. The problem of **indivisibilities** is made worse when different machines, each of which is part of the production process, are of a different size. For example, if there are two types of machine, one producing 6 units a day, the other packaging 4 units a day, a minimum of 12 units per day will have to be produced, involving two production machines and three packaging machines, if all machines are to be fully utilised.

The 'container principle'.   Any capital equipment that contains things (blast furnaces, oil tankers, pipes, vats, etc.) will tend to cost less per unit of output, the larger its size. The reason has to do with the relationship between a container's volume and its surface area. A container's cost will depend largely on the materials used to build it and hence roughly on its *surface area*. Its output will depend largely on its *volume*. Large containers have a bigger volume relative to surface area than do small containers. For example, a container with a bottom, top and four sides, with each side measuring 1 metre, has a volume of 1 cubic metre and a surface area of 6 square metres (6 surfaces of 1 square metre each). If each side were now to be doubled in length to 2 metres, the volume would be 8 cubic metres and the surface area 24 square metres (6 surfaces of 4 square metres each). Thus an eightfold increase in capacity has been gained at only a fourfold increase in the container's surface area, and hence an approximate fourfold increase in cost.

Greater efficiency of large machines.   Large machines may be more efficient, in the sense that more output can be gained for a given amount of inputs. For example, only one worker may be required to operate a machine whether it be large or small. Also, a large machine may make more efficient use of raw materials.

By-products.   With production on a large scale, there may be sufficient waste products to enable them to make some by-product.

Multi-stage production.   A large factory may be able to take a product through several stages in its manufacture. This saves time and cost moving the semi-finished product from one firm or factory to another. For example, a large cardboard-manufacturing firm may be able to convert trees or waste paper into cardboard and then into cardboard boxes in a continuous sequence.

All the above are examples of **plant economies of scale**. They are due to an individual factory or workplace or machine being large. There are other economies of scale that are associated with the business itself being large – perhaps with many factories.

Organisational.   With a large business, individual plants can specialise in particular functions. There can also be centralised administration of the plants. Often, after a merger between two firms, savings can be made by **rationalising** their activities in this way.

Spreading overheads.   Some expenditures are economic only when the *business* is large, such as research and development: only a large business can afford to set up a research laboratory. This is another example of indivisibilities, only this time at the level of the whole business rather than the plant. The greater the business's output, the more these **overhead costs** are spread.

Financial economies.   Large businesses may be able to obtain finance at lower interest rates than small ones. They may be able to obtain certain inputs cheaper by buying in bulk.

Economies of scope.   Often a business is large because it produces a range of products. This can result in each individual product being produced more cheaply than if it was produced in a single-product firm. The reason for these **economies of scope** is that various overhead costs and financial and organisational economies can be shared between the products. For example, a firm that produces a whole range of CD players, cassette recorders, amplifiers and tuners can benefit from shared marketing and distribution costs and the bulk purchase of electronic components.

Definition

Plant economies of scale
Economies of scale that arise because of the large size of the factory.

Rationalisation
The reorganising of production (often after a merger) so as to cut out waste and duplication and generally to reduce costs.

Overheads
Costs arising from the general running of an organisation, and only indirectly related to the level of output.

Economies of scope
When increasing the range of products produced by a firm reduces the cost of producing each one.

Pause for thought

Which of the economies of scale we have considered are due to increasing returns to scale and which are due to other factors?

Diseconomies of scale

Definition

Diseconomies of scale
Where costs per unit of output increase as the scale of production increases.

Long-run average cost curve
A curve that shows how average cost varies with output on the assumption that *all* factors are variable.

When businesses get beyond a certain size, costs per unit of output may start to increase. There are several reasons for such **diseconomies of scale**:

■ Management problems of coordination may increase as the business becomes larger and more complex, and as lines of communication get longer. There may be a lack of personal involvement by management.

■ Workers may feel 'alienated' if their jobs are boring and repetitive, and if they feel an insignificantly small part of a large organisation. Poor motivation may lead to shoddy work.

■ Industrial relations may deteriorate as a result of these factors and also as a result of the more complex interrelationships between different categories of worker.

■ Production-line processes and the complex interdependencies of mass production can lead to great disruption if there are hold-ups in any one part of the business.

Whether businesses experience economies or diseconomies of scale will depend on the conditions applying in each individual one.

Long-run average cost

We turn now to *long-run* cost curves. Since there are no fixed inputs in the long run, there are no long-run fixed costs. For example, a firm may rent more land in order to expand its operations. Its rent bill therefore goes up as it expands its output. All costs, then, in the long run are variable costs.

Although it is possible to draw long-run total, marginal and average cost curves, we will concentrate on **long-run average cost (*LRAC*) curves**. These can take various shapes, but a typical one is shown in Figure 4.2.

It is often assumed that, as a firm expands, it will initially experience economies of scale and thus face a downward-sloping *LRAC* curve. After a point, however, all such economies will have been achieved and thus the curve will flatten out. Then (possibly after a period of constant *LRAC*), the firm will get so large that it will start experiencing diseconomies of scale and thus a rising *LRAC*. At this stage, production and financial economies begin to be offset by the managerial problems of running a giant organisation.

Assumptions behind the long-run average cost curve

We make three key assumptions when constructing long-run average cost curves.

Input prices are given. At each output, a firm will be faced with a given set of input prices. If input prices *change*, therefore, both short- and long-run cost curves will shift. Thus an increase in wages would shift the curves upwards.

However, input prices might be different at *different* levels of output. For example, one of the economies of scale that many firms enjoy is the ability to obtain bulk discount on raw materials and other supplies. In such cases the curve does *not* shift. The different input prices are merely experienced at different points along the curve, and are reflected in the shape of the curve. Input prices are still given for any particular level of output.

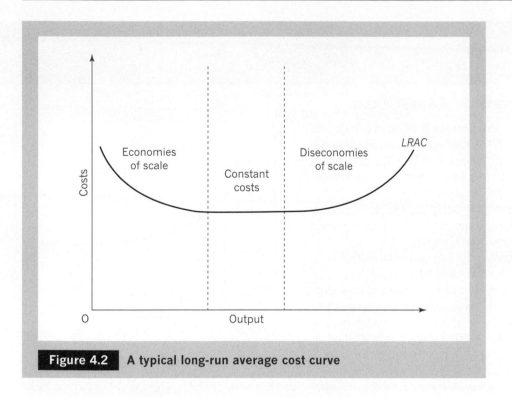

Figure 4.2   **A typical long-run average cost curve**

The state of technology and input quality are given.   These are assumed to change only in the *very* long run. If a firm gains economies of scale, it is because it is being able to exploit *existing* technologies and make better use of the existing availability of inputs.

Firms operate efficiently.   The assumption here is that firms operate efficiently: that they choose the cheapest possible way of producing any level of output. If the firm did not operate efficiently, it would be producing at a point above the LRAC curve.

Recap

- In the long run, a firm is able to vary the quantity it uses of all inputs. There are no fixed inputs and hence there are no fixed costs.

- If it increases all inputs by the same proportion, it may experience constant, increasing or decreasing returns to scale.

- Economies of scale occur when costs per unit of output fall as the scale of production increases. This can be due to a number of factors, some of which are directly caused by increasing (physical) returns to scale. These include the benefits of specialisation and division of labour, the use of larger and more efficient machines, and the ability to have a more integrated system of production. Other economies of scale arise from the financial and administrative benefits of large-scale organisations.

- Typically, *LRAC* curves are drawn as L-shaped or as saucer-shaped. As output expands, initially there are economies of scale. When these are exhausted, the curve will become flat. When the firm becomes very large, it may begin to experience diseconomies of scale. If this happens, the *LRAC* curve will begin to slope upward again.

Box 4.1

Minimum efficient scale

The extent of economies of scale in practice

Two of the most important studies of economies of scale have been those made by C. F. Pratten[1] in the late 1980s and by a group advising the European Commission[2] in 1997. Both studies found strong evidence that many firms, especially in manufacturing, experienced substantial economies of scale.

In a few cases long-run average costs fell continuously as output increased. For most firms, however, they fell up to a certain level of output and then remained constant.

The extent of economies of scale can be measured by looking at a firm's *minimum efficient scale* (*MES*). The *MES* is the size beyond which no significant additional economies of scale can be achieved: in other words, the point where the *LRAC* curve flattens off. In Pratten's studies he defined this level as the minimum scale above which any possible doubling in scale would reduce average costs by less than 5 per cent (i.e. virtually the bottom of the *LRAC* curve). In the diagram *MES* is shown at point a.

The *MES* can be expressed in terms either of an individual factory or of the whole firm. Where it refers to the minimum efficient scale of an individual factory, the *MES* is known as the *minimum efficient plant size* (*MEPS*).

The *MES* can then be expressed as a percentage of the total size of the market or of total domestic production. Table (a), based on the Pratten study, shows *MES* for plants and firms in various industries. The first column shows *MES* as a percentage of total UK production. The second column shows *MES* as a percentage of total EU production. Table (b), based on the 1997 study, shows *MES* for various plants as a percentage of total EU production.

Expressing *MES* as a percentage of total output gives an indication of how competitive the industry could be. In some industries (such as footwear and carpets), economies of scale were exhausted (i.e. *MES* was reached) with plants or firms that were still small relative to total UK production and even smaller relative to total EU production. In such industries there would be room for many firms and thus scope for considerable competition.

In other industries, however, even if a single plant or firm were large enough to produce the whole output of the industry in

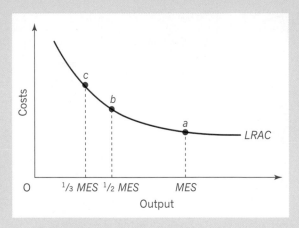

the UK, it would still not be large enough to experience the full potential economies of scale: the *MES* is greater than 100 per cent. Examples from Table (a) include factories producing cellulose fibres, and car manufacturers. In such industries there is no possibility of competition. In fact, as long as the *MES* exceeds 50 per cent there will not be room for more than one firm large enough to gain full economies of scale. In this case the industry is said to be a *natural monopoly*. As we shall see in the next few chapters, when competition is lacking consumers may suffer by firms charging prices considerably above costs.

A second way of measuring the extent of economies of scale is to see how much costs would increase if production were reduced to a certain fraction of *MES*. The normal fractions used are $\frac{1}{2}$ or $\frac{1}{3}$ *MES*. This is illustrated in the diagram. Point b corresponds to $\frac{1}{2}$ *MES*; point c to $\frac{1}{3}$ *MES*. The greater the percentage by which *LRAC* at point b or c is higher than at point a, the greater will be the economies of scale to be gained by producing at *MES* rather than at $\frac{1}{2}$ *MES* or $\frac{1}{3}$ *MES*. For example, in the table there are greater economies of scale to be gained from moving from $\frac{1}{2}$ *MES* to *MES* in the production of electric motors than in cigarettes.

Table (a)

Product	MES as % of production UK	MES as % of production EU	% additional cost at ½ MES
Individual plants			
Cellulose fibres	125	16	3
Rolled aluminium semi-manufactures	114	15	15
Refrigerators	85	11	4
Steel	72	10	6
Electric motors	60	6	15
TV sets	40	9	9
Cigarettes	24	6	1.4
Ball-bearings	20	2	6
Beer	12	3	7
Nylon	4	1	12
Bricks	1	0.2	25
Tufted carpets	0.3	0.04	10
Shoes	0.3	0.03	1
Firms			
Cars	200	20	9
Lorries	104	21	7.5
Mainframe computers	>100	n.a.	5
Aircraft	100	n.a.	5
Tractors	98	19	6

Sources: C. F. Pratten (1988); M. Emerson, *The Economics of 1992* (Oxford University Press, 1988)

The main purpose of the studies was to determine whether the single EU market is big enough to allow both economies of scale and competition. The tables suggest that in all cases, other things being equal, the EU market is large enough for firms to gain the full economies of scale *and* for there to be enough firms for the market to be competitive.

Table (b)

Plants	MES as % of total EU production
Aerospace	12.19
Tractors and agricultural machinery	6.57
Electric lighting	3.76
Steel tubes	2.42
Shipbuilding	1.63
Rubber	1.06
Radio and TV	0.69
Footwear	0.08
Carpets	0.03

Source: see footnote 2 below

The second study also found that 47 of the 53 manufacturing sectors analysed had scope for further exploitation of economies of scale.

Questions

1. Why might a firm operating with one plant achieve *MEPS* and yet not be large enough to achieve *MES*? (Clue: are all economies of scale achieved at plant level?)

2. Why might a firm producing bricks have an *MES* which is only 0.2 per cent of total EU production and yet face little effective competition from other EU countries?

---

[1] C. F. Pratten, 'A survey of the economies of scale', in *Research on the 'Costs of Non-Europe'*, vol. 2 (Office for Official Publications of the European Communities, 1988)

[2] European Commission/Economists Advisory Group Ltd, 'Economies of Scale', *The Single Market Review, Subseries V, Volume 4*. Office for official publications of the European Communities, Luxembourg, 1997

4.4   Profit maximisation

We are now in a position to put costs and revenue together to find the output at which profit is maximised, and also to find out how much that profit will be. First we need to look a little more precisely at what we mean by the term 'profit'.

The meaning of 'profit'

One element of cost is the opportunity cost to the owners of the firm incurred by being in business. This is the minimum return that the owners must make on their capital in order to prevent them from eventually deciding to close down and perhaps move into some alternative business. It is a *cost* since, just as with wages, rent, etc., it has to be covered if the firm is to continue producing. This opportunity cost to the owners is sometimes known as **normal profit**, and is included in the cost curves.

What determines this normal rate of profit? It has two components. First, someone setting up in business invests capital in it. There is thus an opportunity cost. This is the interest that could have been earned by lending it in some riskless form (e.g. by putting it in a savings account in a bank). Nobody would set up a business unless they expected to earn at least this rate of profit. Running a business is far from riskless, however, and hence a second element is a return to compensate for risk. Thus:

Normal profit (%) = rate of interest on a riskless loan + a risk premium

The risk premium varies according to the line of business. In those with fairly predictable patterns, such as food retailing, it is relatively low. Where outcomes are very uncertain, such as mineral exploration or the manufacture of fashion garments, it is relatively high.

Thus if owners of a business earn normal profit, they will (just) be content to remain in that industry.

Any excess of profit over normal profit is known as **supernormal profit**. If firms earn supernormal profit, they will clearly prefer to stay in this business. Such profit will also tend to attract new firms into the industry, since it will give them a better return on capital than elsewhere. If firms earn *less* than normal profit, however, then after a time they will consider leaving and using their capital for some other purpose.

Short-run profit maximising

In the **short run**, we assume that the number of firms in an industry cannot be increased: there is simply not time for new firms to enter the market.

Figure 4.4 shows a short-run equilibrium for an industry and the profit-maximising position for a firm under perfect competition. Both parts of the diagram have the same scale for the vertical axis. The horizontal axes have totally different scales, however. For example, if the horizontal axis for the firm were measured in, say, thousands of units, the horizontal axis for the whole industry might be measured

Definition

Normal profit
The opportunity cost of being in business. It consists of the interest that could be earned on a riskless asset, plus a return for risk taking in this particular industry. It is counted as a cost of production.

Supernormal profit
The excess of total profit above normal profit.

The short run under perfect competition
The period during which there is too little time for new firms to enter the industry.

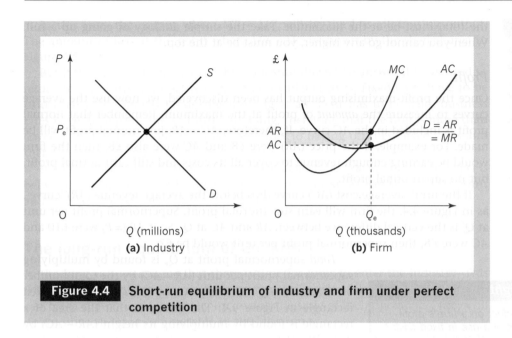

Figure 4.4   **Short-run equilibrium of industry and firm under perfect competition**

in millions or tens of millions of units, depending on the number of firms in the industry.

Let us examine the determination of price, output and profit in turn.

Price

The price is determined in the industry by the intersection of demand and supply. The firm faces a horizontal demand (or average revenue) 'curve' at this price. It can sell all it can produce at the market price (P_e), but nothing at a price above P_e.

Output

The firm will maximise profit where marginal cost equals marginal revenue ($MR = MC$), at an output of Q_e. In fact this **profit-maximising rule** will apply to firms in all types of market.

But why are profits maximised when $MR = MC$? The simplest way of answering this is to see what the position would be if MR did not equal MC.

Referring to Figure 4.4, at a level of output below Q_e, MR exceeds MC. This means that by producing more units there will be a bigger addition to revenue (MR) than to cost (MC). Total profit will *increase*. As long as MR exceeds MC, profit can be *increased by increasing production*.

At a level of output above Q_e, MC exceeds MR. All levels of output above Q_e thus add more to cost than to revenue and hence *reduce* profit. As long as MC exceeds MR, *profit can be increased by cutting back on production*.

Profits are thus maximised where $MC = MR$: at an output of Q_e.

Students worry sometimes about the argument that profits are maximised when $MR = MC$. Surely, they say, if the last unit is making no profit, how can profit be at a *maximum*? The answer is very simple. If you cannot add anything more to a total,

> **Definition**
>
> **Profit-maximising rule**
> Profit is maximised where marginal revenue equals marginal cost.

Does the firm benefit from operating under perfect competition?

Under perfect competition the firm faces a constant battle for survival. If it becomes less efficient than other firms, it will make less than normal profits and be driven out of business. If it becomes more efficient, it will earn supernormal profits. But these supernormal profits will not last for long. Soon other firms, in order to survive themselves, will be forced to copy the more efficient methods of the new firm.

It is the same with the development of new products. If a firm is able to produce a new product that is popular with consumers, it will be able to gain a temporary

---

Box 4.2

E-commerce

A modern form of perfect competition?

The relentless drive towards big business in recent decades has seen markets become more concentrated and increasingly dominated by large producers. And yet forces are at work that are undermining this dominance, and bringing more competition to markets. One of these forces is *e-commerce*.

In this case study, we shall first review the model of perfect competition and then consider how e-commerce is returning 'power to the people'.

A perfectly competitive market

As we have seen, under perfect competition firms are price takers: they have to accept the price as given by the market. Firms are faced with a constant battle for survival. The effect is to drive costs down. With firms freely entering the industry, only normal profits will be made in the long run. So only the fittest will survive, and the fittest will be in a constant struggle to produce at a lower cost.

So what conditions are necessary for the market for a particular good to be perfectly competitive and thus for firms to be price takers? In addition to freedom of entry to the market for new firms, consumers must have knowledge of the quality, availability and price of the good. There must be also be a large number of firms in the market. Only that way will competition be sufficient to ensure that no firm has any power over prices, and thus faces a perfectly elastic demand curve.

E-commerce and competition

How does e-commerce make markets more competitive and even, in some cases, become virtually perfectly competitive?

Consumer knowledge. There are various ways in which e-commerce is adding to the consumer's knowledge. There is greater price transparency, with consumers able to compare prices online. Search engines can quickly locate a list of alternative suppliers. There is greater information on product availability and quality. Virtual shopping malls, full of e-retailers, place the high street retailer under intense competitive pressure.

The pressure is even greater in the market for intermediate products. Many firms are constantly searching for cheaper sources of supply, and the Internet provides a cheap and easy means of conducting such searches.

Large number of firms. The growth of e-commerce has led to many new firms starting up in business. It's not just large firms like Amazon.com that are providing increased competition for established firms, but the thousands of small online companies that are being established every day. Many of these firms are selling directly to us as consumers. This is known as 'B2C' e-commerce (business-to-consumers). But many more are selling to other firms ('B2B'). More and more companies, from the biggest to the smallest, are transferring their purchasing to the Web and are keen to get value for money.

advantage over its rivals. But again, any supernormal profits will last only as long as it takes other firms to respond. Soon the increase in supply of the new product will drive the price down and eliminate these supernormal profits. Similarly, the firm must be quick to copy new products developed by its rivals. If it does not, it will soon make a loss and be driven out of the market.

Thus being in perfect competition is a constant battle for survival. It might benefit the consumer, but most firms in such an environment would love to be able to gain some market power: power to be able to restrict competition and to retain supernormal profits into the long run. Market power is the subject of the next chapter.

> **Pause for thought**
>
> *Why is it highly unlikely that an industry where firms can gain substantial economies of scale can also be perfectly competitive?*

The reach of the Web is global. This means that firms, whether conventional or Web-based, are having to keep an eye on the prices and products of competitors in the rest of the world, not just in the local neighbourhood. Firms' demand curves are thus becoming very price elastic. This is especially so for goods that are cheap to transport, or for services such as insurance and banking.

Freedom of entry.   Internet companies often have lower start-up costs than their conventional rivals. Their premises are generally much smaller, with no 'shop-front' costs and lower levels of stock holding. Marketing costs can also be relatively low, especially given the ease with which companies can be located with search engines. Internet companies are often smaller and more specialist, relying on Internet 'outsourcing' (buying parts, equipment and other supplies through the Internet), rather than making everything themselves. They are also more likely to use delivery firms rather than having their own transport fleet.

All this makes it relatively cheap for new firms to set up and begin trading over the Internet.

The limits to e-commerce

In 20 years, will we be doing all our shopping on the net? Will the only shopping malls be virtual ones? Although e-commerce is revolutionising some markets, it is unlikely that things will go anything like that far.

The benefits of 'shop shopping' are that you get to see the good, touch it and use it. You can buy the good there and then, and take instant possession of it: you don't have to wait. Shopping is also an enjoyable experience. Many people like wandering round the shops, meeting friends, seeing what takes their fancy, trying on clothes, browsing through CDs and so on. 'Retail therapy' for many is an important means of 'de-stressing'.

Online shopping is limited by the screen; Internet access may be slow and frustrating; 'surfing' may instead become 'wading'; you have to wait for goods to be delivered; and what if deliveries are late or fail completely?

Also, costs might not be as low as expected. How efficient is it to have many small deliveries of goods? How significant are the lost cost savings from economies of scale that larger producers or retailers are likely to generate?

Nevertheless, e-commerce has made many markets, both retail and B2B, more competitive. This is especially so for services and for goods whose quality is easy to identify online. Many firms are being forced to face up to having their prices determined by the market.

? Questions

1. Why may the Internet work better for replacement buys than for new purchases?
2. Give three examples of products that are particularly suitable for selling over the Internet and three that are not. Explain your answer.

Recap

■ Normal profit is the minimum profit that must be made to persuade a firm to stay in business in the long run. It is counted as part of the firm's costs. Supernormal profit is any profit over and above normal profit.

■ The maximum-profit output is where marginal revenue equals marginal cost. Having found this output, the level of maximum (supernormal) profit can be found by finding the average (supernormal) profit ($AR - AC$) and then multiplying it by the level of output.

■ For a firm that cannot make a profit at any level of output, the point where $MR = MC$ represents the loss-minimising output. In the short run, a firm will close down if it cannot cover its variable costs. In the long run, it will close down if it cannot make normal profits.

■ In the short run, there is not time for new firms to enter the market, and thus supernormal profits can persist. In the long run, however, any supernormal profits will be competed away by the entry of new firms.

QUESTIONS

1. Are all explicit costs variable costs? Are all variable costs explicit costs?

2. Up to roughly how long is the short run in the following cases?

   (a) A mobile disco firm;

   (b) Electricity power generation;

   (c) A small grocery retailing business;

   (d) 'Superstore Hypermarkets plc'.

   In each case, specify your assumptions.

3. The following are some costs incurred by a shoe manufacturer. Decide whether each one is a fixed cost or a variable cost or has some element of both.

   (a) The cost of leather;

   (b) The fee paid to an advertising agency;

   (c) Wear and tear on machinery;

   (d) Business rates on the factory;

   (e) Electricity for heating and lighting;

   (f) Electricity for running the machines;

   (g) Basic minimum wages agreed with the union;

   (h) Overtime pay;

   (i) Depreciation of machines as a result purely of their age (irrespective of their condition).

4. Why does the marginal cost curve pass through the bottom of the average cost curve?

5. What economies of scale is a large department store likely to experience?

6. Why are many firms likely to experience economies of scale up to a certain size and then diseconomies of scale after some point beyond that?

7. Normal profits are regarded as a cost (and are included in the cost curves). Explain why.

8. What determines the size of normal profit? Will it vary with the general state of the economy?

9. A firm will continue producing in the short run even if it is making a loss, providing it can cover its variable costs. Explain why. Just how long will it be willing to continue making such a loss?

10. Would there ever be a point in a firm attempting to continue in production if it could not cover its *long-run* average (total) costs?

11. The price of pocket calculators and digital watches fell significantly in the years after they were first introduced and at the same time demand for them increased substantially. Use cost and revenue diagrams to illustrate these events. Explain the reasoning behind the diagram(s) you have drawn.

12. Illustrate on a diagram similar to Figure 4.6 what would happen in the long run if price were initially below P_L.

Additional Part B case studies on the Economic Environment of Business Website (www.booksites.net/sloman)

B.1 **The housing market.** A case study of the operation of markets, examining the causes of changes in demand and supply for houses over the past 30 years and how house prices have responded.

B.2 **The measurement of elasticity.** This examines how to work out the value for elasticity using the 'mid-point' method.

B.3 **Any more fares?** Pricing on the buses: an illustration of the relationship between price and total revenue.

B.4 **Elasticities of demand for various foodstuffs.** An examination of the evidence about price and income elasticities of demand for food in the UK.

B.5 **Adjusting to oil price shocks.** A case study showing how demand and supply analysis can be used to examine the price changes in the oil market since 1973.

B.6 **The role of the speculator.** This assesses whether the activities of speculators are beneficial or harmful to the rest of society.

B.7 **The demand for butter.** An examination of a real-world demand function.

B.8 **Diminishing returns in the bread shop.** An illustration of the law of diminishing returns.

B.9 **Advertising and the long run.** How advertising affects consumer demand and the firm's profits over the long term.

B.10 **The fallacy of using historic costs.** A demonstration of how it is important to use opportunity costs and not historic costs when working out prices and output.

B.11 **The relationship between averages and marginals.** An examination of the rules showing how an average curve relates to a marginal curve.

B.12 **Short-run cost curves in practice.** Why *AVC* and *MC* curves may have a flat bottom.

Websites relevant to Part B

Numbers and sections refer to websites listed in the Web Appendix and hotlinked from this book's website at www.booksites.net/sloman/

■ For news articles relevant to Part B, see the *Economics News Articles* link from the book's website.

■ For general news on markets, demand and supply see websites in section A of the Web Appendix, and particularly A2, 3, 4, 5, 8, 9, 11, 12, 18, 20–26, 35, 36. See also site A42 for links to economics news articles from newspapers worldwide.

■ For links to sites on markets, see the relevant sections of I4, 7, 11, 17.

■ For data, information and sites on products and marketing, see sites B2, 10; I7, 11, 13, 17.

■ For data on advertising, see site E37.

■ For links to sites on various aspects of advertising and marketing, see section *Industry and Commerce > Consumer Protection > Advertising* in sites I7 and 11.

■ For links to sites on various aspects of production and costs, see section *Microeconomics > Production* in sites I7 and 11.

■ For a case study examining costs, see site D2.

■ For student resources relevant to Part B, see sites C1–7, 9, 10, 14, 19, 20; D3.

■ For sites favouring the free market, see C17 and E34.

PART C

The microeconomic environment of business

Whatever the aims of firms, if they are to be successful in pursuing them, they must take account of the environment in which they operate. In Part C we look at the microeconomic environment of firms: i.e. the market conditions that firms face in their particular industry.

Most firms are not price takers; they can choose the prices they charge. But in doing do they must take account of the reactions of their rivals. We look at pricing and output decisions in Chapter 5 and see how firms' aims affect these decisions.

And it is not just in terms of pricing and output decisions that firms must take account of rivals. They must also do so in planning out their longer-term strategy – in making decisions about developing and launching new products, how quickly and how much to expand, the methods of production to use, their supply chain, the balance of what should be produced in-house and what should be 'out-sourced' (i.e. bought in from other firms), their sources of finance, and whether to target international markets or to confine themselves to producing and selling domestically. These strategic decisions are the subject of Chapter 6.

In Chapter 7 we turn to the labour market environment of business. What power does the firm have in setting wages; what is the role of trade unions; how flexibly can the firm use labour? These issues all affect the profitability of business, its organisation and its choice of techniques.

Finally, in Chapter 8 we look at the impact of government policy towards business and how this in turn impacts on firms' decision making. How much does government legislation constrain business activity? How much can government force firms to behave in the society's interests and how much will firms choose to take a socially responsible attitude towards things such as ethical trading, the environment, product standards and conditions for their workforce?

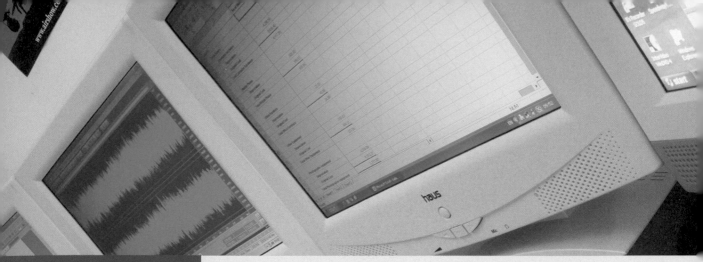

Business issues covered in this chapter

■ What determines the degree of market power of a firm?

■ How do firms get to become monopolies and remain so?

■ At what price and output will a monopolist maximise profits and how much profit will it make?

■ How well or badly do monopolies serve the consumer?

■ How are firms likely to behave when there are just a few of them competing ('oligopolies')? Will they engage in all-out competition or will they collude with each other?

■ What strategic games are oligopolists likely to play in their attempt to out-do their rivals?

■ Does oligopoly serve the consumer's interests?

■ Why may managers pursue goals other than maximising profit? What other goals might they pursue and what will be the effect on price and output?

■ How are prices determined in practice?

■ Why do firms sometimes charge different prices to different customers for the same product (e.g. seats on a plane)?

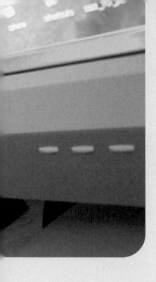

CHAPTER 5

Pricing and output decisions in imperfectly competitive markets

In the previous chapter we looked at price-taking firms. In this chapter we examine firms that face a downward-sloping demand curve. Such firms are said to have 'market power'. In other words, they have the power to raise their price. Of course, if they do so, their sales will fall, and clearly they will have to trade off the benefit of higher prices against the cost of lower sales.

The degree of a firm's market power depends on the price elasticity of demand for its product. The less elastic the demand, the less will sales fall for any given rise in price, and the greater, therefore, is the firm's market power.

Market power benefits the powerful at the expense of others.

When firms have market power over prices, they can use this to raise prices and profits above the perfectly competitive level. Other things being equal, the firm will gain at the expense of the consumer. Similarly, if consumers or workers have market power they can use this to their own benefit.

Key Idea 13

The most extreme case of market power is **monopoly**. This is where there is just one firm in the industry, and hence no competition from *within* the industry. Normally the monopoly will have effective means of keeping other firms out of the industry. We look at monopoly in section 5.1.

Where firms face a downward-sloping demand curve but are not monopolies, we call this situation **imperfect competition**. The vast majority of firms in the real world operate under imperfect competition.

Imperfect competition is normally divided into two types. The more competitive of the two is **monopolistic competition**. This involves quite a lot of firms competing and there is freedom for new firms to enter the industry. As a result, if existing firms are making supernormal profits, new firms will enter the industry (given time). Thus, as under perfect competition, this will have the effect of driving profits down to the normal level.

Examples of monopolistic competition can be found by flicking through the Yellow Pages. Taxi companies, restaurants, small retailers, small builders, plumbers, electrical contractors, etc. all normally operate under monopolistic competition. As a result, their profits are kept down by the intense competition in the industry. Competition is not perfect, however, as the firms are all trying to differentiate their product or service from their rivals'. They have *some* power over prices: their demand curve, whilst relatively elastic, is not horizontal.

Definition

Monopoly
A market structure where there is only one firm in the industry.

Imperfect competition
The collective name for monopolistic competition and oligopoly.

Monopolistic competition
A market structure where, like perfect competition, there are many firms and freedom of entry into the industry, but where each firm produces a differentiated product and thus has some control over its price.

Table 5.1 Features of the four market structures

Type of market	Number of firms	Freedom of entry	Examples of product	Implication for demand curve for firm's product
Perfect competition	Very many	Unrestricted	Fresh fruit and vegetables, shares	Horizontal. The firm is a price taker
Monopolistic competition	Many/several	Unrestricted	Builders, restaurants	Downward sloping, but relatively elastic. The firm has some control over price
Oligopoly	Few	Restricted	Cars, electrical appliances	Downward sloping, relatively inelastic, but depends on reactions of rivals to a price change
Monopoly	One	Restricted or completely blocked	Local water company, many prescription drugs	Downward sloping; more inelastic than oligopoly. Firm has considerable control over price

---

Pause for thought

Give one more example in each of the four market categories in Table 5.1.

The other type of imperfect competition is known as **oligopoly**. This literally means 'few sellers'. As under monopoly, the entry of new firms is restricted. We examine oligopoly in section 5.2.

Table 5.1 summarises the features of the four different types of market structure.

5.1 Monopoly

What is a monopoly?

This may seem a strange question because the answer seems obvious. A monopoly exists when there is only one firm in the industry.

But whether an industry can be classed as a monopoly is not always clear. It depends how narrowly the industry is defined. For example, a textile company may have a monopoly on certain types of fabric, but it does not have a monopoly on fabrics in general. The consumer can buy fabrics other than those supplied by the company. A rail company may have a monopoly over rail services between two cities, but it does not have a monopoly over public transport between these two cities. People can travel by coach or air. They could also use private transport.

To some extent, the boundaries of an industry are arbitrary. What is more important for a firm is the amount of monopoly *power* it has, and that depends on the closeness of substitutes produced by rival industries. The Post Office in the UK

Definition

Oligopoly
A market structure where there are few enough firms to enable barriers to be erected against the entry of new firms.

has a monopoly over the delivery of letters, but it faces competition in communications from telephone, faxes and e-mail.

Barriers to entry

For a firm to maintain its monopoly position, there must be barriers to the entry of new firms. Barriers also exist under oligopoly, but in the case of monopoly they must be high enough to block the entry of new firms. Barriers can take various forms.

Economies of scale. If the monopolist's costs go on falling significantly up to the output that satisfies the whole market, the industry may not be able to support more than one producer. This case is known as **natural monopoly**. It is particularly likely if the market is small. For example, two bus companies might find it unprofitable to serve the same routes, each running with perhaps only half-full buses, whereas one company with a monopoly of the routes could make a profit. Electricity transmission via a national grid is another example of a natural monopoly.

Even if a market could support more than one firm, a new entrant is unlikely to be able to start up on a very large scale. Thus the monopolist which is already experiencing economies of scale can charge a price below the cost of the new entrant and drive it out of business. If, however, the new entrant is a firm already established in another industry, it may be able to survive this competition.

Economies of scope. A firm that produces a range of products is also likely to experience a lower average cost of production. For example, a large pharmaceutical company producing a range of drugs and toiletries can use shared research, marketing, storage and transport facilities across its range of products. These lower costs make it difficult for a new single-product entrant to the market, since the large firm will be able to undercut its price and drive it out of the market.

Product differentiation and brand loyalty. If a firm produces a clearly differentiated product, where the consumer associates the product with the brand, it will be very difficult for a new firm to break into that market. Rank Xerox invented, and patented, the plain paper photocopier. After this legal monopoly (see below) ran out, people still associated photocopiers with Rank Xerox. It is still not unusual to hear someone say that they are going to 'Xerox the article' or, for that matter, 'Hoover their carpet'. Other examples of strong brand image include Guinness, Kellogg's Cornflakes, Coca-Cola, Nescafé and Sellotape.

Lower costs for an established firm. An established monopoly is likely to have developed specialised production and marketing skills. It is more likely to be aware of the most efficient techniques and the most reliable and/or cheapest suppliers. It is likely to have access to cheaper finance. It is thus operating on a lower cost curve. New firms would therefore find it hard to compete and would be likely to lose any price war.

Ownership of, or control over, key inputs or outlets. If a firm governs the supply of vital inputs (say, by owning the sole supplier of some component part), it can deny access to these inputs to potential rivals. On a world scale, the de Beers company has a monopoly in fine diamonds because all diamond producers market their diamonds through de Beers.

> **Definition**
>
> **Natural monopoly**
> A situation where long-run average costs would be lower if an industry were under monopoly than if it were shared between two or more competitors.

Similarly, if a firm controls the outlets through which the product must be sold, it can prevent potential rivals from gaining access to consumers. For example, Birds Eye Wall's used to supply freezers free to shops on the condition that they stocked only Wall's ice cream in them.

Legal protection. The firm's monopoly position may be protected by patents on essential processes, by copyright, by various forms of licensing (allowing, say, only one firm to operate in a particular area) and by tariffs (i.e. customs duties) and other trade restrictions to keep out foreign competitors. Examples of monopolies protected by patents include most new medicines developed by pharmaceutical companies (e.g. anti-AIDS drugs), Microsoft's Windows operating systems and agro-chemical companies, such as Monsanto, with various genetically modified plant varieties and pesticides.

Mergers and takeovers. The monopolist can put in a takeover bid for any new entrant. The sheer threat of takeovers may discourage new entrants.

Profit maximising under monopoly

The rule for profit maximising under monopoly is the same as for a firm under perfect competition. It should produce the output where marginal cost equals marginal revenue. The costs curves for a monopolist will look similar to those for a firm under perfect competition. The revenue curves, however, will look different.

Average and marginal revenue

Compared with other market structures, demand under monopoly will be relatively inelastic at each price. The monopolist can raise its price and consumers have no alternative supplier to turn to within the industry. They either pay the higher price, or go without the good altogether.

Because the firm faces a downward-sloping demand curve, its average and marginal revenue curves will also be downward sloping. This is illustrated in Figure 5.1, which is based on Table 5.2.

Note that, as in the case of a price-taking firm, the demand curve and the AR curve lie along exactly the same line. The reason for this is simple: $AR = P$, and thus the curve relating price to quantity (the demand curve) must be the same as that relating average revenue to quantity (the AR curve).

When a firm faces a downward-sloping demand curve, marginal revenue will be less than average revenue, and may even be negative. But why?

If a firm is to sell more per time period, it must lower its price (assuming it does not advertise). This will mean lowering the price not just for the extra units it hopes to sell, but also for those units it would have sold had it not lowered the price.

Thus the marginal revenue is the price at which it sells the last unit, *minus* the loss in revenue it has incurred by reducing the price on those units it could otherwise have sold at the higher price. This can be illustrated with Table 5.2.

Assume that price is currently £7. Two units are thus sold. The firm now wishes to sell an extra unit. It lowers the price to £6. It thus gains £6 from the sale of the third unit, but loses £2 by having to reduce the price by £1 on the two units it could otherwise have sold at £7. Its net gain is therefore £6 − £2 = £4. This is the marginal revenue: it is the extra revenue gained by the firm from selling one more unit.

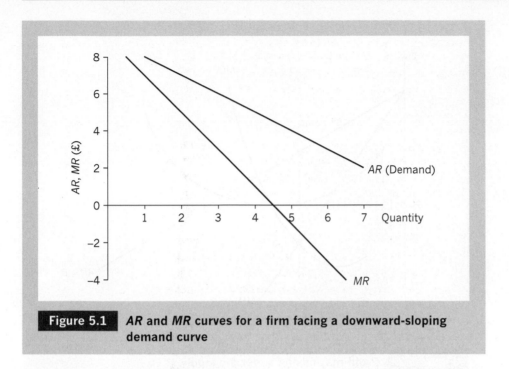

Figure 5.1   *AR* and *MR* curves for a firm facing a downward-sloping demand curve

Table 5.2   Revenue for a monopolist

Q (units)	P = AR (£)	TR (£)	MR (£)
			8
1	8	8	
2	7	14	6
3	6	18	4
4	5	20	2
5	4	20	0
6	3	18	−2
7	2	14	−4

Profit-maximising output and price

We can now put cost and revenue curves together on one diagram. This is done in Figure 5.2 (overleaf). Profit is maximised at an output of Q_m, where $MC = MR$. The price is given by the demand curve. Thus at Q_m the price is $AR = P$ (point *a* on the demand curve). Average cost (*AC*) is found at point *b*. Supernormal profit per unit is $AR - AC$. Total supernormal profit is shown by the shaded area.

These profits will tend to be larger, the less elastic is the demand curve (and hence the steeper is the *MR* curve), and thus the bigger is the gap between *MR* and price (*AR*). The actual elasticity will depend on whether reasonably close substitutes are available in *other* industries. The demand for a rail service will be much less elastic (and the potential for profit greater) if there is no bus service to the same destination.

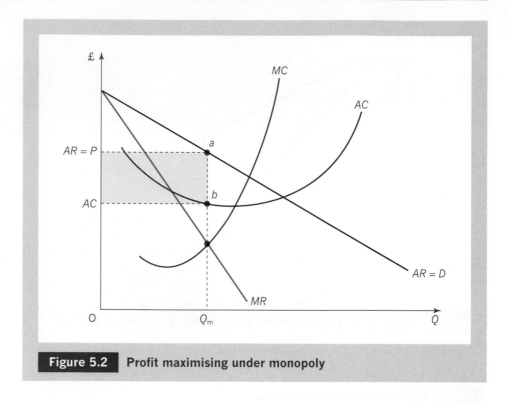

Figure 5.2 Profit maximising under monopoly

Comparing monopoly with perfect competition

Because it faces a different type of market environment, the monopolist will produce a quite different output and at a quite different price from a perfectly competitive industry. Typically a monopolist will charge a price above the market price of an equivalent industry under perfect competition. There are three main reasons for this.

■ Under perfect competition price equals marginal cost (see Figure 4.4 on page 95). Under monopoly, however, price is above marginal cost (see Figure 5.2). The less elastic the demand curve, the higher will price be above marginal cost.

■ Since there are barriers to the entry of new firms, a monopolist's supernormal profits will not be competed away in the long run. There is no competition to drive the price down. The monopolist is not forced to operate at the bottom of the *LRAC* curve. Thus, other things being equal, long-run prices will tend to be higher, and hence output lower, under monopoly.

■ The monopolist's cost curves may be higher. The sheer survival of a firm in the long run under perfect competition requires that it uses the most efficient known technique, and develops new techniques wherever possible. The monopolist, however, sheltered by barriers to entry, can still make large profits even if it is not using the most efficient technique. It has less incentive, therefore, to be efficient.

Pause for thought

If the shares in a monopoly (such as a water company) were very widely distributed among the population, would the shareholders necessarily want the firm to use its monopoly power to make larger profits?

It is possible, however, that a monopolist will operate with *lower* costs than an equivalent industry under perfect competition. The monopoly may be able to achieve substantial economies of scale due to larger plant, centralised administration and the avoidance of unnecessary duplication (e.g. a monopoly water company would eliminate the need for several sets of rival water mains under each street). If this results in an *MC* curve substantially below that of the same industry under perfect competition, the monopoly may even produce a *higher* output at a *lower* price.

Another reason why a monopolist may operate with lower costs is that it can use part of its supernormal profits for research and development and investment. It may not have the same *incentive* to become efficient as the perfectly competitive firm which is fighting for survival, but it may have a much greater *ability* to become efficient than has the small firm with limited funds.

Although a monopoly faces no competition in the goods market, it may face an alternative form of competition in financial markets. A monopoly, with potentially low costs, which is currently run inefficiently, is likely to be subject to a takeover bid from another company. This **competition for corporate control** may thus force the monopoly to be efficient in order to prevent it being taken over.

Finally, the promise of supernormal profits, protected perhaps by patents, may encourage the development of new (monopoly) industries producing new products. It is this chance of making monopoly profits that encourages many people to take the risks of going into business.

Definition

Competition for corporate control
The competition for the control of companies through takeovers.

Recap

- There are four alternative market structures under which firms operate. In ascending order of firms' market power, they are: perfect competition, monopolistic competition, oligopoly and monopoly.

- A monopoly is where there is only one firm in an industry. In practice, it is difficult to determine where a monopoly exists because it depends on how narrowly an industry is defined.

- Barriers to the entry of new firms will normally be necessary to protect a monopoly from competition. Such barriers include economies of scale (making the firm a natural monopoly or at least giving it a cost advantage over new, smaller, competitors), control over supplies of inputs or over outlets, patents or copyright, and tactics to eliminate competition (such as takeovers or aggressive advertising).

- The demand curve (*AR* curve) for a monopolist is downward sloping. The *MR* curve is below it and steeper.

- Profits for the monopolist (as for other firms) are maximised where $MC = MR$.

- If demand and cost curves are the same in a monopoly and a perfectly competitive industry, the monopoly will produce a lower output and at a higher price than the perfectly competitive industry.

- On the other hand, any economies of scale will in part be passed on to consumers in lower prices, and the monopolist's high profits may be used for research and development and investment, which in turn may lead to better products at possibly lower prices.

Box 5.1

Windows cleaning

Microsoft, the Internet and the US Justice Department

On 18 May 1998, the US government initiated its biggest competition case for 20 years: it sued Microsoft, the world's largest software company. It accused Microsoft of abusing its market power and seeking to crush its rivals.

The case against Microsoft had been building for many years, but it was with the release of Windows 98 that the US government decided to act. Windows, owned by Microsoft, is the operating system installed on more than 90 per cent of the world's personal computers. With Windows 98, Microsoft integrated its own Internet browser, Internet Explorer, into the Windows system. But it was in this area of Internet browsers that Microsoft faced stiff competition from Netscape Communications, which at the time controlled over 60 per cent of the market. US officials argued that the integration of Microsoft's Internet browser with its operating system would stifle competition in Internet software. In other words, by controlling the operating software, Microsoft could force its Internet browser on to consumers and computer manufacturers.

The US Justice Department alleged that Microsoft had committed the following anti-competitive actions:

■ Back in May 1995, Microsoft attempted to collude with Netscape Communications to divide the Internet browser market. Netscape Communications refused.

■ Microsoft had forced personal computer manufacturers to install Internet Explorer in order to obtain a Windows 95 operating licence.

■ Microsoft insisted that PC manufacturers conformed to a Microsoft front screen for Windows. This included specified icons, one of which was Microsoft's Internet Explorer.

■ It had set up reciprocal advertising arrangements with America's largest Internet service providers, such as America Online (AOL). Here Microsoft would promote AOL via Windows. In return, AOL would not promote Netscape's browsers.

Microsoft, in its defence, argued that the integration of its own browser into the Windows system was a natural part of the process of product innovation and development. If Microsoft were to do nothing with its Windows product, it would, over time, lose its dominant market position, and be replaced by a more innovative and superior product manufactured by a rival software producer.

In this respect, Microsoft could be seen to be operating in the consumer's interest. The argument is that, in an environment where technology is changing rapidly, Microsoft's control over standards gives the user a measure of stability, knowing that any new products and applications will be compatible with existing ones. In other words, new software can be incorporated into existing systems.

Network effects

The key issue in respect to Microsoft, then, was not so much the browser war, but far more fundamentally to do with the operating system, and how Microsoft used its ownership of this system to extend its leverage into other related high-technology markets.

An operating system attracts software developed around that operating system, thereby discouraging new competition

5.2   Oligopoly

Oligopoly occurs when just a few firms between them share a large proportion of the industry. Most oligopolists produce differentiated products (e.g. cars, soap powder, soft drinks, electrical appliances). Much of the competition between such oligopolists is in terms of the marketing of their particular brand.

As with monopoly, there are barriers to the entry of new firms (see above, pages 107–8). The size of the barriers, however, varies from industry to industry. In some cases entry is relatively easy; in others it is virtually impossible.

Interdependence of the firms.   Because there are only a few firms under oligopoly, each firm will have to take account of the others. This means that they are mutually

since any alternative faces not only the challenge of creating a better operating system but competing against a whole array of already existing software applications . . . These so-called 'network effects' give an incredible anti-competitive edge to companies like Microsoft that control so many different parts of the network.[1]

Network effects arise when consumers of a product benefit from it being used by other consumers. The more people that use it, the greater the benefit to each individual user. The problem for the consumer in such a scenario is that these network effects can lead to the establishment of a monopoly producer and hence to higher prices. There is also the problem of whether the best product is being produced by the monopolist. In such an instance, the consumer may be 'locked in' to using an inferior product or technology with limited opportunity (if any) to change.

Microsoft had been able to use consumer lock-in to drive competitors from the market. Where choice did exist, for example in Internet browsers, Microsoft was using its operating system dominance to promote its own product.

Court findings

A verdict was reached on 7 June 2000, when Federal Judge Thomas Penfield Jackson ruled that Microsoft be split in two to prevent it operating as a monopoly. One company would produce and market the Windows operating system; the other would produce and market the applications software, such as Microsoft Office and the Web browser, Internet Explorer.

Microsoft appealed against the judgment to the US Federal Appeals Court, which in June 2001 overturned the ruling and referred the case to a different judge for reconsideration. Judge Colleen Kollar-Kotelly urged both sides (Microsoft and the US Justice Department) to try to reach a settlement and in November 2001 they did just that. They agreed that Microsoft would provide technical information about Windows to other companies to enable them to write software that would compete with Microsoft's own software. Also, Microsoft would not be allowed to retaliate against computer manufacturers that installed rival products or removed icons for Microsoft applications.

Nine states, however, refused to sign up to the agreement and a further year went past before Judge Kollar-Kotelly gave her final ruling. Whilst she agreed with many of Judge Jackson's original findings, she did not require that Microsoft be split into two companies. Instead, she upheld the November 2001 agreement.

? Questions

1. In what ways was Microsoft's behaviour (a) against the public interest; (b) in the public interest?
2. The problem with being locked-in to a product or technology is only a problem if such a product can be clearly shown to be inferior to an alternative. What difficulties might there be in establishing such a case?

[1] N. Newman, From MS Word to MS World: How Microsoft is Building a Global Monopoly (1997), www.netaction.org/msoft/world

---

dependent: they are **interdependent**. Each firm is affected by its rivals' actions. If a firm changes the price or specification of its product or the amount of its advertising, the sales of its rivals will be affected. The rivals may then respond by changing their price, specification or advertising. No firm can therefore afford to ignore the actions and reactions of other firms in the industry.

People often think and behave strategically.
How you think others will respond to your actions is likely to influence your own behaviour. Firms, for example, when considering a price or product change will often take into account the likely reactions of their rivals.

Key Idea 14

Definition

Interdependence (under oligopoly)
One of the two key features of oligopoly. Each firm will be affected by its rivals' decisions. Likewise its decisions will affect its rivals. Firms recognise this interdependence. This recognition will affect their decisions.

It is impossible, therefore, to predict the effect on a firm's sales of, say, a change in its price without first making some assumption about the reactions of other firms. Different assumptions will yield different predictions. For this reason there is no single generally accepted theory of oligopoly. Firms may react differently and unpredictably.

Competition and collusion

Oligopolists are pulled in two different directions:

■ The interdependence of firms may make them wish to *collude* with each other. If they can club together and act as if they were a monopoly, they could jointly maximise industry profits.

■ On the other hand, they will be tempted to *compete* with their rivals to gain a bigger share of industry profits for themselves.

These two policies are incompatible. The more fiercely firms compete to gain a bigger share of industry profits, the smaller these industry profits will become! For example, price competition drives down the average industry price, while competition through advertising raises industry costs. Either way, industry profits fall.

Sometimes firms will collude. Sometimes they will not. The following sections examine first **collusive oligopoly** (both open and tacit), and then **non-collusive oligopoly**.

Collusive oligopoly

When firms under oligopoly engage in collusion, they may agree on prices, market share, advertising expenditure, etc. Such collusion reduces the uncertainty they face. It reduces the fear of engaging in competitive price cutting or retaliatory advertising, both of which could reduce total industry profits.

A cartel

A formal collusive agreement is called a **cartel**. The cartel will maximise profits if it acts like a monopoly: if the members behave as if they were a single firm. This is illustrated in Figure 5.3.

The total market demand curve is shown with the corresponding market MR curve. The cartel's MC curve is the *horizontal* sum of the MC curves of its members (since we are adding the *output* of each of the cartel members at each level of marginal cost). Profits are maximised at Q_1 where $MC = MR$. The cartel must therefore set a price of P_1 (at which Q_1 will be demanded).

Having agreed on the cartel price, the members may then compete against each other using *non-price competition*, to gain as big a share of resulting sales (Q_1) as they can.

Alternatively, the cartel members may somehow agree to divide the market between them. Each member would be given a **quota**. The sum of all the quotas must add up to Q_1. If the quotas exceeded Q_1, either there would be output unsold if price remained fixed at P_1, or the price would fall.

In many countries cartels are illegal, being seen by the government as a means of driving up prices and profits and thereby as being against the public interest. Government policy towards cartels is examined in section 8.3.

Definition

Collusive oligopoly
When oligopolists agree (formally or informally) to limit competition between themselves. They may set output quotas, fix prices, limit product promotion or development, or agree not to 'poach' each other's markets.

Non-collusive oligopoly
When oligopolists have no agreement between themselves – formal, informal or tacit.

Cartel
A formal collusive agreement.

Quota
(set by a cartel)
The output that a given member of a cartel is allowed to produce (production quota) or sell (sales quota).

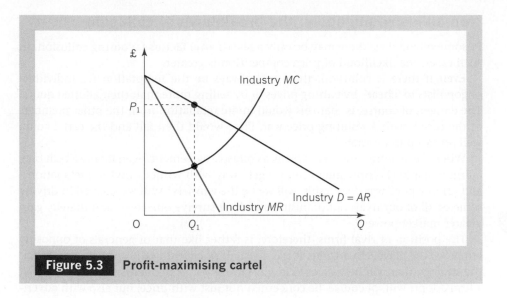

Figure 5.3   **Profit-maximising cartel**

Tacit collusion

Where open collusion is illegal, firms may simply break the law, or get round it. Alternatively, firms may stay within the law, but still *tacitly* collude by watching each other's prices and keeping theirs similar. Firms may tacitly 'agree' to avoid price wars or aggressive advertising campaigns.

One form of **tacit collusion** is where firms keep to the price that is set by an established leader. Such **price leadership** is more likely when there is a dominant firm in the industry, normally the largest.

Factors favouring collusion

Collusion between firms, whether formal or tacit, is more likely when firms can clearly identify with each other or some leader and when they trust each other not to break agreements. It will be easier for firms to collude if the following conditions apply:

■ There are only very few firms, all well known to each other.

■ They are open with each other about costs and production methods.

■ They have similar production methods and average costs, and are thus likely to want to change prices at the same time and by the same percentage.

■ They produce similar products and can thus more easily reach agreements on price.

■ There is a dominant firm.

■ There are significant barriers to entry and thus there is little fear of disruption by new firms.

■ The market is stable. If industry demand or production costs fluctuate wildly, it will be difficult to make agreements, partly due to difficulties in predicting and partly because agreements may frequently have to be amended. There is a particular problem in a declining market where firms may be tempted to undercut each other's price in order to maintain their sales.

■ There are no government measures to curb collusion.

Definition

Tacit collusion
When oligopolists take care not to engage in price cutting, excessive advertising or other forms of competition. There may be unwritten 'rules' of collusive behaviour such as price leadership.

Price leadership
When firms (the followers) choose the same price as that set by a one of the firms in the industry (the leader). The leader will normally be the largest firm.

Non-collusive oligopoly: the breakdown of collusion

In some oligopolies, there may be only a few (if any) factors favouring collusion. In such cases, the likelihood of price competition is greater.

Even if there is collusion, there will always be the temptation for individual oligopolists to 'cheat', by cutting prices or by selling more than their allotted quota. The danger, of course, is that this would invite retaliation from the other members of the cartel, with a resulting price war. Price would then fall and the cartel could well break up in disarray.

When considering whether to break a collusive agreement, even if only a tacit one, a firm will ask: (1) 'How much can we get away with without inviting retaliation?' and (2) 'If a price war does result, will we be the winners? Will we succeed in driving some or all of our rivals out of business and yet survive ourselves, and thereby gain greater market power?'

The position of rival firms, therefore, is rather like that of generals of opposing armies or the players in a game. It is a question of choosing the appropriate *strategy*: the strategy that will best succeed in outwitting your opponents. The strategy that a firm adopts will, of course, be concerned not just with price, but also with advertising and product development.

The firm's choice of strategy will depend on (a) how it thinks its rivals will react to any price changes or other changes it makes; (b) its willingness to take a gamble. Economists have developed **game theory**, which examines the best strategy that a firm can adopt for each assumption about its rivals' behaviour.

Definition

Game theory (or the theory of games) The study of alternative strategies that oligopolists may choose to adopt, depending on their assumptions about their rivals' behaviour.

Non-collusive oligopoly: game theory

Simple dominant strategy games

The simplest case is where there are just two firms with identical costs, products and demand. They are both considering which of two alternative prices to charge. Table 5.3 shows typical profits they could each make.

Let us assume that at present both firms (X and Y) are charging a price of £2 and that they are each making a profit of £10 million, giving a total industry profit of £20 million. This is shown in the top left-hand box (A).

Now assume they are both (independently) considering reducing their price to £1.80. In making this decision, they will need to take into account what their rival might do, and how this will affect them. Let us consider X's position. In our

Table 5.3 Profits for firms A and B at different prices

	X's price £2.00	X's price £1.80
Y's price £2.00	A £10m each	B £5m for Y, £12m for X
Y's price £1.80	C £12m for Y, £5m for X	D £8m each

simple example there are just two things that its rival, firm Y, might do. Either Y could cut its price to £1.80, or it could leave its price at £2. What should X do?

One alternative is to go for the *cautious* approach and think of the worst thing that its rival could do. If X kept its price at £2, the worst thing for X would be if its rival Y cut its price. This is shown by box C: X's profit falls to £5 million. If, however, X cut its price to £1.80, the worst outcome would again be for Y to cut its price, but this time X's profit only falls to £8 million. In this case, then, if X is cautious, it will *cut its price to £1.80*. Note that Y will argue along similar lines, and if it is cautious, it too will cut its price to £1.80. The result is that the firms end up in box D.

An alternative strategy is to go for the *optimistic* approach and assume that your rivals react in the way most favourable to you. Here the firm will go for the strategy that yields the highest possible profit. In X's case this will be again to cut price, only this time on the optimistic assumption that firm Y will leave its price unchanged. If firm X is correct in its assumption, it will move to box B and achieve the maximum possible profit of £12 million. Note that again the same argument applies to Y, which will also cut its price. Again, the result is that the firms end up in box D.

Given that in this 'game' *both* approaches, cautious and optimistic, lead to the *same* strategy (namely, cutting price), this is known as a **dominant strategy game**. The result is that the firms will end up in box D, earning a lower profit (£8 million each) than if they had charged the higher price (£10 million each in box A).

The equilibrium outcome of a game where there is no collusion between the players (box D in this game) is known as a **Nash equilibrium**, after John Nash, a US mathematician (and subject of the film *A Beautiful Mind*) who introduced the concept in 1951.

In our example, collusion rather than a price war would have benefited both firms. Yet, even of they did collude, both would still be tempted to cheat and cut prices. This is known as the **prisoners' dilemma**: the dilemma faced by suspects of a crime who are in custody and wondering whether to 'shop' their fellow suspects in the hope of getting a lighter sentence. The police rely on the fact that suspects are tempted to own up in case their fellow prisoners do so first. The result is that everyone owns up, even though collusion to keep quiet would have been in all the suspects' interests.

More complex games with no dominant strategy

More complex 'games' can be devised with more than two firms, many alternative prices, differentiated products and various forms of non-price competition (e.g. advertising). In such cases, the cautious strategy may suggest a different policy (e.g. do nothing) from the high-risk (optimistic) strategy (e.g. cut prices substantially).

In many situations, firms will have a number of different options open to them and a number of possible reactions by rivals. In such cases, the choice facing firms may be many. They may opt for a compromise strategy between the optimistic and the cautious approaches. This could be a strategy that is more risky than the cautious one, but with the chance of a higher profit; but not as risky as the optimistic one, but where the maximum profit possible is not so high.

The importance of threats and promises

In many situations, an oligopolist will make a threat or promise that it will act in a certain way. As long as the threat or promise is **credible** (i.e. its competitors believe it), the firm can gain and it will influence its rivals' behaviour.

Definition

Dominant strategy game
Where the *same* policy is suggested by different strategies.

Nash equilibrium
The position resulting from everyone making their optimal decision based on the assumptions about their rivals' decisions. Without collusion, there is no incentive to move from this position.

Prisoners' dilemma
Where two or more firms (or people), by attempting independently to choose the best strategy for whatever the other(s) are likely to do, end up in a worse position than if they had cooperated in the first place.

Credible threat (or promise)
One that is believable to rivals because it is in the threatener's interests to carry it out.

Take the simple situation where a large oil company, such as Esso, states that it will match the price charged by any competitor within a given radius. Assume that competitors believe this 'price promise' but also that Esso will not try to *undercut* their price. In the simple situation where there is only one other filling station in the area, what price should it charge? Clearly it should charge the price which would maximise its profits, assuming that Esso will charge the *same* price. In the absence of other filling stations in the area, this is likely to be a relatively high price.

Now assume that there are several filling stations in the area. What should the company do now? Its best bet is probably to charge the same price as Esso and hope that no other company charges a lower price and forces Esso to cut its price. Assuming that Esso's threat is credible, other companies are likely to reason in a similar way.

> ### Pause for thought
>
> Assume that there are two major oil companies operating filling stations in an area. The first promises to match the other's prices. The other promises to sell at 1p per litre cheaper than the first. Describe the likely sequence of events in this 'game' and the likely eventual outcome. Could the promise of the second company be seen as credible?

The importance of timing: decision trees

Most decisions by oligopolists are made by one firm at a time rather than simultaneously by all firms. Sometimes a firm will take the initiative. At other times it will respond to decisions taken by other firms.

Take the case of a new generation of large passenger aircraft which can fly further without refuelling. Assume that there is a market for a 500-seater version of this type of aircraft and a 400-seater version, but that the market for each sized aircraft is not big enough for the two manufacturers, Boeing and Airbus, to share it profitably. Let us also assume that the 400-seater market would give an annual profit of £50 million to a single manufacturer and the 500-seater would give an annual profit of £30 million, but that if both manufacturers produced the same version, they would each make an annual loss of £10 million.

Assume that Boeing announces that it is building the 400-seater plane. What should Airbus do? The choice is illustrated in Figure 5.4. This diagram is called a **decision tree** and shows the sequence of events. The small square at the left of the diagram is Boeing's decision point (point A). If it had decided to build the 500-seater plane, we would move up the top branch. Airbus would now have to make a decision (point B_1). If it too built the 500-seater plane, we would move to outcome 1: a loss of £10m for both manufacturers. Clearly, with Boeing building a 500-seater plane, Airbus would choose the 400-seater plane: we would move to outcome 2, with Boeing making a profit of £30m and Airbus a profit £50m. Airbus would be very pleased!

Boeing's best strategy at point A, however, would be to build the 400-seater plane. We would then move to Airbus's decision point B_2. In this case, it is in Airbus's interests to build the 500-seater plane. Its profit would be only £30m (outcome 3), but this is better than a £10m loss if it too built the 400-seater plane (outcome 4). With Boeing deciding first, the Nash equilibrium will thus be outcome 3.

There is clearly a **first-mover advantage** here. Once Boeing has decided to build the more profitable version of the plane, Airbus is forced to build the less profitable one. Naturally, Airbus would like to build the more profitable one and be the first mover. Which company succeeds in going first depends on how advanced they are in their research and development and in their production capacity.

> ### Definition
>
> **Decision tree (or game tree)**
> A diagram showing the sequence of possible decisions by competitor firms and the outcome of each combination of decisions.
>
> **First-mover advantage**
> When a firm gains from being the first to take action.

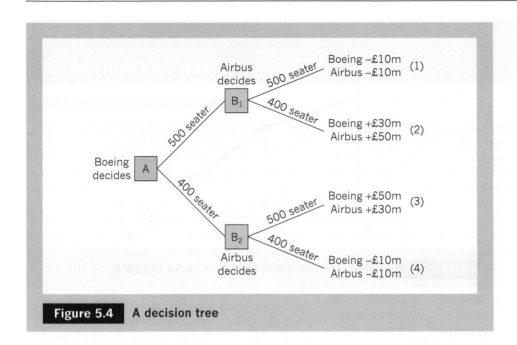

Figure 5.4   **A decision tree**

More complex decision trees. The aircraft example is the simplest version of a decision tree, with just two companies and each one making only one key decision. In many business situations, much more complex trees could be constructed. The 'game' would be more like one of chess, with many moves and several options on each move. If there were more than two companies, the decision tree would be more complex still.

> **Pause for thought**
>
> *Give an example of decisions that two firms could make in sequence, each one affecting the other's next decision.*

The kinked demand curve

Even when oligopolists do not collude over price, the price is often relatively stable. The reason is that oligopolists may believe that they face a **kinked demand curve**. But why? The firm makes two key assumptions:

- If it cuts its price, its rivals will feel forced to follow suit and cut theirs, to prevent losing customers to the first firm.

- If it raises its price, however, its rivals will *not* follow suit since, by keeping their prices the same, they will thereby gain customers from the first firm.

On these assumptions, the oligopolist's perceived demand curve is *kinked* at the current price and output (see Figure 5.5 – overleaf). It believes that if it raises its price, this will lead to a large fall in sales as customers switch to the now lower-priced rivals. The firm will thus be reluctant to raise its price. Demand is relatively elastic above the kink. On the other hand, it believes that if it reduces price, this will bring only a modest increase in sales, since rivals will lower their prices too and therefore customers do not switch. The firm will thus also be reluctant to reduce its price. Demand is relatively inelastic below the kink. Thus oligopolists will be reluctant to change prices at all.

> **Definition**
>
> **Kinked demand theory**
>
> The theory that oligopolists face a demand curve that is kinked at the current price: demand being significantly more elastic above the current price than below. The effect of this is to create a situation of price stability.

Recap

- An oligopoly is where there are just a few firms in the industry with barriers to the entry of new firms. Firms recognise their mutual dependence.

- Whether oligopolists compete or collude depends on the conditions in the industry. They are more likely to collude if there are few of them; if they are open with each other; if they have similar products and cost structures; if there is a dominant firm; if there are significant entry barriers; if the market is stable; and if there is no government legislation to prevent collusion.

- A formal collusive agreement is called a 'cartel'. A cartel aims to act as a monopoly. It can set price and leave the members to compete for market share, or it can assign quotas. There is always a temptation for cartel members to 'cheat' by undercutting the cartel price if they think they can get away with it and not trigger a price war.

- Tacit collusion can take the form of price leadership.

- Non-collusive oligopolists will have to work out a price strategy. This will depend on their attitudes towards risk and on the assumptions they make about the behaviour of their rivals.

- Game theory examines various strategies that firms can adopt when the outcome of each is not certain. They can adopt a cautious strategy of choosing the policy that has the least possible worst outcome, or a high-risk optimistic strategy of choosing the policy with the best possible outcome, or some compromise. Either way, a 'Nash' equilibrium is likely to be reached which is not in the best interests of the firms collectively. It will entail a lower level of profit than if they had colluded.

- A firm may gain a strategic advantage over its rivals by being the first one to take action (e.g. launch a new product).

- Because may firms perceive that they face a kinked demand curve, they are likely to keep their prices stable unless there is a large shift in costs or demand.

- Whether consumers benefit from oligopoly depends on the particular oligopoly and how competitive it is; whether the firms engage in extensive advertising and of what type; whether product differentiation results in a wide range of choice for the consumer; and how much of the profits are ploughed back into research and development.

5.3 Alternative aims of the firm

The traditional profit-maximising theories of the firm have been criticised for being unrealistic. They assume that it is the *owners* of the firm that make price and output decisions. It is reasonable to assume that owners will want to maximise profits: this much most of the critics of the traditional theory accept. But as we saw in Chapter 1, in public limited companies there is generally a separation of ownership and control of companies. *Managers* are the decision makers and may well be motivated by objectives other than maximising profits. Different managers in the same firm may well pursue different aims.

Managers will still have to ensure that *sufficient* profits are made to keep shareholders happy, but that may be very different from *maximising* profits.

Alternative theories of the firm to those of profit maximisation, therefore, tend to assume that large firms are **profit satisficers**. That is, managers strive hard for a minimum target level of profit, but are less interested in profits above this level.

Definition

Profit satisficing
Where decision makers in a firm aim for a target level of profit rather than the absolute maximum level.

Such theories fall into two categories: first, those that assume that firms attempt to maximise some other aim, provided that sufficient profits are achieved; and second, those that assume that firms pursue a number of potentially conflicting aims, of which sufficient profit is merely one. We examine each in turn.

Alternative maximising aims

Sales revenue maximisation

Perhaps the most famous of all alternative theories of the firm is the theory of **sales revenue maximisation**. So why should managers want to maximise their firm's sales revenue? The answer is that the success of managers, and especially sales managers, may be judged according to the level of the firm's sales. Sales figures are an obvious barometer of the firm's health. Managers' salaries, power and prestige may depend directly on sales revenue. The firm's sales representatives may be paid commission on their sales. Thus sales revenue maximisation may be a more dominant aim in the firm than profit maximisation, particularly if it has a dominant sales department.

Total sales revenue (TR) will be maximised at a higher output and lower price than will profits. This is illustrated in Figure 5.6. Profits are maximised at output Q_1 and price P_1, where $MC = MR$. Sales revenue, however, is maximised at the higher output Q_2 and lower price P_2, where $MR = 0$. The reason is that if MR equals zero, nothing more can be added to total revenue (TR) by producing extra and thus TR must be at the maximum. Indeed, by producing above Q_2, MR would be negative and thus TR would fall.

Sales revenue maximisation tends to involve more advertising than does profit maximisation. Ideally the profit-maximising firm will advertise up to the point

Definition

Sales revenue maximisation
An alternative theory of the firm which assumes that managers aim to maximise the firm's short-run total revenue.

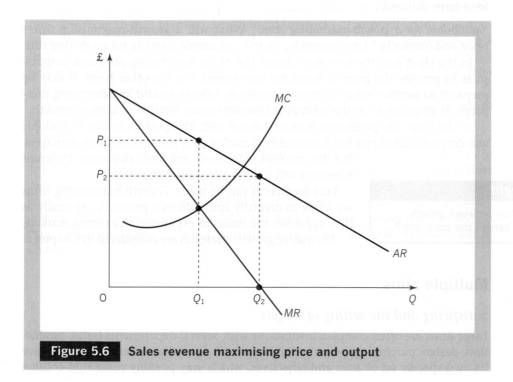

Figure 5.6   **Sales revenue maximising price and output**

Recap

- In large companies shareholders (the owners) may want maximum profits, but it is the managers who make the decisions, and managers are likely to aim to maximise their own self-interest rather than that of the shareholders. This leads to profit 'satisficing'. This is where managers aim to achieve sufficient profits to keep shareholders happy, but this is a secondary aim to one or more alternative aims.

- Some alternative theories assume that there is a single alternative aim that firms seek to maximise. Others assume that managers have a series of (possibly conflicting) aims.

- Managers may seek to maximise sales revenue. The output of a sales-revenue-maximising firm will be higher than that of a profit-maximising one. Its level of advertising will also tend to be higher.

- Many managers aim for maximum growth of their organisation, believing that this will help their salaries, power, prestige, etc. It is difficult, however, to predict the price and output strategies of a growth-maximising firm. Much depends on the judgements of particular managers about growth opportunities.

- In large firms, decisions are taken by, or influenced by, a number of different people, including various managers, shareholders, workers, customers, suppliers and creditors. If these different stakeholders have different aims, then a conflict between them is likely to arise. A firm cannot maximise more than one of these conflicting aims. The alternative is to seek to achieve a satisfactory target level of a number of aims.

- If targets were easily achieved last year, they are likely to be made more ambitious next year. If they were not achieved, a search procedure will be conducted to identify how to rectify the problem. This may mean adjusting targets downwards, in which case there will be some form of bargaining process between managers.

- Life is made easier for managers if conflict can be avoided. This will be possible if slack is allowed to develop in various parts of the firm. If targets are not being met, the slack can then be taken up without requiring adjustments in other targets.

5.4 Setting price

How are prices determined in practice? Do firms construct marginal cost and marginal revenue curves (or equations) and find the output where they are equal? Do they then use an average revenue curve (or equation) to work out the price at that output?

The problem is that firms often do not have the information to do so, even if they wanted to. In practice, firms look for rules of pricing that are relatively simple to apply.

Definition

Average cost or **Mark-up pricing**
Where firms set the price by adding a profit mark-up to average costs.

Cost-based pricing

One approach is **average cost** or **mark-up pricing**. Here producers work out the price by simply adding a certain percentage (mark-up) for profit on top of average costs (average fixed costs plus average variable costs).

$$P = AFC + AVC + \text{Profit mark-up}$$

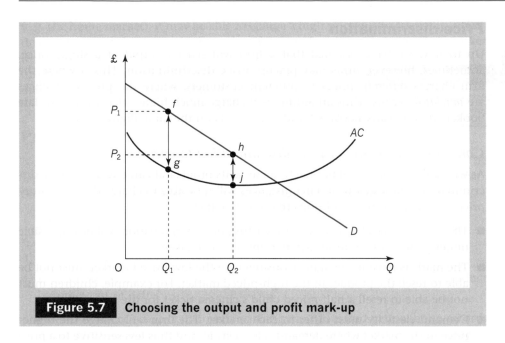

Figure 5.7   **Choosing the output and profit mark-up**

Choosing the mark-up

The level of profit mark-up on top of average cost will depend on the firm's aims: whether it is aiming for high or even maximum profits, or merely a target based on previous profit. It will also depend on the likely actions of rivals and their responses to changes in this firm's price and how these responses will affect demand.

If a firm could estimate its demand curve, it could then set its output and profit mark-up at levels to avoid a shortage or surplus. Thus in Figure 5.7 it could choose a lower output (Q_1) with a higher mark-up (fg), or a higher output (Q_2) with a lower mark-up (hj). If a firm could not estimate its demand curve, then it could adjust its mark-up and output over time by a process of trial and error, according to its success in meeting profit and sales aims.

> **Pause for thought**
>
> *If a firm has a typical-shaped average cost curve and sets prices 10 per cent above average cost, what will its supply curve look like?*

Variations in the mark-up

In most firms, the mark-up is not rigid. In expanding markets, or markets where firms have monopoly/oligopoly power, the size of the mark-up is likely to be greater. In contracting markets, or under conditions of rising costs and constant demand, a firm may well be forced to accept lower profits and thus reduce the mark-up.

The firm is likely to take account of the actions and possible reactions of its competitors. It may well be unwilling to change prices when costs or demand change, for fear of the reactions of competitors (see the kinked demand curve theory on pages 119–20). If prices are kept constant and yet costs change, either due to a movement along the *AC* curve in response to a change in demand, or due to a shift in the *AC* curve, the firm must necessarily change the size of the mark-up.

All this suggests that, whereas the mark-up may well be based on a target profit, firms are often prepared to change their target and hence their mark-up.

> **Pause for thought**
>
> *If the firm adjusts the size of its mark-up according to changes in demand and the actions of competitors, could its actions approximate to setting price and output where MC = MR?*

Business issues covered in this chapter

- What are the objectives of strategic management?

- What are the key competitive forces affecting a business?

- What choices of strategy towards competitors are open to a business?

- What internal strategic choices are open to a business and how can it make best use of its core competencies when deciding on its internal organisation?

- By what means can a business grow and how can growth be financed?

- Should businesses seek to raise finance through the stock market?

- Under what circumstances might a business want to merge with another?

- What are the advantages and problems of remaining a small business?

CHAPTER 6
Business growth and strategy

6.1   Strategic analysis

For most of the time most managers are concerned with routine day-to-day activities of the business, such as dealing with personnel issues, checking budgets and looking for ways to enhance efficiency. In other words, they are involved in the detailed operational activities of the business.

Some managers, however, especially those high up in the business organisation, such as the managing director, will be busy in a different way, thinking about big, potentially complex issues, which affect the whole company. For example, they might be analysing the behaviour of competitors, or evaluating the company's share price or considering ways to expand the business. In other words, these managers are involved in the *strategic* long-term activities of the business. This is known as **strategic management**.

Strategic management involves *analysing* the alternative long-term courses of action for the firm and then *making choices* of what strategy to pursue.

The strategic choices that are made depend on the aims of the firm. Most firms have a 'mission statement' which sets out the broad aims, but as we saw in the last chapter, the aims in practice might be difficult to establish, given the number of different stakeholders in the business. It is thus in the *actual* decisions that are taken that the firm's aims can best be judged. In practice these aims are often complex, with economic objectives, such as profit, market share, product development and growth being mixed with broader social, ethical and environmental objectives.

We look at strategic analysis in this section and strategic choices in section 6.2.

Definition

Strategic management
The management of the strategic long-term decisions and activities of the business.

Strategic analysis of the external business environment

In Chapter 1 we considered the various dimensions of the business environment and how they shape and influenced business activity. We divided the business environment into four distinct sets of factors: political, economic, social and technological. Such factors comprise what we call a PEST analysis. In this section we will take our analysis of the business environment forward and consider more closely those factors that are likely to influence the competitive advantage of the organisation.

The extent of competitive rivalry. As we saw in the previous two chapters, the degree of competition a firm faces is a crucial element in shaping its strategic analysis. Competitive rivalry will be enhanced when there is the potential for new firms to enter the market, when there is a real threat from substitute products and when buyers and suppliers have some element of influence over the firm's performance. In addition to this, competitive rivalry is likely to be enhanced in the following circumstances:

- There are many competitors and of a similar size. This is a particular issue when firms are competing in a global market.

- Markets are growing slowly. This makes it difficult to acquire additional sales without taking market share from rivals.

- Product differentiation is difficult to achieve; hence switching by consumers to competitors' products is a real threat.

- There exist high exit costs. When a business invests in non-transferable fixed assets, such as highly specialist capital equipment, it may be reluctant to leave a market. It may thus compete fiercely to maintain its market position. On the other hand, high exit costs may deter firms from entering a market in the first place and thus reduce the threat of competition.

- There exists the possibility for merger and acquisition. This competition for corporate control may have considerable influence on the firm's strategy.

Pause for thought

Given that the stronger the competitive forces the lower the profit potential for firms, describe what five-force characteristics an attractive and unattractive industry might have.

Porter's model is designed to analyse the competitive factors influencing the firm. Often, however, success might be achievable not via competition but rather through cooperation and collaboration. For example, a business might set up close links with one of its major buyers; or businesses in an industry might collaborate over research and development, thereby saving on costs.

Internal strategic analysis: analysing the value chain

It is not enough to analyse the competitive environment the business faces. If it is to develop an advantage over its rivals, a business needs to be organised effectively. Strategic analysis, therefore, also involves managers assessing the internal workings of the business, right from the purchase and delivery of inputs, to the production process, to delivering and marketing the product, to providing after-sales service.

Definition

Value chain
The stages or activities that help to create product value.

Value-chain analysis, also developed by Michael Porter, is concerned with how each of these various operations adds value to the product and contributes to the competitive position of the business. Ultimately it is these value-creating activities that shape a firm's strategic capabilities. A firm's value chain can be split into two separate sets of activities: primary and support (see Figure 6.2).

Primary activities

Primary activities cover those that involve the product's physical creation or delivery, its sale and distribution and its after-sales service. Such primary activities can be grouped into five categories:

- *Inbound logistics.* Here we are concerned with the handling of inputs, and the storage and distribution of such inputs throughout the business.

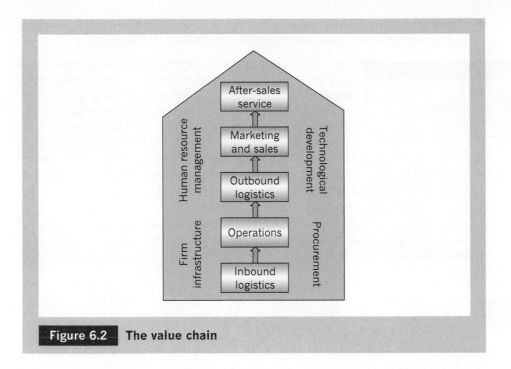

Figure 6.2   **The value chain**

- *Operations.* These activities involve the conversion of inputs into the final product or service. Operations might include manufacturing, packaging and assembly.

- *Outbound logistics.* These are concerned with transferring the final product to the consumer. Such activities would include warehousing and transport.

- *Marketing and sales.* This section of the value chain is concerned with bringing the product to the consumer's attention and would involve product advertising and promotion.

- *Service.* This can include activities such as installation and repair, as well as customer requirements such as training.

A business might attempt to add value to its activities by improving its performance in one or more of the above categories. For example, it might attempt to lower production costs or be more efficient in outbound logistics.

Support activities

Such primary activities are underpinned by support activities. These are activities that do not add value directly to any particular stage within the value chain. They do, however, provide support to such a chain and ensure that its various stages are undertaken effectively. Support activities include:

- *Procurement.* This involves the acquisition of inputs by the firm.

- *Technological development.* This includes activities within the business that support new product and process developments, such as the use of research departments.

- *Human resource management.* Activities in this category include things such as recruitment, training and wage negotiation and determination.

■ *Firm infrastructure.* This category includes activities such as financial planning and control systems, quality control and information management.

Pause for thought

Is it possible to add value to the firm by improving any or all of these support activities?

As well as creating value directly themselves, most firms buy in certain value-chain activities, such as employing another firm to do its advertising, or using an external delivery firm to distribute its products. The outsourcing of these activities might prove to be far more beneficial to a business than providing the activities itself. You can employ the best advertisers or the most reliable distributors. It may also be cheaper than doing things in-house. The companies you employ are likely to have economies of scale in their specialist activity (see page 87) and therefore be able to offer the service at a lower cost than you could achieve.

With the background to strategic analysis defined, we can now shift our focus to consider strategic choice and implementation. What strategies are potentially open to businesses and how do they choose the right ones and set about implementing them?

Recap

■ Strategic management differs from operational management (the day-to-day running of the business) as it focuses on issues which affect the whole business, usually over the long term.

■ In conducting strategic analysis the business should assess its external and internal environment.

■ The Five Forces Model of the external environment identifies those factors that are most likely to influence the competition faced by a business. The five forces are: the bargaining power of suppliers, the bargaining power of buyers, the threat of potential new entrants, the threat of substitutes, and the extent of competitive rivalry.

■ The internal environment can be assessed by value-chain analysis. The value chain can be split into primary and support activities. Primary activities are those that directly create value, such as operations and marketing and sales. Support activities are those that underpin value creation in other areas, such as procurement and human resource management.

6.2 Strategic choice

As with strategic analysis, strategic choices fall into two main categories. The first concerns choices to do with the external business environment: for example, choices of how to compete and what markets to target. The second concerns choices about the internal organisation of the firm and how to use its resources.

Environment- or market-based strategic choices

As with many other areas in this field, our analysis of market-based choices starts with the observations of Michael Porter. As an extension of his Five Forces Model of competition, Porter argued that there are three fundamental (or 'generic') strategies that a business might adopt:

- cost leadership;
- differentiation;
- focus.

In order to identify which of these was the most appropriate strategy, a business would need to establish two things: (a) the basis of its competitive advantage – whether it lies in lower costs or differentiation; (b) the nature of the target market – is it broad or a distinct market niche?

Cost leadership

As the title implies, a business that is a low-cost leader is able to manufacture and deliver its product more cheaply than its rivals, thereby gaining competitive advantage. The strategic emphasis here is on driving out inefficiency at every stage of the value chain. 'No-frills' budget airlines, such as easyJet and Ryanair, are classic examples of companies that pursue a cost-leadership strategy.

A strategy based upon cost leadership may require a fundamentally different use of resources or organisational structure if the firm is to stay ahead of its rivals. Wal-Mart's hub and spoke distribution system would be an example in point. Here the company distributes its products to shops from regional depots in order to minimise transport costs.

In addition, firms that base their operations on low costs in order to achieve low prices (although that may not necessarily be the aim of low costs) are unlikely to have a high level of brand loyalty. In other words, if customer choice is going to be driven largely by price, demand is likely to be relatively price elastic. Other virtues of the product that might tie in buyers, such as quality or after-sales service, are largely absent from such firms' strategic goals.

Differentiation

A differentiation strategy aims to emphasise and promote the uniqueness of the firm's product: to make demand less elastic. As such, high rather than low prices are often attached to such products. Product characteristics such as quality, design and reliability are the basis of the firm's competitive advantage. Hence a strategy that adds to such differences and creates value for the customer needs to be identified.

Such a strategy might result in higher costs, especially in the short term, as the firm pursues constant product development through innovation, design and research. However, with the ability to charge premium prices, revenues may increase more than costs: i.e. the firm may achieve higher profits. Games console manufacturers, such as Sony with its PlayStation and Microsoft with its X Box, are a good example. Even though they are in fierce competition with each other, both manufacturers focus their strategy on trying to differentiate their products from their rival's. This differentiation is in terms of features and performance, not price. Processor speed, online capabilities, software support and product image are all characteristics used in the competitive battle.

Focus strategy

Rather than considering a whole market as a potential for sales, a focus strategy involves identifying market niches and designing and promoting products for them. In doing so a business may be able to exploit some advantage over its rivals, whether in terms of costs, or product difference. An example is Häagen-Dazs ice cream (a division of General Mills). The mass low-cost ice-cream market is served by a other large multinational food manufacturers and processors (such as Unilever, with its Wall's brand), and by supermarkets' own brands, but the existence of niche high-quality ice-cream markets offers opportunities for companies like

Box 6.1

Sashimi Theory

Business the Samsung way

The following extracts are taken from two articles from *BusinessWeek*. They sketch an outline of some of the strategic initiatives undertaken by one of the most successful consumer electronic firms of recent times, Samsung.

Samsung's recent success is quite an achievement, given the massive financial problems it was left facing following the Asian financial crisis in the late 1990s. Since that time it has managed not only to shake off its debts and post significant improvements in profits, but to reposition itself upmarket within the consumer electronics industry.

How has Samsung achieved this? What have been the keys to its success? The following extracts are from Samsung's 'Sashimi Theory' of Success (11 June 2003).

Yun Jong Yong has a vivid way of describing his survival strategy in today's hypercompetitive consumer-electronics market, where today's hot-selling novelty can become a cheap commodity within months. The vice-chairman and CEO of Samsung Electronics calls it the 'sashimi theory.' When prime fish is first caught, it's very expensive at a top-notch Japanese restaurant. If some of the fish is left over, it sells the next day for half the price at a second-tier restaurant. By the third day, it goes for one-fourth the price. 'After that,' Yun says, 'it's dried fish.'

So the secret to success in consumer electronics is getting the most advanced products onto retail shelves ahead of the competition. That way, you can charge premium prices – until the rest of the pack catches up and the product is no longer fresh. 'In our business, there's money to be made if you can reduce the lead time to customers,' Yun says. 'If I can reduce that time by one week, it makes a big difference. If you're two months late to the market, the game is finished.'

Few electronics companies are doing a better job than Samsung at keeping their products from turning into yesterday's sashimi. Samsung has been consistently hitting global markets with cutting-edge cell phones, wide-screen TVs, memory chips, and video cameras ahead of its main rivals, enabling it to charge some of the highest prices in the industry.

It's a dramatic change for a company that just six years ago was in perilous financial shape and whose brand was mainly associated with low-end TVs and air conditioners. . . .

Yun took aggressive measures to clean up Samsung's finances. He laid off 24 000 employees – about 30% of Samsung Electronics' payroll – and sold off $2 billion worth of corporate assets. In another break from tradition, Yun ordered Samsung's consumer-appliance factories shut for several months. . . .

Samsung had always been obsessed with boosting production and sales volume. After the Asia crisis, it took careful stock of where all the output went and discovered it had four months' worth of inventory of TVs, computers, and other products sitting in offshore warehouses. The value of the excess inventory was more than $2 billion. . . .

[A major step was] reducing inventory cycles. At one point in 1996, prices of DRAMs – which then accounted for 60% of Samsung's exports – were dropping by 1% every week, or by 50% each year. The longer the chips sat in inventory, the lower the price they fetched on the market. By dramatically shrinking the period between which an electronics product is made and the time it's sold, therefore, Samsung was able to reap higher average prices. . . .

Another key to the turnaround was Samsung's decision to recreate itself as an up-market brand. Not only would it spend heavily on more sophisticated marketing and focus on producing high-end phones and appliances but Yun also declared that Samsung would completely abandon low-end products, even if that meant passing up easy opportunities for big sales.

Häagen-Dazs and Ben & Jerry's. By focusing on such consumers they are able to sell and market their product at premium prices.

Niche markets, however profitable, are by their nature small and as such limited in their growth potential. There is also the possibility that niches might shift over time or even disappear. This would require a business to be flexible in setting out its strategic position.

The following extracts are from The Samsung Way (16 June 2003)

A few measures of Samsung's progress: It has become the biggest maker of digital mobile phones using code division multiple access (CDMA) technology – and while it still lags No. 2 Motorola Inc. in handsets sold, it has just passed it in overall global revenues. A year ago, you'd have been hard pressed to find a Samsung high-definition TV in the U.S. Now, Samsung is the best-selling brand in TVs priced at $3000 and above – a mantle long held by Sony and Mitsubishi Corp. In the new market for digital music players, Samsung's three-year-old Yepp is behind only the Rio of Japan's D&M Holdings Inc. and Apple Computer Inc.'s iPod. Samsung has blown past Micron Technology, Infineon Technologies, and Hynix Semiconductor in dynamic random-access memory (DRAM) chips – used in all PCs – and is gaining on Intel in the market for flash memory, used in digital cameras, music players, and handsets. In 2002, with most of techdom reeling, Samsung earned $5.9 billion on sales of $33.8 billion. . . .

Rather than outsource manufacturing, the company sinks billions into huge new factories. Instead of bearing down on a few 'core competencies,' Samsung remains diversified and vertically integrated – Samsung chips and displays go into its own digital products. . . .

Yet the industrial history of the past two decades suggests that this model does not work in the long run. The hazard – as many Japanese, U.S., and European companies learned in the 1980s and '90s – is that Samsung must keep investing heavily in R&D and new factories across numerous product lines. Samsung has sunk $19 billion over five years into new chip facilities. Rivals can buy similar technologies from other vendors without tying up capital or making long-term commitments. What's more, the life cycle of much hardware is brutally short and subject to relentless commoditization. The average price of a TV set has dropped 30% in five years; a

DVD player goes for less than a quarter. The Chinese keep driving prices ever lower, leveraging supercheap wages and engineering talent. Meanwhile, the Japanese are building their own Chinese factories to lower costs. No wonder Samsung exited the low-margin market for TV sets 27 inches and under.

Faced with these perils, Samsung needs a constant stream of well-timed hits to stay on top. . . .

Samsung's strategy to win is pretty basic, but it's executing it with ferocious drive over a remarkably broad conglomerate. . . .

Samsung managers who have worked for big competitors say they go through far fewer layers of bureaucracy to win approval for new products, budgets, and marketing plans, speeding up their ability to seize opportunities. . . .

Second, Samsung often forces its own units to compete with outsiders to get the best solution. In the liquid-crystal-display business, Samsung buys half of its color filters from Sumitomo Chemical Co. of Japan and sources the other half internally, pitting the two teams against each other. . . .

The next step is to customize as much as possible. Even in memory chips, the ultimate commodity, Samsung commands prices that are 17% above the industry average. A key reason is that 60% of its memory devices are custom-made for products like Dell servers, Microsoft Xbox game consoles, and even Nokia's cell phones. . . .

The final ingredient is speed. Samsung says it takes an average of five months to go from new product concept to rollout, compared to 14 months six years ago. . . .

Questions

1. Identify the main features of Samsung's business strategy.
2. What core competencies does Samsung have? (You might justify a core competence in terms of *all* four of the criteria given on page 144.)

Internal resource-based strategic choices

Resource-based strategy focuses on exploiting a firm's internal organisation and production processes in order to develop its competitive advantage. It is important that the firm does certain things better or more cheaply than its rivals. What the firm will seek to exploit or to develop is one or more 'core competencies'.

Core competencies

Definition

Core competences
The key skills of a business that underpin its competitive advantage.

Core competencies are those skills, knowledge and technologies that underpin the organisation's competitive advantage. These competencies are likely to differ from one business to another, reflecting the uniqueness of each individual organisation, and ultimately determining its potential for success. The business should seek to exploit these competencies, whether in the design of the product or in its methods of production.

In many cases, however, firms do not have any competencies that give them a distinctive competitive advantage, even though they may still be profitable. In such instances, strategy often focuses either on *developing* such competencies or simply on more effectively using the resources the firm already has.

What defines a core competence?

A core competence (or core resource) must satisfy the following four capabilities to serve as a source of competitive advantage for the business. It must be:

- *valuable*: a competence that helps the firm deal with threats or contributes to business opportunities;
- *rare*: a competence or resource that is not possessed by competitors;
- *costly to imitate*: a competence or resource that other firms find difficult to develop and copy;
- *non-substitutable*: a competence or resource for which there is no alternative.

Recap

- Strategic choice often involves a consideration of both external and internal factors.

- External environment- or market-based strategies are of three types: cost leadership strategy, where competitiveness is achieved by lower costs; differentiation strategy, where the business promotes the uniqueness of its product; focus strategy, where competitiveness is achieved by identifying market niches and tailoring products for different groups of consumers.

- Internal strategy normally involves identifying core competencies as the key to a business's compeitive advantage. A core competence will be valuable, rare, costly to imitate and non-substitutable.

Growth strategy   6.3

Whether businesses wish to grow or not, many are forced to. The dynamic competitive process of the market drives producers on to expand in order to remain in the marketplace. If a business fails to grow, this may benefit its more aggressive rivals. They may secure a greater share of the market, leaving the first firm with reduced profits. Thus business growth is often vital if a firm is to survive.

In this section we consider the various growth strategies open to firms and assess their respective advantages and disadvantages. Growth may be achieved by one or both of the following:

- **Internal expansion**. This is where a business looks to expand its productive capacity by adding to existing plant or by building new plant.

- **External expansion**. This is where a business grows by merging with other firms or by taking them over.

Whether the business embarks upon internal or external expansion, a number of alternative growth paths are open to the business. Figure 6.3 shows these various routes.

> **Definition**
>
> **Internal expansion**
> Where a business adds to its productive capacity by adding to existing or by building new plant.
>
> **External expansion**
> Where business growth is achieved by merging with or taking over businesses within a market or industry.

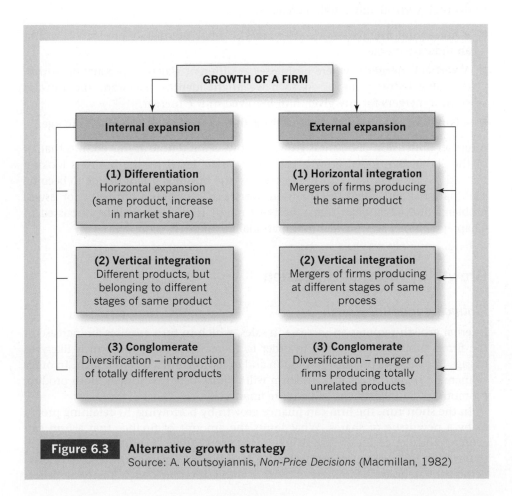

Figure 6.3   Alternative growth strategy
Source: A. Koutsoyiannis, *Non-Price Decisions* (Macmillan, 1982)

Definition

Product differentiation

In the context of growth strategies, this is where a business upgrades existing products or services so as to make them different from those of rival firms.

Vertical integration

A business growth strategy that involves expanding within an existing market, but at a different stage of production. Vertical integration can be 'forward', such as moving into distribution or retail, or 'backward', such as expanding into extracting raw materials or producing components.

Diversification

A business growth strategy in which a business expands into new markets outside of its current interests.

Horizontal merger

Where two firms in the same industry at the same stage of the production process merge.

Vertical merger

Where two firms in the same industry at different stages in the production process merge.

Conglomerate merger

Where two firms in different industries merge.

Internal expansion

In order to achieve additional sales, the business must seek new demand in order to justify investment in additional capacity. There are three main ways of doing this:

■ The firm can expand or **differentiate its product** within existing markets, by, for example, updating or restyling its product, or improving its technical characteristics.

■ Alternatively, the business might seek to expand via **vertical integration**. This involves the firm expanding within the same product market, but at a different stage of production. For example, a car manufacturer might wish to produce its own components ('backward vertical integration') or distribute and sell its own car models ('forward vertical integration').

■ As a third option, the business might seek to expand outside of its current product range, and move into new markets. This is known as a process of **diversification**.

External expansion (growth through mergers and takeovers)

Similar growth paths can be pursued via external expansion. However, in this case the business does not create the productive facilities itself, but purchases existing production. As Figure 6.3 identifies, we can distinguish three types of merger: horizontal, vertical and conglomerate.

■ A **horizontal merger** is where two firms at the same stage of production within an industry merge.

■ A **vertical merger** is where businesses at different stages of production within the same industry merge. As such we might identify backward and forward vertical mergers for any given firm involved in the merger.

■ A **conglomerate merger** is where firms in totally unrelated industries merge.

A further dimension of business growth that we should note at this point is that all of the above-mentioned growth paths can be achieved by the business looking beyond its national markets. In other words, the business might decide to become multinational and invest in expansion overseas. This raises a further set of issues, problems and advantages that a business might face. These will be discussed in Chapter 12 when we consider multinational business.

Growth by internal expansion

Financing internal growth

Internal growth requires an increase in sales, which in turn requires an increase in the firm's productive capacity. In order to increase its *sales*, the firm is likely to engage in extensive product promotion and to try to launch new products. In order to increase *productive capacity*, the firm will require new investment. Both product promotion and investment will require finance.

In the short run, the firm can finance growth by borrowing, by retaining profits or by a new issue of shares. What limits the amount of finance that a firm can acquire, and hence the rate at which it can grow? If the firm *borrows* too much, the interest payments it incurs will make it difficult to maintain the level of dividends to shareholders. Similarly, if the firm *retains* too much *profit*, there will be less available to pay out in dividends. Also, if it attempts to raise capital by a *new issue of shares*, the distributed profits will have to be divided between a larger number of shares. Whichever way it finances investment, therefore, the more it invests, the more the dividends on shares in the short run will probably fall.

This could lead shareholders to sell their shares, unless they are confident that *long-run* profits and hence dividends will rise again, thus causing the share price to remain high in the long run. If shareholders do sell their shares, this will cause share prices to fall. If they fall too far, the firm runs the risk of being taken over and of certain managers losing their jobs. The **takeover constraint** therefore requires that the growth-maximising firm distribute sufficient profits to avoid being taken over.

In the long run, a rapidly growing firm may find its profits increasing, especially if it can achieve economies of scale and a bigger share of the market. These profits can then be used to finance further growth.

> **Definition**
>
> **Takeover constraint**
> The effect that the fear of being taken over has on a firm's willingness to undertake projects that reduce distributed profits.

Growth through vertical integration

If market conditions make growth through increased sales difficult, then a firm may choose to grow through vertical integration. This has a number of advantages:

Economies of scale.   These can occur by the business performing *complementary* stages of production within a single business unit. The classic example of this is the steel manufacturer combining the furnacing and milling stages of production, saving the costs that would have been required to reheat the iron had such operations been undertaken by independent businesses. Clearly, for most firms, the performing of more than one stage on a single site is likely to reduce transport costs, as semi-finished products no longer have to be moved from one plant to another.

Reduced uncertainty.   A business that is not vertically integrated may find itself subject to various uncertainties in the marketplace. Examples include: uncertainty over future price movements, supply reliability or access to markets.

Backward vertical integration will enable the business to control its supply chain. Without such integration the firm may feel very vulnerable, especially if there are only a few suppliers within the market. In such cases the suppliers would be able to exert considerable control over price. Alternatively, suppliers may be unreliable.

Forward vertical integration creates greater certainty in so far as it gives the business guaranteed access to distribution and retailing on its own terms. As with supply, forward markets might be dominated by large buyers, which are able not only to dictate price, but also to threaten market foreclosure (being shut out from a market). Forward vertical integration can remove the possibility of such events occurring.

Barriers to entry.   Vertical integration may give the firm greater power in the market by enabling it to erect entry barriers to potential competitors. For example, a firm that undertakes backward vertical integration and acquires a key input resource can effectively close the market to potential new entrants, either by simply refusing to supply a competitor, or by charging a very high price for the input such that new firms face an absolute cost disadvantage.

> **Pause for thought**
>
> *See if you can identify two companies that are vertically integrated and what advantages they have from such integration.*

The major problem with vertical integration is that it may reduce the firm's ability to respond to changing market demands. A business that integrates, either backward or forward, ties itself to particular supply sources or particular retail outlets. If, by contrast, it were free to choose between suppliers, inputs might be obtained at a lower price than the firm could achieve by supplying itself. Equally, the ability to shift between retail outlets would allow the firm to locate in the best market positions. This may not be possible if it is tied to its own retail network.

Many firms are finding that it is better *not* to be vertically integrated but to focus on their core competencies and to outsource their supplies, their marketing and many other functions. That way they put alternative suppliers and distributors in competition with each other.

An alternative is to be *partially* vertically integrated, through a process known as **tapered vertical integration**.

Tapered vertical integration.   This involves firms making part of a given input themselves and subcontracting the production of the remainder to one or more other firms. For example, Coca-Cola and Pepsi are large vertically integrated enterprises. They have, as part of their operations, wholly-owned bottling subsidiaries. However, in certain markets they subcontract to independent bottlers both to produce and to market their product.

By making a certain amount of an input itself, the firm is less reliant on suppliers, but does not require as much capital equipment as if it produced all the input itself. A policy of tapered vertical integration suits many multinational companies. In certain countries, they produce the inputs themselves; in others, they rely on local suppliers, drawing on the supplier's competitive advantage in that local market.

Growth through diversification

An alternative internal growth strategy to vertical integration is that of diversification. A good example of a highly diversified company is Virgin. As we saw in Box 3.2 (page 73), Virgin's interests include planes, trains, cars, finance, music, mobile phones, holidays, wine, cinemas, radio, cosmetics, publishing and even space travel.

If the current market is saturated, stagnant or in decline, diversification might be the only avenue open to the business if it wishes to maintain a high growth performance. In other words, it is not only the level of profits that may be limited in the current market, but also the growth of sales.

Diversification also has the advantage of spreading risks. So long as a business produces a single product in a single market, it is vulnerable to changes in that market's conditions. If a farmer produces nothing but potatoes, and the potato harvest fails, the farmer is ruined. If, however, the farmer produces a whole range of vegetable products, or even diversifies into livestock, then he or she is less subject to the forces of nature and the unpredictability of the market.

Growth through merger

A **merger** is a situation in which, as a result of mutual agreement, two firms decide to bring together their business operations. A merger is distinct from a takeover in so far as a **takeover** involves one firm bidding for another's shares (often against the will of the directors of the target firm). One firm thereby acquires another.

In order to avoid confusion at this stage, we will use the term 'merger' to refer to *both* mergers ('mutual agreements') and takeovers ('acquisitions').

Definition

Tapered vertical integration
Where a firm is partially integrated with an earlier stage of production: where it produces *some* of an input itself and buys some from another firm.

Merger
The outcome of a mutual agreement made by two firms to combine their business activities.

Takeover
Where one business acquires another. A takeover may not necessarily involve mutual agreement between the two parties. In such cases, the takeover might be viewed as 'hostile'.

Why merge?

Why do firms want to merge with or take over others? Is it purely that they want to grow: are mergers simply evidence of the hypothesis that firms are growth maximisers? Or are there other motives that influence the predatory drive?

Merger for growth.   Mergers provide a much quicker means to growth than does internal expansion. Not only does the firm acquire new capacity, but also it acquires additional consumer demand. Building up this level of consumer demand by internal expansion might have taken a considerable length of time.

Merger for economies of scale.   Once the merger has taken place, the constituent parts can be reorganised through a process of 'rationalisation'. The result can be a reduction in costs. For example, only one head office will now be needed. On the marketing side, the two parts of the newly merged company may now share distribution and retail channels, benefiting from each other's knowledge and operation in distinct market segments or geographical locations.

The merger of Airbus Industries' partners, Aerospatiale-Matra of France, DaimlerChrysler Aerospace of Germany and Construcciones Aeronauticas of Spain, is estimated to have saved, through rationalisation, hundreds of millions of pounds annually. The newly created firm European Aeronautics Space and Defence Company (EADS) owns 80 per cent of Airbus, while BAe Systems of the UK owns the remaining 20 per cent. The rationalisation process was seen by many as necessary if Airbus was effectively to challenge its main rival Boeing of the USA.

In fact, the evidence on costs suggests that most mergers result in few if any cost savings: either potential economies of scale are not exploited due to a lack of rationalisation, or diseconomies result from the disruptions of reorganisation. New managers installed by the parent company are often seen as unsympathetic, and morale may go down.

Merger for monopoly power.   Here the motive is to reduce competition and thereby gain greater market power and larger profits. This applies mainly to horizontal mergers. With less competition, the firm will face a less elastic demand and be able to charge a higher percentage above marginal cost. What is more, the new more powerful company will be in a stronger position to regulate entry into the market by erecting effective entry barriers, thereby enhancing its monopoly position yet further.

> **Pause for thought**
>
> *Which of the three types of merger (horizontal, vertical and conglomerate) are most likely to lead to (a) reductions in average costs; (b) increased market power?*

Merger for increased market valuation.   A merger can benefit shareholders of *both* firms if it leads to an increase in the stock market valuation of the merged firm. If both sets of shareholders believe that they will make a capital gain on their shares, then they are more likely to give the go-ahead for the merger.

In practice, however, there is little evidence to show that mergers lead to a capital gain. One possible reason for this is the lack of reduction in costs referred to above. In fact, a survey by *BusinessWeek* in 2002 showed that 61 per cent of mergers undertaken in the USA during the merger boom in Spring 1998 actually *reduced* shareholder value.

Merger to reduce uncertainty.   Firms face uncertainty at two levels. The first is in their own markets. The behaviour of rivals may be highly unpredictable. Mergers, by reducing the number of rivals, can correspondingly reduce uncertainty. At the same time, they can reduce the *costs* of competition (e.g. reducing the need to advertise).

The second source of uncertainty is the economic environment. In a period of rapid change, such as often accompanies a boom, firms may seek to protect themselves by merging with others.

Other motives.   Other motives for mergers include:

■ Getting bigger so as to become less likely to be taken over oneself.

■ Merging with another firm so as to defend it from an unwanted predator (the 'White Knight' strategy).

■ Asset stripping. This is where a firm takes over another and then breaks it up, selling off the profitable bits and probably closing down the remainder.

■ Empire building. This is where owners or managers favour takeovers because of the power or prestige of owning or controlling several (preferably well-known) companies.

■ Geographical expansion. The motive here is to broaden the geographical base of the company by merging with a firm in a different part of the country or the world.

Mergers, especially horizontal ones, will generally have the effect of increasing the market power of those firms involved. This could lead to less choice and higher prices for the consumer. For this reason, mergers have become the target for government competition policy. Such policy is the subject of Chapter 8.

Growth through strategic alliances

One means of achieving growth is through the formation of **strategic alliances** with other firms. They are a means whereby business operations can be expanded relatively quickly and at relatively low cost, and are a common way in which firms can deepen their involvement in global markets.

There are many types of strategic alliance between businesses, covering a wide range of alternative collaborative arrangements.

Joint ventures.   A **joint venture** is where two or more firms decide to create, and jointly own, a new independent organisation. The creation of Cellnet by BT and Securicor is an example of such a strategy.

Consortia.   In recent years, many consortia have been created. Camelot, the company that runs the UK National Lottery, and Trans Manche Link, the company that built the Channel Tunnel, are two examples. A **consortium** is usually created for very specific projects, such as a large civil engineering work. As such, they have a very focused objective and once the project is completed the consortium is usually dissolved.

Franchising.   A less formal strategic alliance is where a business agrees to **franchise** its operations to third parties. McDonald's and Coca-Cola are good examples of businesses that use a franchise network. In such a relationship the franchisee is

Definition

Strategic alliance
Where two firms work together, formally or informally, to achieve a mutually desirable goal.

Joint venture
Where two or more firms set up and jointly own a new independent firm.

Consortium
Where two or more firms work together on a specific project and create a separate company to run the project.

Franchise
A formal agreement whereby a company uses another company to produce or sell some or all of its product.

responsible for manufacturing and/or selling, and the franchiser retains responsibility for branding and marketing.

Subcontracting. Like franchising, **subcontracting** is a less formal source of strategic alliance, where companies maintain their independence. When a business subcontracts, it employs an independent business to manufacture or supply some service rather conduct the activity itself. Car manufacturers are major subcontractors. Given the multitude and complexity of components that are required to manufacture a car, the use of subcontractors to supply specialist items, such as brakes and lights, seems a logical way to organise the business.

Networks. **Networks** are less formal than any of the above alliances. A network is where two or more businesses work collaboratively but without any formal relationship binding one to the other. Such a form of collaboration is highly prevalent in Japan. Rather than a formal contract regulating the behaviour of the partners to the agreement, their relationship is based upon an understanding of trust and loyalty.

> **Definition**
>
> **Subcontracting**
> Where a firm employs another firm to produce part of its output or some of its input(s).
>
> **Network**
> An informal arrangement between businesses to work together towards some common goal.

Why form strategic alliances?

As a business expands, possibly internationally, it may well be advantageous to join with an existing player in the market. Such a business would have local knowledge and an established network of suppliers and distributors.

In addition, strategic alliances allow firms to share risk. The Channel Tunnel and the consortium of firms that built it is one such example. The construction of the Channel Tunnel was a massive undertaking and far too risky for any single firm to embark upon. With the creation of a consortium, risk was spread, and the various consortium members were able to specialise in their areas of expertise.

They also allow firms to pool capital. Projects that might have prohibitively high start-up costs, or running costs, may become feasible if firms cooperate and pool their capital. In addition, an alliance of firms, with their combined assets and credibility, may find it easier to generate finance, whether from investors in the stock market or from the banking sector.

The past 20 years have seen a flourishing of strategic alliances. They have become a key growth strategy for business both domestically and internationally. They are seen as a way of expanding business operations quickly without the difficulties associated with the more aggressive approach of acquisition or the more lengthy process of merger.

Growth through going global

In many respects a firm's global strategy is simply an extension of its strategy within its own domestic market. However, opening up to global markets can provide an obvious means for a business to expand its markets and spread its risks. It also is a means of reducing costs, whether through economies of scale or from accessing cheap sources of supply or low-wage production facilities.

A firm's global growth strategy may involve simply exporting or opening up factories abroad, or it may involve merging with businesses abroad or forming strategic alliances. As barriers to trade and the international flow of capital have

The role of the Stock Exchange

The London Stock Exchange operates as both a primary and secondary market in capital.

Definition

Primary market in capital

Where shares are sold by the issuer of the shares (i.e. the firm) and where, therefore, finance is channelled directly from the purchasers (i.e. the shareholders) to the firm.

Secondary market in capital

Where shareholders sell shares to others. This is thus a market in 'second-hand' shares.

As a **primary market** it is where public limited companies (see page 7) can raise finance by issuing new shares, whether to new shareholders or to existing ones. To raise finance on the Stock Exchange a business must be 'listed'. The Listing Agreement involves directors agreeing to abide by a strict set of rules governing behaviour and levels of reporting to shareholders. A company must have at least three years' trading experience and make at least 25 per cent of its shares available to the public. In 2004, there were over 1500 UK and nearly 400 international companies on the Official List. During 2002/03, 202 companies raised £17.9 billion's worth of new capital by selling equity (ordinary shares) and fixed-interest securities on the London Stock Exchange.

As well as those on the Official List, there are some 750 companies on what is known as the Alternative Investment Market (AIM). Companies listed here tend to be young but with growth potential, and do not have to meet the strict criteria or pay such high costs as companies on the Official List.

As a **secondary market**, the Stock Exchange operates as a market where investors can sell existing shares to one another. In 2003, on an average day's trading, £7.5 billion's worth of trading in UK equities and £7.0 billion's worth of trading in international equities took place.

The advantages and disadvantages of using the stock market to raise capital

As a market for raising capital the stock market has a number of advantages:

- It brings together those that wish to invest and those that seek investment. It thus represents a way that savings can be mobilised to create output, and does so in a relatively low-cost way.

- Firms that are listed on the Stock Exchange are subject to strict regulations. This is likely to stimulate investor confidence, making it easier for business to raise finance.

- The process of merger and acquisition is facilitated by having a share system. It enables business more effectively to pursue this as a growth strategy.

The main weaknesses of the stock market for raising capital are:

- The cost to a business of getting listed can be immense, not only in a financial sense, but also in being open to public scrutiny. Directors' and senior managers' decisions will often be driven by how the market is likely to react, rather by what they perceive to be in the business's best interests. They always have to think about the reactions of those large shareholders in the City that control a large proportion of their shares.

- It is often claimed that the stock market suffers from *short-termism*. Investors on the Stock Exchange are more concerned with a company's short-term performance and its share value. In responding to this, the business might neglect its long-term performance and potential.

Is the stock market efficient?

One of the arguments made in favour of the stock market is that it acts as an arena within which share values can be accurately or efficiently priced. If new information comes on to the market concerning a business and its performance, this will be quickly and rationally transferred into the business's share value. This is known as the **efficient market hypothesis**. So for example, if an investment analyst found that, in terms of its actual and expected dividends, a particular share was under-priced and thus represented a 'bargain', the analyst would advise investors to buy. As people then bought the shares, their price would rise, pushing their value up to their full worth. So by attempting to gain from inefficiently priced securities, investors will encourage the market to become more efficient.

> **Efficient capital markets.**
>
> Capital markets are efficient when the prices of shares accurately reflect information about companies' current and expected future performance.
>
> **Key Idea 15**

If the market were perfectly efficient in this sense, then no gain could be made from studying a company's performance and prospects, as any such information would *already* be included in the current share price. In selecting shares, you would do just as well by pinning the financial pages of a newspaper on the wall, throwing darts at them, and buying the shares the darts hit!

If the stock market were perfectly efficient, it would only be unanticipated information that would cause share prices to deviate from that which reflected expected average yields. Such information must, by its nature, be random, and as such would cause share prices to deviate randomly from their expected price, or follow what we call a **random walk**. Evidence suggests that share prices do tend to follow random patterns.

Definition

Efficient (capital) market hypothesis
The hypothesis that new information about a company's current or future performance will be quickly and accurately reflected in its share price.

Random walk
Where fluctuations in the value of a share away from its 'correct' value are random. When charted over time, these share price movements would appear like a 'random walk' – like the path of someone staggering along drunk.

Recap

- Business finance can come from internal and external sources. Sources external to the firm include borrowing and the issue of shares.

- The stock market operates as both a primary and secondary market in capital. As a primary market it channels finance to companies as people purchase new shares. It is also a market for existing shares.

- It helps to stimulate growth and investment by bringing together companies and people who want to invest in them. By regulating firms and by keeping transaction costs of investment low, it helps to ensure that investment is efficient.

- It does impose costs on firms, however. It is expensive for firms to be listed and the public exposure may make them too keen to 'please' the market. It can also foster short-termism.

- The stock market is relatively efficient. It achieves efficiency by allowing share prices to respond quickly and fully to publicly available information.

Box 6.2

The Dyson Dual Cyclone vacuum cleaner

A small business redefining the Hoover

In 1995, Dyson Appliances recorded turnover of £55 million. Just one year later, with sales of 30 000 vacuum cleaners and a turnover of £8 million a month, Dyson Appliances was outperforming the market's major players, Hoover and Electrolux.

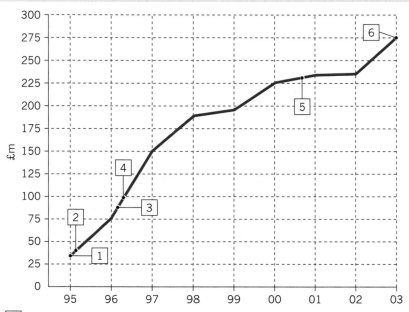

1	**1995** – Currys and Comet agree to sell Dyson
2	**Feb 1995** – Dyson DC-01 becomes best-selling upright cleaner
3	**Feb 1996** – R&D centre opens
4	**Mar 1996** – Dyson DC-02 becomes best-selling cylinder cleaner
5	**Oct 2000** – High Court injunction bans sale of Hoover's bagless cleaner
6	**2003** – Dyson secures distribution network of 3000 shops in USA

Dyson's turnover 1995–2003
Source: Dyson and *Dyson's domestic dilemma* BBC News Online, 2 October 2003

The tale of the Dyson Dual Cyclone vacuum cleaner records the successful and dramatic rise of James Dyson. As a budding entrepreneur, in the early 1980s he invented a revolutionary bagless vacuum cleaner, which worked, in effect, by creating a mini cyclone, whereby a high-speed air vortex pushed dust particles to the side of a collector. Without a bag, the suction power of the cleaner would not diminish over time, unlike conventional vacuums. When he initially developed this product (there were 5000 prototypes before a marketable product was finalised), neither Electrolux nor Hoover was interested – largely because of the profits they made from selling bags!

After an early and unsuccessful attempt to launch the project, Dyson managed to secure a deal with a Japanese company to produce and sell his product in Japan, where his vacuum retailed for a staggering £1200. At this price, it was unlikely to yield the mass sales Dyson hoped for, even given the superiority of the product. Thus Dyson set out to manufacture the product himself.

Finding it difficult to raise capital and find backers, Dyson reinvested his profits from the Japanese sales, and managed to raise the £4.5 million required to design and patent his product, to establish a network of subcontractor suppliers, and to create an assembly plant in the UK. With his vacuum cleaner priced at £200, Dyson hoped to enter the market at an affordable price.

Today, Dyson's vacuum cleaner has 50 per cent of the UK market and accounts for one-fifth of all vacuum cleaner sales across Western Europe.

Not content to sit on his success, James Dyson, at the end of 1999, launched his robot cleaner, a £5 million project which he hopes will have the same impact on the cleaner market as his bagless vacuum. He is hoping that by 2005 worldwide sales from the robot vacuum will be in the region of £2 billion, a substantial increase over the £400 million that the company currently earns.

The Dyson Dual Cyclone vacuum cleaner is a classic example of how a small business with a revolutionary product can have a massive impact on a market, and within a short period of time become established as a market leader.

In recognition of his contribution to innovation, the Trade and Industry Secretary, Patricia Hewitt, in 2003 named James Dyson as her 'innovation tsar'.

The Dyson story has not, however, been all good news for the UK: in 2002, Dyson shifted production from its Malmesbury plant in the UK to Malaysia, with the loss of 560 UK jobs. Dyson countered criticisms of the move by arguing that fierce competition from competitors, who were selling bagless cleaners for half the price of Dysons, forced the company to relocate its manufacturing to a country where labour was much cheaper and which was close to suppliers of parts.

Also, Dyson has created over 100 new jobs in the UK in R&D and is working on a whole range of new innovative products. His philosophy of investing in new technology and new products remains his core strategy for business success.

Questions

1. What conditions existed to enable James Dyson's small business to do so well in such a short period of time?
2. In retrospect, were Electrolux and Hoover correct not to produce the new type of vacuum cleaner? Should they do so now?

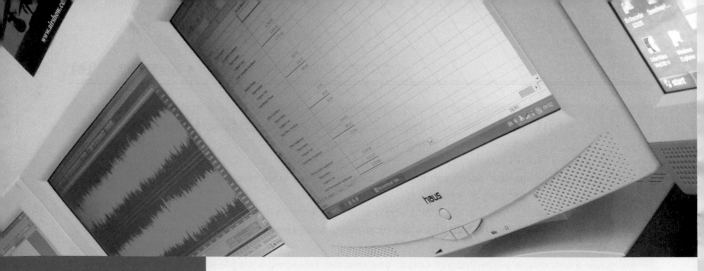

Business issues covered in this chapter

- How has the UK labour market changed over the years?

- How are wage rates determined in a perfect labour market?

- What are the determinants of the demand and supply of labour and their respective elasticities?

- What forms of market power exist in the labour market and what determines the power of employers and labour?

- What effects do powerful employers and trade unions have on wages and employment?

- How has the minimum wage affected business and employment?

- What is meant by a 'flexible' labour market and how has increased flexibility affected working practices, employment and wages?

CHAPTER 7

Labour and employment

In this chapter we consider how labour markets affect business. In particular, we will focus on the determination of wage rates in different types of market: ones where employers are wage takers, ones where they can choose the wage rate, and ones where wage rates are determined by a process of collective bargaining.

We start by examining some of the key trends in the structure of the labour market.

7.1 The UK labour market

The labour market has undergone great change in recent years. Advances in technology, changes in the pattern of output, a need to be competitive in international markets and various social changes have all contributed to changes in work practices and in the structure and composition of the workforce.

Major changes in the UK include the following:

■ A shift from agricultural and manufacturing to service-sector employment. Figure 7.1 (overleaf) reveals that employment in agriculture has been falling over a long historical period. The fall in manufacturing employment, however, has been more recent, starting in the 1960s and gathering pace through the 1970s, 1980s and 1990s. By contrast, employment in the service industries has grown steadily since 1946. In fact since 1979, it has expanded by over 5 million jobs.

■ A rise in part-time employment, and a fall in full-time employment. In 1971 one in six workers was part time; by 2003 this had risen to one worker in four. In the EU as a whole, the figure is one in six. The growth in part-time work reflects the growth in the service sector, where many jobs are part time. Since 1979 part-time employment has risen by over 2.2 million.

■ A rise in female participation rates. Women now constitute approximately half of the paid labour force. The rise in participation rates is strongly associated with the growth in the service sector and the creation of part-time positions. Nearly half of all female workers, about 6.3 million, are in part-time work.

■ A rise in the proportion of workers employed on fixed-term contracts, or on a temporary or casual basis. Many firms nowadays prefer to employ only their core workers/managers on a permanent ('continuing') basis. They feel that it gives them more flexibility to respond to changing market conditions to have the remainder of their workers employed on a short-term basis and, perhaps, to make use of agency staff or to contract out work.

- the number of qualified people;
- the non-wage benefits or costs of the job, such as the pleasantness or otherwise of the working environment, job satisfaction or dissatisfaction, status, power, the degree of job security, holidays, perks and other fringe benefits;
- the wages and non-wage benefits in alternative jobs.

> **Pause for thought**
>
> *Which way will the supply curve shift if the wage rates in alternative jobs rise?*

A change in the wage rate will cause a movement along the supply curve. A change in any of these other three determinants will shift the whole curve.

The elasticity of the market supply of labour

How *responsive* will the supply of labour be to a change in the wage rate? If the market wage rate goes up, will a lot more labour become available or only a little? This responsiveness (elasticity) depends on (a) the difficulties and costs of changing jobs and (b) the time period.

Another way of looking at the elasticity of supply of labour is in terms of the **mobility of labour**: the willingness and ability of labour to move to another job, whether in a different location (geographical mobility) or in a different industry (occupational mobility). The mobility of labour (and hence the elasticity of supply of labour) will be higher when there are alternative jobs in the same location, when alternative jobs require similar skills and when people have good information about these jobs.

It is also much higher in the long run, when people have the time to acquire new skills and when the education system has had time to adapt to the changing demands of industry.

> **Definition**
>
> **Mobility of labour**
> The ease with which labour can either shift between jobs (occupational mobility) or move to other parts of the country in search of work (geographical mobility).

The demand for labour: the marginal productivity theory

The market demand curve for labour will typically be downward sloping. To see why, let us examine how may workers an individual firm will want to employ. We will assume for the moment that the firm aims to maximise profits.

The profit-maximising approach

How many workers will a profit-maximising firm want to employ? The firm will answer this question by weighing up the costs of employing extra labour against the benefits. It will use exactly the same principles as in deciding how much output to produce.

In the goods market, the firm will maximise profits where the marginal cost of an extra unit of *goods* produced equals the marginal revenue from selling it: $MC = MR$.

In the labour market, the firm will maximise profits where the marginal cost of employing an extra *worker* equals the marginal revenue that the worker's output earns for the firm: MC of labour = MR of labour. The reasoning is simple. If an extra worker adds more to a firm's revenue than to its costs, the firm's profits will increase. It will be worth employing that worker. But as more workers are employed, diminishing returns to labour will set in (see page 80). Each extra worker will produce less than the previous one, and thus earn less revenue for the firm. Eventually the marginal revenue from extra workers will fall to the level of their marginal cost. At that point the firm will stop employing extra workers. There are no additional profits to be gained. Profits are at a maximum.

Box 7.1

'Telecommuters'

The electronic cottage

One of the causes of inequality of wages has been the geographical immobility of labour. Within countries this manifests itself in different rates of pay between different regions: often, those regions furthest from the capital city pay the lowest rates.

It also applies between countries. Poorer countries pay lower wages because there is not the mobility of labour between countries to counteract it. Nevertheless, within countries people are often prepared to commute long distances in order to earn the higher pay that large cities have to offer. Witness the army of people who travel into London each day from many miles away, getting up early, arriving back late and paying huge sums of money for travelling.

One important development in recent years, however, is helping to reverse this trend. The increasing sophistication of information technology, with direct computer linking, the Internet, fax machines and mobile phones, has meant that many people can work at home. The number of these 'telecommuters' has grown steadily since the information technology revolution of the early 1980s.

It has been found that where 'telecommuting networks' have been established, gains in productivity levels have been significant, when compared with comparable office workers. Most studies indicate rises in productivity of over 35 per cent. With fewer interruptions and less chatting with fellow workers, less working time is lost. Add to this the stress-free environment, free from the strain of commuting, and the individual worker's performance is enhanced.

With further savings in time, in the renting and maintenance of offices (often in high-cost inner city locations) and in heating and lighting costs, the economic arguments in favour of telecommuting seem very persuasive.

Then there are the broader gains to society. Telecommuting opens up the labour market to a wider group of workers who might find it difficult to leave the home – groups such as single parents and the disabled. Also, concerns that managers lose control over their employees, and that the quality of work falls, appear unfounded. In fact the reverse seems to have occurred: the quality of work in many cases has improved.

But do such employees feel isolated? For many people, work is an important part of their social environment, providing them with an opportunity to meet others and to work as a team. For those who are unable to leave the home, however, telecommuting may be the *only* means of earning a living: the choice of travelling to work may simply not be open to them.

Ironically, it appears that whereas the industrial revolution destroyed cottage industries and people's ability to work from home, information technology is doing the reverse, and may in the end contribute to the destruction of the office – at least of large central offices. Small local offices, however, may flourish as the developments in technology (such as video conferencing) mean that people do not have to travel long distances for meetings.

These technological developments have been the equivalent of an increase in labour mobility. Work can be taken to the workers rather than the workers coming to the work. The effect will be to reduce the premium that needs to be paid to workers in commercial centres, such as the City of London.

There is no reason, of course, why telecommuters cannot work in different countries. Increasingly companies in developed countries are employing low-wage workers in the developing world to do data processing, telesales and various 'back-office' work.

However, telecommuters can be exploited. According to the Low Pay Commission, in 2002 up to a quarter of all homeworkers in the UK were paid below £3.60 per hour, and of these nine out of ten were female. Manual homeworkers were particularly affected, with up to 75 per cent paid below £3.60. The problem with homeworking is its largely hidden nature, which makes it difficult to ensure that minimum wages are paid. Maybe, along with the flexibility, some of the less desirable elements of the cottage industry are also returning!

? Questions

1. What effects are such developments likely to have on (a) trade union membership; (b) trade union power?
2. How are the developments referred to in this box likely to affect relative house prices between capital cities and the regions?

Measuring the marginal cost and revenue of labour

Marginal cost of labour (MC_L). This is the extra cost of employing one more worker. Under perfect competition the firm is too small to affect the market wage. It faces a horizontal supply curve. In other words, it can employ as many workers as it chooses at the market wage rate. Thus the additional cost of employing one more person will simply be the wage rate: $MC_L = W$.

Marginal revenue of labour (MRP_L). The marginal revenue that the firm gains from employing one more worker is called the **marginal revenue product of labour** (MRP_L). The MRP_L is found by multiplying two elements – the *marginal physical product* of labour (MPP_L) and the marginal revenue gained by selling one more unit of output (MR).

$$MRP_L = MPP_L \times MR$$

The MPP_L is the extra output produced by the last worker. Thus if the last worker produces 100 tonnes of output per week (MPP_L), and if the firm earns an extra £2 for each additional tonne sold (MR), then the worker's MRP is £200. This extra worker is adding £200 to the firm's revenue.

Definition

Marginal revenue product of labour
The extra revenue a firm earns from employing one more unit of labour.

The profit-maximising level of employment for a firm

The MRP_L curve is illustrated in Figure 7.3. As more workers are employed, there will come a point when diminishing returns set in (point *x*). Thereafter the MRP_L curve slopes downwards. The figure also shows the MC_L 'curve' at the current market wage W_e.

Profits are maximised at an employment level of Q_e, where MC_L (i.e. W) = MRP_L. Why? At levels of employment below Q_e, MRP_L exceeds MC_L. The firm will increase profits by employing more labour. At levels of employment above Q_e, MC_L exceeds MRP_L. In this case the firm will increase profits by reducing employment.

Derivation of the firm's demand curve for labour

No matter what the wage rate is, the quantity of labour demanded will be found from the intersection of W and MRP_L (see Figure 7.4). At a wage rate of W_1, Q_1

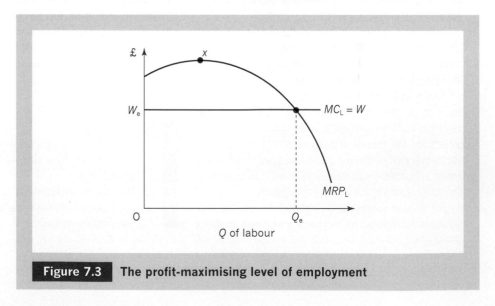

Figure 7.3 **The profit-maximising level of employment**

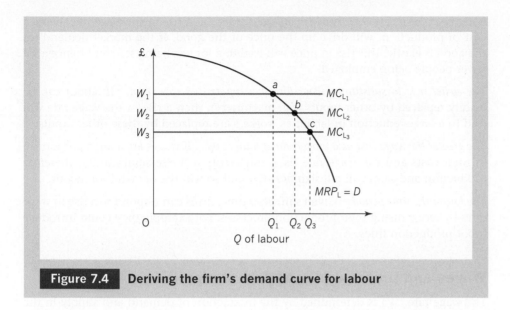

Figure 7.4   Deriving the firm's demand curve for labour

labour is demanded (point *a*); at W_2, Q_2 is demanded (point *b*); at W_3, Q_3 is demanded (point *c*).

Thus the MRP_L curve shows the quantity of labour employed at each wage rate. But this is just what the demand curve for labour shows. Thus the MRP_L curve is the demand curve for labour.

There are three determinants of the demand for labour:

■ The wage rate. This determines the position *on* the demand curve. (Strictly speaking, we would refer here to the wage determining the 'quantity demanded' rather than the 'demand'.)

■ The productivity of labour (MPP_L). This determines the position *of* the demand curve.

■ The demand for the good. The higher the market demand for the good, the higher will be its market price, and hence the higher will be the *MR*, and thus the MRP_L. This too determines the position of the demand curve. It shows how the demand for labour (and other factors) is a **derived demand**: i.e. one derived from the demand for the good. For example, the higher the demand for houses, and hence the higher their price, the higher will be the demand for bricklayers.

A change in the wage rate is represented by a movement *along* the demand curve for labour. A change in the productivity of labour or in the demand for the good *shifts* the curve.

Definition

Derived demand
The demand for a factor of production depends on the demand for the good that uses it.

Pause for thought

If the productivity of a group of workers rises by 10 per cent, will the wage rate they are paid also rise by 10 per cent? Explain why or why not.

Market demand and its elasticity

For the same reason that the firm's demand for labour is downward sloping, so the whole market demand for labour will be downward sloping. At higher wage rates, firms in total will employ less labour. The *elasticity* of this market demand for labour (with respect to changes in the wage rate) depends on various factors. Elasticity will be greater:

The greater the price elasticity of demand for the good. A rise in the wage rate, being a cost of production, will drive up the price of the good. If the market demand for the good is elastic, this rise in price will lead to a lot less being sold and hence a lot fewer people being employed.

The easier it is to substitute labour for other inputs and vice versa. If labour can be readily replaced by other inputs (e.g. machinery), then a rise in the wage rate will lead to a large reduction in labour as workers are replaced by these other inputs.

The greater the wage cost as a proportion of total costs. If wages are a large proportion of total costs and the wage rate rises, total costs will rise significantly; therefore production and sales will fall significantly, and so will the demand for labour.

The longer the time period. Given sufficient time, firms can respond to a rise in wage rates by reorganising their production processes. For example they could introduce robot production lines.

Wages and profits under perfect competition

The wage rate (W) is determined by the interaction of demand and supply in the labour market. This will be equal to the value of the output that the last person produces (MRP_L).

Profits to the individual firm will arise from the fact that the MRP_L curve slopes downward (diminishing returns). Thus the last worker adds less to the revenue of firms than previous workers already employed.

If *all* workers in the firm receive a wage equal to the *MRP* of the *last* worker, everyone but the last worker will receive a wage *less* than their *MRP*. This excess of MRP_L over W of previous workers provides a surplus to the firm over its wages bill (see Figure 7.5). Part of this will be required for paying non-wage costs; part will be the profits for the firm.

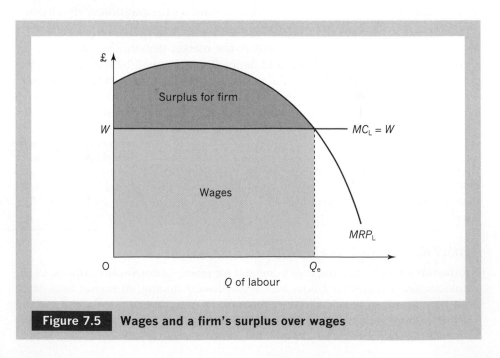

Figure 7.5 **Wages and a firm's surplus over wages**

Perfect competition between firms will ensure that profits are kept down to *normal* profits. If the surplus over wages is such that *supernormal* profits are made, new firms will enter the industry. The price of the good (and hence MRP_L) will fall, and the wage will be bid up, until only normal profits remain.

Recap

- Wages in a competitive labour market are determined by the interaction of demand and supply. The market supply of labour in any labour market is likely to be upward sloping.

- The elasticity of labour supply will depend largely upon the geographical and occupational mobility of labour. The more readily labour can transfer between jobs and regions, the more elastic the supply.

- The demand for labour is traditionally assumed to be based upon labour's productivity. Marginal productivity theory assumes that the employer will demand labour up to the point where the cost of employing one additional worker (MC_L) is equal to the revenue earned from the output of that worker (MRP_L). The firm's demand curve for labour is its MRP_L curve.

- The elasticity of demand for labour is determined by: the price elasticity of demand for the good that labour produces; the substitutability of labour for other factors; the proportion of wages to total costs; and time.

Power in the labour market **7.3**

Firms with power

In the real world, many firms have the power to influence wage rates: they are not wage takers. This is one of the major types of labour market 'imperfection'.

When a firm is the only employer of a particular type of labour, this situation is called a **monopsony**. The Post Office is a monopsony employer of postal workers. Another example is when a factory is the only employer of certain types of labour in that district. It therefore has local monopsony power. When there are just a few employers, this is called **oligopsony**.

Monopsonists (and oligopsonists too) are 'wage setters', not 'wage takers'. Thus a large employer in a small town may have considerable power to resist wage increases or even to force wage rates down.

Such firms face an upward-sloping supply curve of labour. This is illustrated in Figure 7.6 (overleaf). If the firm wants to take on more labour, it will have to pay a higher wage rate to attract workers away from other industries. But conversely, by employing less labour it can get away with paying a lower wage rate.

The supply curve shows the wage that must be paid to attract a given quantity of labour. The wage it pays is the *average cost* to the firm of employing labour (AC_L): i.e. the cost per worker. The supply curve is also therefore the AC_L curve.

The *marginal* cost of employing one more worker (MC_L) will be above the wage (AC_L): see Figure 7.6. The reason is that the wage rate has to be raised to attract extra workers. The MC_L will thus be the new higher wage paid to the new employee *plus* the small rise in the total wages bill for existing employees: after all, they will be paid the higher wage too.

Definition

Monopsony
A market with a single buyer or employer.

Oligopsony
A market with just a few buyers or employers.

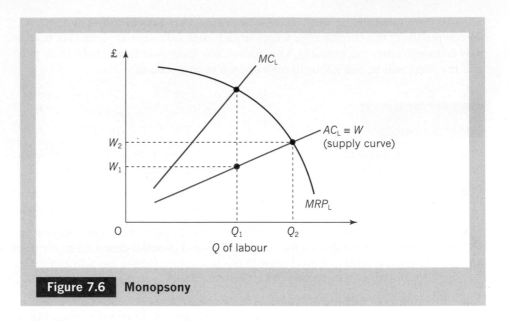

Figure 7.6 Monopsony

The profit-maximising employment of labour would be at Q_1, where $MC_L = MRP_L$. The wage (found from the AC_L curve) would thus be W_1.

If this had been a perfectly competitive labour market, employment would have been at the higher level Q_2, with the wage rate at the higher level W_2, where $W = MRP_L$. What in effect the monopsonist is doing, therefore, is forcing the wage rate down by restricting the number of workers employed.

The role of trade unions

How can unions influence the determination of wages, and what might be the consequences of their actions?

The extent to which unions will succeed in pushing up wage rates depends on their power and militancy. It also depends on the power of firms to resist and on their ability to pay higher wages. In particular, the scope for unions to gain a better deal for their members depends on the sort of market in which the employers are producing.

Unions facing competitive employers

If the employers are producing in a highly competitive goods market, unions can raise wages only at the expense of employment. Firms are likely to be earning little more than normal profit. Thus if unions force up wages, the marginal firms will go bankrupt and leave the industry. Fewer workers will be employed. The fall in output will lead to higher prices. This will enable the remaining firms to pay a higher wage rate.

Figure 7.7 illustrates these effects. If unions force the wage rate up from W_1 to W_2, employment will fall from Q_1 to Q_2. There will be a surplus of people ($Q_3 - Q_2$) wishing to work in this industry for whom no jobs are available.

The union is in a doubly weak position. Not only will jobs be lost as a result of forcing up the wage rate, but also there is a danger that these unemployed people could undercut the union wage, unless the union can prevent firms employing non-unionised labour.

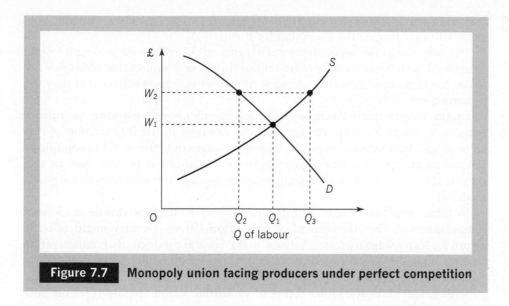

Figure 7.7   **Monopoly union facing producers under perfect competition**

In a competitive market, then, the union is faced with the choice between wages and jobs. Its actions will depend on its objectives.

Wages can be increased without a reduction in the level of employment only if, as part of the bargain, the productivity of labour is increased. This is called a **productivity deal**. The *MRP* curve, and hence the demand curve in Figure 7.7, shifts to the right.

> **Pause for thought**
>
> At what wage rate in Figure 7.7 would employment be maximised: (a) W_1; (b) a wage rate above W_1; (c) a wage rate below W_1?

Bilateral monopoly

What happens when a union monopoly faces a monopsony employer? What will the wage rate be? What will the level of employment be? Unfortunately, economic theory cannot give a precise answer to these questions. There is no 'equilibrium' level as such. Ultimately, the wage rate and level of employment will depend on the relative bargaining strengths and skills of unions and management.

Strange as it may seem, unions may be in a stronger position to make substantial gains for their members when they are facing a powerful employer. There is often considerable scope for them to increase wage rates *without* this leading to a reduction in employment, or even for them to increase both the wage rate *and* employment. The reason is that if firms have power in the *goods* market too, and are making supernormal profit, then there is scope for a powerful union to redistribute some of these profits to wages.

The actual wage rate under bilateral monopoly is usually determined through a process of negotiation or 'collective bargaining'. The outcome of this bargaining will depend on a wide range of factors, which vary substantially from one industry or firm to another.

> **Definition**
>
> **Productivity deal**
> Where, in return for a wage increase, a union agrees to changes in working practices that will increase output per worker.

Collective bargaining

Sometimes when unions and management negotiate, *both* sides can gain from the resulting agreement. For example, the introduction of new technology may allow higher wages, improved working conditions and higher profits. Usually, however,

Definition

Picketing
Where people on strike gather at the entrance to the firm and attempt to dissuade workers or delivery vehicles from entering.

Working to rule
Workers do no more than they are supposed to, as set out in their job descriptions.

Lock-outs
Union members are temporarily laid off until they are prepared to agree to the firm's conditions.

Efficiency wage hypothesis
A hypothesis that states that a worker's productivity is linked to the wage he or she receives.

one side's gain is the other's loss. Higher wages mean lower profits. Either way, both sides will want to gain the maximum for themselves.

The outcome of the negotiations will depend on the relative bargaining strengths of both sides. In bargaining there are various threats or promises that either side can make. For these to be effective, of course, the other side must believe that they will be carried out.

Union *threats* might include strike action, **picketing**, **working to rule** or refusing to cooperate with management, for example in the introduction of new technology. Alternatively, in return for higher wages or better working conditions, unions might *offer* no strike agreements (or an informal promise not to take industrial action), increased productivity, reductions in the workforce or long-term deals over pay.

In turn, employers might threaten employees with plant closure, **lock-outs**, redundancies or the employment of non-union labour. Or they might offer, in return for lower wage increases, various 'perks' such as productivity bonuses, profit-sharing schemes, better working conditions, more overtime, better holidays or security of employment.

Strikes, lock-outs and other forms of industrial action impose costs on both unions and firms. Unions lose pay. Firms lose revenue. It is usually in both sides' interests, therefore, to settle by negotiation. Nevertheless, to gain the maximum advantage, each side must persuade the other that it will carry out its threats if pushed.

The approach described so far has essentially been one of confrontation. The alternative is for both sides to concentrate on increasing the total net income of the firm by cooperating on ways to increase efficiency or the quality of the product. This approach is more likely when unions and management have built up an atmosphere of trust over time.

Efficiency wages

We have seen that a union may be able to force an employer to pay a wage above the market-clearing rate. But it may well be in employers' interests to do so, even in non-unionised sectors.

One explanation for this phenomenon is the **efficiency wage hypothesis**. This states that the productivity of workers rises as the wage rate rises. As a result, employers are frequently prepared to offer wage rates above the market-clearing level, attempting to balance increased wage costs against gains in productivity. But why may higher wage rates lead to higher productivity? There are three main explanations.

Less 'shirking'.   In many jobs it is difficult to monitor the effort that individuals put into their work. Workers may thus get away with shirking or careless behaviour. This is an example of the principal–agent problem (see page 9). The worker, as an agent of the employer (the principal), is not necessarily going to act in the principal's interest.

The business could attempt to reduce shirking by imposing a series of sanctions, the most serious of which would be dismissal. The greater the wage rate currently received, the greater will be the cost to the individual of dismissal, and the less likely it is that workers will shirk. The business will benefit not only from the additional output, but also from a reduction in the costs of having to monitor workers' performance. As a consequence, the **efficiency wage rate** for the business will lie above the market-determined wage rate.

Reduced labour turnover. If workers receive on-the-job training or retraining, then to lose a worker once the training has been completed is a significant cost to the business. Labour turnover, and hence its associated costs, can be reduced by paying a wage above the market-clearing rate. By paying such a wage, the business is seeking a degree of loyalty from its employees.

Morale. A simple reason for offering wage rates above the market-clearing level is to motivate the workforce – to create the feeling that the firm is a 'good' employer that cares about its employees. As a consequence, workers might be more industrious and more willing to accept the introduction of new technology (with the reorganisation that it involves).

The paying of efficiency wages above the market-clearing wage will depend upon the type of work involved. Workers who occupy skilled positions, especially where the business has invested time in their training (thus making them costly to replace), are likely to receive efficiency wages considerably above the market wage. By contrast, workers in unskilled positions, where shirking can be easily monitored, little training takes place and workers can be easily replaced, are unlikely to command an 'efficiency wage premium'. In such situations, rather than keeping wage rates high, the business will probably try to pay as little as possible.

Definition

Efficiency wage rate
The profit-maximising wage rate for the firm after taking into account the effects of wage rates on worker motivation, turnover and recruitment.

> **Pause for thought**
>
> *Give some examples of things an employer could do to increase the morale of the workforce other than raising wages. How would you assess whether they were in the interests of the employer?*

Recap

- In an imperfect labour market, where a business has monopoly power in employing labour, it is known as a monopsonist. Such a firm will employ workers to the point where $MRP_L = MC_L$. Since the wage is below the MC_L, the monopsonist, other things being equal, will employ fewer workers at a lower wage than would be employed in a perfectly competitive labour market.

- If a union has monopoly power, its power to raise wages will be limited if the employer operates in a highly competitive goods market. A rise in wage rates will force the employer to cut back on employment, unless there is a corresponding rise in productivity.

- In a situation of bilateral monopoly (where a monopoly union faces a monopsony employer), the union may have considerable scope to raise wages above the monopsony level, without the employer wishing to reduce the level of employment. There is no unique equilibrium wage. The wage will depend on the outcome of a process of collective bargaining between union and management.

- The efficiency wage hypothesis states that business might hold wages above the market-clearing wage rate so as to: reduce shirking; reduce labour turnover; improve the quality of labour recruited; and stimulate worker morale. The level of efficiency wage will be determined largely by the type of job the worker does, and the level and scarcity of skill they possess.

Recap

- Statutory minimum wage rates have been adopted in many countries.

- In a perfect labour market, where employers are forced to accept the wage as determined by the market, any attempt to impose a minimum wage above this level will create unemployment. Amounts of additional unemployment are likely to be low, however, because the demand and supply of labour are relatively inelastic to changes in wage rates that apply to *all* firms.

- In an imperfect labour market, where an employer has some monopsonistic power, the impact of a minimum wage is uncertain. The impact will depend largely upon how much workers are currently paid below their *MRP* and whether a higher wage encourages them to work more productively.

7.5　The flexible firm and the market for labour

The past 25 years have seen sweeping changes in the ways that firms organise their workforce. Two world recessions combined with rapid changes in technology have led many firms to question the wisdom of appointing workers on a permanent basis to specific jobs. Instead, they want to have the greatest flexibility possible to respond to new situations. If demand falls, they want to be able to 'shed' labour without facing large redundancy costs. If demand rises, they want rapid access to additional labour supplies. If technology changes, say with the introduction of new computerised processes, they want to have the flexibility to move workers around, or to take on new workers in some areas and lose workers in others.

What many firms seek, therefore, is flexibility in employing and allocating labour. What countries are experiencing is an increasingly flexible labour market, as workers and employment agencies respond to the new 'flexible firm'.

There are three main types of flexibility in the use of labour:

- **Functional flexibility.** This is where an employer is able to transfer labour between different tasks within the production process. It contrasts with traditional forms of organisation where people were employed to do a specific job, and then stuck to it. A functionally flexible labour force will tend to be multiskilled and relatively highly trained.

- **Numerical flexibility.** This is where the firm is able to adjust the size and composition of its workforce according to changing market conditions. To achieve this, the firm is likely to employ a large proportion of its labour on a part-time or casual basis, or even subcontract out specialist requirements, rather than employing such labour skills itself.

- **Financial flexibility.** This is where the firm has flexibility in its wage costs. In large part it is a result of functional and numerical flexibility. Financial flexibility can be achieved by rewarding individual effort and productivity rather than paying a given rate for a particular job. Such rates of pay are increasingly negotiated at the local level rather than being nationally set. The result is not only a widening of pay differentials between skilled and unskilled workers, but also growing differentials in pay between workers within the same industry but in different parts of the country.

Definition

Functional flexibility
Where employers can switch workers from job to job as requirements change.

Numerical flexibility
Where employers can change the size of their workforce as their labour requirements change.

Financial flexibility
Where employers can vary their wage costs by changing the composition of their workforce or the terms on which workers are employed.

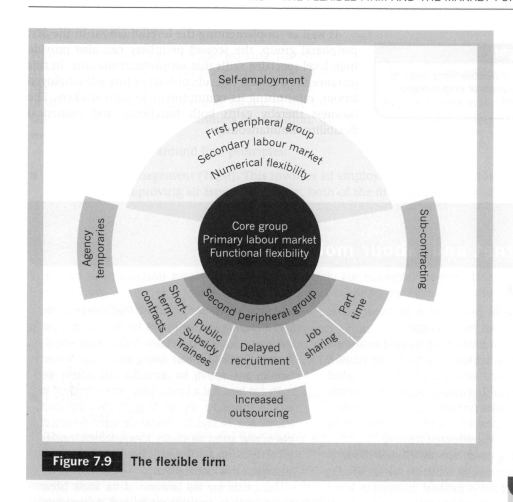

Figure 7.9   The flexible firm

Figure 7.9 shows how these three forms of flexibility are reflected in the organisation of a **flexible firm**, an organisation quite different from that of the traditional firm. The most significant difference is that the labour force is segmented. The core group, drawn from the **primary labour market**, will be composed of *functionally* flexible workers, who have relatively secure employment and are generally on full-time permanent contracts. Such workers will be relatively well paid and receive wages reflecting their scarce skills.

The periphery, drawn from the **secondary labour market**, is more fragmented than the core, and can be subdivided into a first and a second peripheral group. The first peripheral group is composed of workers with a lower level of skill than those in the core, skills that tend to be general rather than firm specific. Thus workers in the first peripheral group can usually be drawn from the external labour market. Such workers may be employed on full-time contracts, but they will generally face less secure employment than those workers in the core.

The business gains a greater level of numerical flexibility by drawing labour from the second peripheral group. Here workers are employed on a variety of short-term, part-time contracts, often through a recruitment agency. Some of these workers may be working from home, or online from another country, such as India, where wage rates are much lower. Workers in the second peripheral group have little job security.

Definition

Flexible firm
A firm that has the flexibility to respond to changing market conditions by changing the composition of its workforce.

Primary labour market
The market for permanent full-time core workers.

Secondary labour market
The market for peripheral workers, usually employed on a temporary or part-time basis, or a less secure 'permanent' basis.

QUESTIONS

1. If a firm faces a shortage of workers with very specific skills, it may decide to undertake the necessary training itself. If on the other hand it faces a shortage of unskilled workers it may well offer a small wage increase in order to obtain the extra labour. In the first case it is responding to an increase in demand for labour by attempting to shift the supply curve. In the second case it is merely allowing a movement along the supply curve. Use a demand and supply diagram to illustrate each case. Given that elasticity of supply is different in each case, do you think that these are the best policies for the firm to follow?

2. The wage rate a firm has to pay and the output it can produce varies with the number of workers as follows (all figures are hourly):

Number of workers	1	2	3	4	5	6	7	8
Wage rate (AC_L) (£)	3	4	5	6	7	8	9	10
Total output (TPP_L)	10	22	32	40	46	50	52	52

Assume that output sells at £2 per unit.

(a) Copy the table and add additional rows for TC_L, MC_L, TRP_L and MRP_L. Put the figures for MC_L and MRP_L in the spaces between the columns.

(b) How many workers will the firm employ in order to maximise profits?

(c) What will be its hourly wage bill at this level of employment?

(d) How much hourly revenue will it earn at this level of employment?

(e) Assuming that the firm faces other (fixed) costs of £30 per hour, how much hourly profit will it make?

(f) Assume that the workers now form a union and that the firm agrees to pay the negotiated wage rate to all employees. What is the maximum to which the hourly wage rate could rise without causing the firm to try to reduce employment below that in (b) above? (See Figures 7.6 and 7.8.)

(g) What would be the firm's hourly profit now?

3. For what types of reason does the marginal revenue product differ between workers in different jobs?

4. If, unlike a perfectly competitive employer, a monopsonist has to pay a higher wage to attract more workers, why, other things being equal, will a monopsonist pay a lower wage than a perfectly competitive employer?

5. The following are figures for a monopsonist employer:

Number of workers (1)	Wage rate (£) (2)	Total cost of labour (£) (3)	Marginal cost of labour (£) (4)	Marginal revenue product (£) (5)
1	100	100		230
2	105	210	110	240
3	110	230	120	240
4	115			230
5	120			210
6	125			190
7	130			170
8	135			150
9	140			130
10	145			

Fill in the missing figures for columns (3) and (4). How many workers should the firm employ if it wishes to maximise profits?

6. To what extent could a trade union succeed in gaining a pay increase from an employer with no loss in employment?

7. Do any of the following contradict the theory that the demand for labour equals the marginal revenue product: wage scales related to length of service (incremental scales), nationally negotiated wage rates, discrimination, firms taking the lead from other firms in determining this year's pay increase?

8. What is the efficiency wage hypothesis? Explain what employers might gain from paying wages above the market-clearing level.

9. 'Statutory minimum wages will cause unemployment.' Is this so?

10. Identify the potential costs and benefits of the flexible firm to (a) employers and (b) employees.

Business issues covered in this chapter

- To what extent does business meet the interests of consumers and society in general?

- In what sense are perfect markets 'socially efficient' and why do most markets fail to achieve social efficiency?

- How do business ethics influence business behaviour?

- In what ways do governments intervene in markets and attempt to influence business behaviour?

- What forms do government environmental policies take, and how do they affect business?

- How does the government attempt to prevent both the abuse of monopoly power and collusion by oligopolists?

- How are privatised industries regulated and how has competition been increased in these industries?

CHAPTER 8

Government, the firm and the market

Despite the fact that most countries today can be classified as 'market economies', governments nevertheless intervene substantially in the activities of business in order to protect the interests of consumers, workers or the environment.

Firms might collude to fix prices, use misleading advertising, create pollution, produce unsafe products, or use unacceptable employment practices. In such cases, government is expected to intervene to correct for the failings of the market system: e.g. by outlawing collusion, by establishing advertising standards, by taxing or otherwise penalising polluting firms, by imposing safety standards on firms' behaviour and products, or by protecting employment rights.

In this chapter we examine the ways in which markets might fail to protect people's interests, whether as consumers or simply as members of society. We also look at the different types of policy the government can adopt to correct these 'market failures'.

8.1 Markets and the role of government

Definition

Marginal social benefit (MSB)
The additional benefit gained by society of producing or consuming one more unit of a good.

Marginal social cost (MSC)
The additional cost incurred by society of producing or consuming one more unit of a good.

Social efficiency
Production and consumption at the point where $MSB = MSC$.

Government intervention and social objectives

One of the key arguments for government intervention in the behaviour of business is that, if left to its own devices, the private enterprise system will fail to achieve 'social efficiency'.

So what is meant by social efficiency? If the extra benefits to society – or **marginal social benefit** (MSB) – of producing more of any given good or service exceed the extra costs to society – or **marginal social cost** (MSC) – then it is said to be socially efficient to produce more. For example, if people's gains from having additional motorways exceed *all* the additional costs to society (both financial and non-financial) then it is socially efficient to construct more motorways.

If, however, the marginal social cost of producing more of any good or service exceeds the marginal social benefit, then it is socially efficient to produce less.

It follows that if the marginal social benefit of any activity is equal to the marginal social cost, then the current level is the optimum. To summarise: for **social efficiency** in the production of any good or service:

$$MSB > MSC \rightarrow \text{produce more}$$
$$MSC > MSB \rightarrow \text{produce less}$$
$$MSB = MSC \rightarrow \text{keep production at its current level}$$

Similar rules apply to consumption. For example, if the marginal social benefit of consuming more of any good or service exceeds the marginal social cost, then society would benefit from more of the good being consumed.

Social efficiency.

This is achieved where no further net social gain can be made by producing more or less of a good. This will occur where marginal social benefit equals marginal social cost.

Key Idea 16

In the real world, the market rarely leads to social efficiency: the marginal social benefits from the production of most goods and services do not equal the marginal social costs. In this section we examine why the free market fails to lead to social efficiency and what the government can do to rectify the situation.

Types of market failure

Externalities

The market will not lead to social efficiency if the actions of producers or consumers affect people *other than themselves*. These effects on other people are known as **externalities**: they are the side-effects, or 'third-party' effects, of production or consumption. Externalities can be either desirable or undesirable. Whenever other people are affected beneficially, there are said to be **external benefits**. Whenever other people are affected adversely, there are said to be **external costs**.

Externalities are spillover costs or benefits.

Where these exist, even an otherwise perfect market will fail to achieve social efficiency.

Key Idea 17

Thus the full cost to society (the **social cost**) of the production of any good or service is the private cost faced by firms plus any externalities of production (positive or negative). Likewise the full benefit to society (the **social benefit**) from the consumption of any good is the private benefit enjoyed by consumers plus any externalities of consumption (positive or negative).

External costs produced by business. Let us take the case of a chemical firm that dumps waste in a river or pollutes the air. In such a case, the community bears costs additional to those borne by the firm. The marginal social cost (*MSC*) of chemical production exceeds the marginal private cost (*MC*). Diagrammatically, the *MSC* curve is above the *MC* curve. This is shown in Figure 8.1, which assumes that the firm in other respects is operating in a perfect market, and is therefore a price taker (i.e. faces a horizontal demand curve).

The firm maximises profits at Q_1: the output where marginal cost equals price (see section 4.4 on page 94). The price is what people buying the good are prepared to pay for one more unit (if it wasn't they wouldn't buy it) and therefore reflects

---

Definition

Externalities
Costs or benefits of production or consumption experienced by society but not by the producers or consumers themselves. Sometimes referred to as 'spillover' or 'third-party' costs or benefits.

External benefits
Benefits from production (or consumption) experienced by people *other* than the producer (or consumer).

External costs
Costs of production (or consumption) borne by people *other* than the producer (or consumer).

Social cost
Private cost plus externalities in production.

Social benefit
Private benefit plus externalities in consumption.

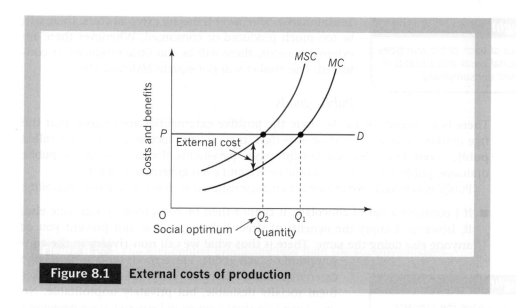

Figure 8.1   **External costs of production**

their marginal benefit. We assume no externalities from consumption, and therefore the marginal benefit to consumers is the same as the marginal *social* benefit (*MSB*).

The socially optimum output would be Q_2, where P (i.e. MSB) = MSC. The firm, however, produces Q_1, which is more than the optimum. Thus external costs lead to *overproduction* from society's point of view.

The problem of external costs arises in a free-market economy because no one has legal ownership of the air or rivers and no one, therefore, can prevent or charge for their use as a dump for waste. Such a 'market' is missing. Control must, therefore, be left to the government or local authorities.

Other examples of firms producing external costs include extensive farming that destroys hedgerows and wildlife, acid rain caused by smoke from coal-fired power stations, and nuclear waste from nuclear power stations.

Other examples of externalities.   Sometimes firms' actions *benefit* people other than consumers. An example is research and development. If other firms have access to the results of the research, then clearly the benefits extend beyond the firm that finances it. Since the firm only receives the private benefits, it will conduct a less than optimal amount of research. Similarly, a forestry company planting new woodlands will not take into account the beneficial effect on the atmosphere.

Externalities occur in consumption too. For example, when people use their cars, other people suffer from their exhaust, the added congestion, the noise, etc. These 'negative externalities' make the marginal social benefit of using cars less than the marginal private benefit (i.e. marginal utility to the car user). Other examples of negative externalities of consumption include noisy radios in public places, the smoke from cigarettes, and litter.

Consumption externalities could be positive. For example, when people travel by train rather than by car, other people benefit by there being less congestion and exhaust and fewer accidents on the roads. Thus the marginal social benefit of rail travel is greater than the marginal private benefit (i.e. the marginal utility to the rail passenger). Other examples of positive externalities of consumption include deodorants, vaccinations and attractive gardens in front of people's houses.

Definition

Corporate social responsibility

Where a business takes into account the interests and concerns of a community rather than just its shareholders.

Business ethics

The values and principles that shape business behaviour.

Stakeholder

An individual affected by the operations of a business.

Environmental scanning

Where a business surveys social and political trends in order to take account of changes in its decision-making process.

Business ethics and corporate social responsibility

It is often assumed that firms are simply concerned to maximise profits: that they are not concerned with broader issues of **corporate social responsibility**. Indeed, many forms of market failure can be attributed directly to business practices that could not be classified as 'socially responsible': advertising campaigns that seek to misinform, or in some way deceive the consumer; monopoly producers exploiting their monopoly position through charging excessively high prices; the conscious decision to ignore water and air pollution limits, knowing that the chances of being caught are slim.

To some extent, however, the role of modern business has changed, and society expects business to adhere to certain moral and social principles. Indeed, social responsibility is a key component in many companies' **business ethics**.

Modern businesses often see themselves as more than economic institutions, as they are actively involved in society's social, political and legal environments. As such, all businesses are responsible not only to their shareholders but to all **stakeholders**. Stakeholders are all those affected by the business's operations: not only shareholders, but workers, customers, suppliers, creditors and people living in the neighbourhood. Given the far-reaching environmental effects of many businesses, stakeholding might extend to the whole of society.

In many top corporations, **environmental scanning** is now an integral part of the planning process. This involves the business surveying changing social and political trends in order to remain in tune with consumer concerns. For example, the general public's growing concern over 'green' issues has significantly influenced many businesses' product development programmes and R&D strategies. The more successful a business is in being able to associate the image of 'environmentally friendly' to a particular product or brand, the more likely it is to enhance its sales or establish a measure of brand loyalty, and thereby to strengthen its competitive position.

A reputation for social responsibility may also help the firm in raising finance and attracting trading partners. Investment in ethically screened investment funds has grown rapidly in recent years. This has been driven not only by the demands of shareholders for ethical funds, but also by a realisation from investors generally that socially responsible business has the potential to be hugely profitable.

Socially responsible companies also may find it easier to recruit and hold on to their employees. In a number of surveys of graduate employment intentions, students have claimed that they would be prepared to take a lower salary in order to work for a business with high ethical standards and a commitment to socially responsible business practices.

Social responsibility appears not only to bring a range of benefits to business and society, but also to be generally profitable. It is likely to enhance business performance, strengthen brand image, reduce employee turnover and increase access to stock market funds. Box 8.1 gives an example of a company that has built its reputation of being socially and environmentally responsible – The Body Shop.

It is nevertheless the case that there are still many firms that care little about the social or natural environment. There is thus a strong case for government intervention to correct market failures.

Box 8.1

The Body Shop

Embodying social responsibility

The Body Shop shot to fame in the 1980s. It stood for environmental awareness and an ethical approach to business. But its success had as much to do with what it sold as what it stood for. It sold natural cosmetics, Raspberry Ripple Bathing Bubbles and Camomile Shampoo, products that were immensely popular with consumers.

Its profits increased from a little over £1 million in 1985 to £24.0 million in 2003 (although they had been as high as £38.0 million in 1998). Sales, meanwhile, grew even more dramatically, from £4.9 million to £697.1 million in 2003.

What makes this success so remarkable is that The Body Shop does virtually no advertising. Its promotion has largely stemmed from the activities and environmental campaigning of its founder Anita Roddick, and the company's uncompromising claims that it sells only 'green' products and conducts its business operations with high ethical standards. It actively supports green causes such as saving whales and protecting rainforests, and it refuses to allow its products to be tested on animals. Perhaps most surprising in the world of big business has been its high-profile initiative 'trade not aid', whereby it claimed to pay 'fair' prices for its ingredients, especially those supplied from people in developing countries, who were open to exploitation by large companies.

The growth strategy of The Body Shop, since its founding in 1976, has focused on developing a distinctive and highly innovative product range, and at the same time identifying such products with major social issues of the day, such as the environment and animal rights.

In the 1990s, sales growth was less rapid and in 2000 Roddick announced that she was planning to leave the company. The day after the announcement, the following article appeared in the *Financial Times*.

> . . . At the beginning it was a green fairy tale, the company's commitment to fair trade and the environment and its stance on animal testing was a combination that caught the imagination in the newly affluent 1980s. For over a decade sales and profits continued to grow, on average by 50 per cent a year. Franchises sprang up like mushrooms

and following its flotation in 1984 the share price rose from just 5p to a high of 370p in 1992.

> With a new shop opening every two and a half days it seemed as if nothing could go wrong for the Roddicks, that is, until they hit America. In 1988 they launched into the US market. Initially the venture was successful. The once successful franchising of the company soon began to disintegrate. 'We just got everything wrong,' said Ms Roddick, who was criticised for conducting no market research, paying scant attention to marketing and giving little thought to where the shops appeared.

> By 1998 the company's earnings had collapsed by 90 per cent and the share price fell to under 117p.

> In the City there was a certain amount of *schadenfreude*. Many investors were not impressed with Roddick's cuddly hippie attitude to business and analysts criticised the company for developing new products too quickly.

> They were also unimpressed with Ms Roddick's off-hand attitude to finances, especially her comments that finance 'bored the pants off her' and her frequent denouncements of the 'pin-striped dinosaurs in Throgmorton Street'.

> When she was forced to step down as chief executive in 1998, following shareholder pressure for 'positive and demonstrable change', she compared the experience to handing over a child to complete strangers.

> The day-to-day running of Body Shop was handed over to Patrick Gournay, a former vice president at Groupe Danone and Ms Roddick became joint co-chairman with husband Gordon.

In 2002, Anita Roddick and her husband stepped down as co-chairmen of the company, by which time profits had fallen to £20.4 million.

? **Questions**
1. What assumptions has The Body Shop made about the 'rational consumer'?
2. How would you describe the aims of The Body Shop?

Table 8.1 Types of environmental taxes and charges

Motor fuels	Other goods	Air transport
Leaded/unleaded	Batteries	Noise charges
Diesel (quality differential)	Plastic carrier bags	Aviation fuels
Carbon/energy taxation	Glass containers	**Water**
Sulphur tax	Drink cans	Water charges
Other energy products	Tyres	Sewage charges
Carbon/energy tax	CFCs/halons	Water effluent charges
Sulphur tax or charge	Disposable razors/cameras	Manure charges
NO_2 charge	Lubricant oil charge	**Direct tax provisions**
Methane charge	Oil pollutant charge	Tax relief on green investment
Agricultural inputs	Solvents	Taxation on free company cars
Fertilisers	**Waste disposal**	Employer-paid commuting
Pesticides	Municipal waste charges	expenses taxable
Manure	Waste-disposal charges	Employer-paid parking
Vehicle-related taxation	Hazardous waste charges	expenses taxable
Sales tax depends on car size	Landfill tax or charges	Commuter use of public
Road tax depends on car size	Duties on waste water	transport tax deductible

---

Pause for thought

Assume that production by a firm has beneficial spillover effects: i.e. that there are positive externalities which have the effect of positioning the MSC curve below the MC curve. Illustrate this on a diagram similar to Figure 8.3 and show (a) the profit-maximising level of output; (b) the socially efficient level of output; (c) the optimum level of subsidy.

This is illustrated in Figure 8.3. For simplicity, it is assumed that the firm is a price taker. It produces Q_1 where $P = MC$ (its profit-maximising output), but in doing so takes no account of the external pollution costs it imposes on society. If the government imposes a tax on production equal to the marginal pollution cost, it will effectively 'internalise' the externality. The firm will have to pay an amount equal to the external cost it creates. The firm's MC curve thus shifts upwards to become the same as the MSC curve. It will therefore now maximise profits at Q_2, which is the socially optimum output where $MSB = MSC$.

Advantages of taxes and subsidies

Many economists favour the tax/subsidy solution to market imperfections (especially the problem of externalities) because it still allows the market to operate. It forces firms to take on board the full social costs and benefits of their actions. It also has the flexibility of being adjustable according to the magnitude of the problem. For example, the bigger the external costs of a firm's actions, the bigger the tax can be.

What is more, by taxing firms for polluting, they are encouraged to find cleaner ways of producing. The tax thus acts as an incentive over the longer run to reduce pollution: the more a firm can reduce its pollution, the more taxes it can save.

Likewise, when *good* practices are subsidised, firms are given the incentive to adopt more good practices.

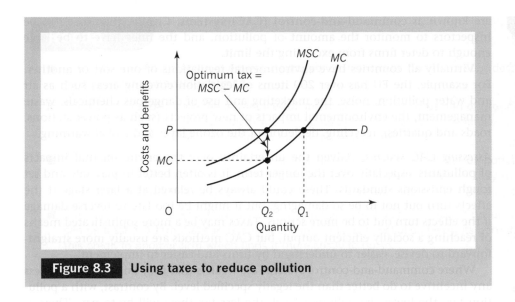

Figure 8.3   **Using taxes to reduce pollution**

Disadvantages of taxes and subsidies

Infeasible to use different tax and subsidy rates.   Each firm produces different levels and types of externality and operates under different degrees of imperfect competition. It would be expensive and administratively very difficult, if not impossible, to charge every offending firm its own particular tax rate (or grant every relevant firm its own particular rate of subsidy).

Lack of knowledge.   Even if a government did decide to charge a tax equal to each offending firm's marginal external costs, it would still have the problem of measuring that cost. The damage from pollution is often extremely difficult to assess. It is also difficult to apportion blame. For example, the damage to lakes and forests from acid rain has been a major concern since the beginning of the 1980s. But just how serious is that damage? What is its current monetary cost? How long lasting is the damage? What will be the position in 20 years? Just what and who are to blame? These are questions that cannot be answered precisely. It is thus impossible to fix the 'correct' pollution tax on, say, a particular coal-fired power station.

Despite these problems, it is nevertheless possible to charge firms by the amount of a particular emission. For example, firms could be charged for chimney smoke by so many parts per million of a given pollutant. Although it is difficult to 'fine-tune' such a system so that the charge reflects the precise number of people affected by the pollutant and by how much, it does go some way to internalising the externality.

> **Pause for thought**
>
> *Why is it easier to use taxes and subsidies to tackle the problem of car exhaust pollution than to tackle the problem of peak-time traffic congestion in cities?*

Laws and regulations

The traditional way of tackling pollution has been to set maximum permitted levels of emission or resource use, or minimum acceptable levels of environmental quality, and then to fine firms contravening these limits. Measures of this type

Box 8.2

The problem of urban traffic congestion

Does London have the answer?

Traffic congestion is a classic example of the problem of externalities. When people use their cars, not only do they incur private costs (petrol, wear and tear on the vehicle, tolls, the time taken to travel, etc.), but also they impose costs on other people. These external costs include the following:

Congestion costs: time.   When a person uses a car on a congested road, it adds to the congestion. This therefore slows down the traffic even more and increases the journey time of other car users.

Congestion costs: monetary.   Congestion increases fuel consumption, and the stopping and starting increases the costs of wear and tear. When a motorist adds to congestion, therefore, there are additional monetary costs imposed on other motorists.

Environmental costs.   When motorists use a road they reduce the quality of the environment for others. Cars emit fumes and create noise. This is bad enough for pedestrians and other car users, but can be particularly distressing for people living along the road. Driving can cause accidents, a problem that increases as drivers become more impatient as a result of delays.

Exhaust gases cause long-term environmental damage and are one of the main causes of the greenhouse effect and of the increased acidity of lakes and rivers and the poisoning of forests. They can also cause long-term health problems (e.g. for asthma sufferers).

The socially efficient level of road usage

These externalities mean that road usage will be above the social optimum. This is illustrated in the diagram. Costs and benefits are shown on the vertical axis and are measured in money terms. Thus any non-monetary costs or benefits (such as time costs) must be given a monetary value. The horizontal axis measures

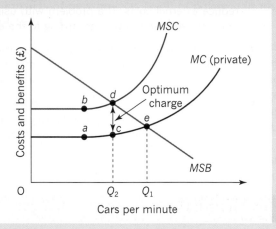

Actual and optimum road usage

road usage in terms of cars per minute passing a specified point on the road.

For simplicity it is assumed that there are no external benefits from car use and that therefore marginal private and marginal social benefits are the same. The *MSB* curve is shown as downward sloping. The reason for this is that different road users put a different value on any given journey. If the marginal (private) cost of making the journey were high, only those for whom the journey had a high marginal benefit would travel along the road. If the marginal cost of making the journey fell, more people would make the journey: people choosing to make the journey as long as the marginal cost of the journey was less than the marginal benefit. Thus the greater the number of cars, the lower the marginal benefit.

The marginal (private) cost curve (*MC*) is likely to be constant up to the level of traffic flow at which congestion begins to

The firm maximises profits at Q, where $MC = MR$. Profits are shown by the shaded area. The greater the firm's market power, the steeper will be the firm's *AR* curve and also the *MR* curve. The bigger will be the gap between price (point *a*) and marginal cost (point *b*). Remember that under perfect competition, price equals marginal cost (see Figure 4.4 on page 95). This is shown by point *c*, which is at a lower price and a higher output.

occur. This is shown as point *a* in the diagram. Beyond this point, marginal cost is likely to rise as time costs increase (i.e. journey times lengthen) and as fuel consumption rises.

The marginal *social* cost curve (*MSC*) is drawn above the marginal private cost curve. The vertical difference between the two represents the external costs. Up to point *b*, external costs are simply the environmental costs. Beyond point *b*, there are also external congestion costs, since additional road users slow down the journey of *other* road users. These external costs get progressively greater as traffic grinds to a halt.

The actual level of traffic flow will be at Q_1, where marginal private costs and benefits are equal (point *e*). The socially efficient level of traffic flow, however, will be at the lower level of Q_2 where marginal social costs and benefits are equal (point *d*). In other words, there will be an excessive level of road usage.

So what can governments do to 'internalise' these externalities? One solution is to impose charges on cars entering a 'congestion zone'. This solution is the one adopted in London.

Congestion charging in London

In London, car drivers must pay £5 per day to enter the inner London area (or 'congestion zone') any time between 7.00 and 18.30, Monday to Friday. Payment can be made by various means, including post, Internet, telephone, mobile phone SMS text message and at various shops and petrol stations. Payment can be in advance or up to 22.00 on the day of travel, or up to midnight for an extra £5. Cars entering the congestion zone have their number plate recorded by camera and a computer check then leads to a fine of £80 being sent to those who have not paid.

The London congestion charging system has reduced traffic in the zone by about 20 per cent and has significantly increased the rate of traffic flow. The charge is not a marginal one, however,

in the sense that it does not vary with the degree of congestion or the amount of time spent or distance travelled by a motorist within the zone. Nevertheless, its simplicity makes it easy to understand and relatively cheap to operate.

More sophisticated electronic road pricing

More sophisticated schemes attempt to relate directly the price charged to the motorist to the specific level of marginal external cost. In Singapore, for example, cars are fitted with a dashboard device into which you must insert a smart card which contains pre-paid units, much as a photocopying or telephone card. The cards can be recharged. On specified roads, overhead gantries read the device and deduct units from the card. Charges vary with the time of day. If a car does not have sufficient funds on its card, the car's details are relayed to a control centre and a fine is sent to the owner.

The most sophisticated scheme, still under development in parts of the world, would involve equipping all cars with a receiver. Their position is located by satellite tracking. Charges are then imposed according to location, distance travelled, time of day and type of vehicle. The charges can operate either through smart cards in a dashboard device or though central computerised billing.

> **? Questions**
> 1. Referring to a town or city with which you are familiar, consider what would be the most appropriate mix of policies to deal with its traffic congestion problems.
> 2. Explain how, by varying the charge to motorists according to the time of day or level of congestion, a socially optimal level of road use can be achieved.

In addition to the problem of a higher price, a lack of competition removes the incentive to become more efficient.

But market power is not necessarily a bad thing. Firms may not fully exploit their position of power – perhaps for fear that very high profits would eventually lead to other firms overcoming entry barriers, or perhaps because they are not aggressive profit maximisers. Even if they do make large supernormal profits, they may still

■ Vertical restraints. This is where a supplying firm imposes conditions on a purchasing firm (or vice versa). For example, a manufacturer may impose rules on retailers about displaying the product or the provision of after-sales service, or it may refuse to supply certain outlets (e.g. perfume manufacturers refusing to supply discount chains, such as Superdrug).

The simple *existence* of any of these practices may not constitute an abuse. The OFT has to decide whether their *effect* is to restrict competition. If the case is not straightforward, the OFT can refer it to the Competition Commission (CC). The CC will then carry out a detailed investigation to establish whether competition is restricted or distorted. If it is, the CC will rule what actions must be taken to remedy the situation.

UK merger policy

Merger policy is covered by the 2002 Enterprise Act. It seeks to prevent mergers that are likely to result in a substantial lessening of competition.

A merger or takeover will be investigated by the OFT if the target company has a turnover of £70 million or more, or if the merger results in the new company having a market share of 25 per cent or more. The OFT conducts a preliminary investigation to see whether competition is likely to be threatened. If it is, and if there are unlikely to be any substantial compensating benefit to consumers, the OFT refers the case to the Competition Commission.

If reference is made to the CC, it conducts a detailed investigation to establish whether the merger is likely to lead to a significant reduction in competition. If so, it can prohibit the merger. Alternatively, it can require the merged firm to behave in certain ways in order to protect consumers' interests. In such cases, the OFT then monitors the firm to ensure that it is abiding by the CC's conditions. CC investigations must normally be completed within 24 weeks.

Recap

■ Competition policy in most countries recognises that monopolies, mergers and restrictive practices can bring both costs and benefits to the consumer. Generally, though, restrictive practices tend to be more damaging to consumers' interests than simple monopoly power or mergers.

■ UK legislation is covered by the 1998 Competition Act and 2002 Enterprise Act. The Office of Fair Trading (OFT) is charged with ensuring that firms abide by the legislation. Where there is doubt, it can refer cases to the Competition Commission for a ruling.

■ Cartel agreements are a criminal offence and certain other types of collusive behaviour can be curtailed by the OFT if they are against the public interest.

■ The abuse of monopoly power by a dominant firm can also be prevented by the OFT. Such abuses include charging excessively high prices.

■ Mergers over a certain size are investigated by the OFT with possible reference to the Competition Commission for a ruling as to whether they should be permitted.

Box 8.3

What price for peace of mind?

Exploiting monopoly power in the sale of extended warranties on electrical goods

If you go into Dixons, Comet, PC World or virtually any other High Street retailer to buy an electrical good, such as a DVD player, a fridge or PC, the sales assistant will probably be very keen to sell you an extended warranty (EW). These EWs are typically for three to five years and sometimes merely extend the product's guarantee against breakdown beyond its normal one- or two-year expiry date. Sometimes they go further and provide cover against other risks, such as accidental damage or theft.

These EWs are highly profitable for the retailer. In 2002 they accounted for approximately 40 per cent of Dixons' profits and 80 per cent of Comet's. It's hardly surprising that retailers are very keen to sell them to you!

In 2002 the Office of Fair Trading (OFT) published a report on EWs and concluded that 'there is insufficient competition and information to ensure that consumers get good value, and that many electrical retailers may make considerable profits on the sale of EWs'.

Research conducted by the OFT indicates that customers can feel pressurised to rush to a decision to buy an extended warranty when they buy their new appliance. A high percentage of consumers had not thought about buying an extended warranty before they arrive at the store.

Buyers should think whether extended warranties offer them value for money. OFT research found that the average washing machine repair costs between £45 to £65. So if a five year extended warranty costs £150 on a £300 washing machine, it would need to break down four times for a consumer to benefit.

A recent 'Which?' report highlights that modern domestic appliances are generally reliable. It found that 81 per cent of washing machines didn't break down at all in the first six years.

. . . Some sales staff are paid commission on each extended warranty they sell, so may be keen for a customer to sign on the dotted line.[1]

The OFT was concerned that retailers were using their market power at the point of sale and benefiting from consumers' ignorance. It decided, therefore, to refer the case to the Competition Commission (CC), which published its report in December 2003.

The CC report found that there was a 'complex monopoly'[2] in the market, worth £900 million per year, which was working against the public interest. It concluded that there had been an abuse of monopoly power, stating that:

> Were this market fully competitive such that the top five EW retailers' returns were no greater than their cost of capital,[3] we estimate that EW prices would have been, on average, up to one-third lower.
>
> . . . Many of the practices that we have identified during the course of our investigation operate or may be expected to operate against the public interest. They result in lack of choice, excessive prices, insufficient information, insufficient competition at point of sale, limited but not insignificant sales pressure, some terms which could be disadvantageous, and lack of information about the scope of protection under service-backed schemes.[4]

Despite these findings, the Competition Commission did not recommend banning shops from bundling warranties with electrical goods at the point of sale, despite many of the EWs being 'unfair and uncompetitive'. Instead, it recommended that retailers should display prices for EWs alongside the price of the goods, both in shops and in advertisements. It also recommended that the shops should provide information about customers' rights and that customers should get a full refund on the EW if they cancelled within 45 days.

The government minister, the Secretary of State for Trade and Industry, Patricia Hewitt, accepted these findings and ruled that they should be implemented.

? Questions

1. What features of the market for EWs distort competition?
2. To what extent will the ruling by the government make the market for EWs competitive?

---

[1] OFT News Release, PN 68/02, October 2002.

[2] A complex monopoly is where several companies separately (i.e. not collusively) are in a position to exploit a particular market advantage to the detriment of the consumer.

[3] A measure of 'normal profit'.

[4] Summary to 'Extended warranties on domestic electrical goods: A report on the supply of extended warranties on domestic electrical goods within the UK', Competition Commission, December 2003, (http://www.competition-commission.org.uk/rep_pub/reports/2003/485xwars.htm#summary)

up to competition (with the exception of water). Thus there are now many producers and sellers of electricity and gas. This is possible because they are given access, by law, to the national and local electricity grids and gas pipelines. The telecommunications market too has become more competitive with the growth of mobile phones and lines supplied by cable operators.

But despite attempts to introduce competition into the privatised industries, they are still dominated by giant companies. Even if they are no longer strictly monopolies, they still have considerable market power and the scope for price leadership or other forms of oligopolistic collusion is great. Thus although regulation through the price formula has been progressively abandoned as elements of competition have been introduced, the regulators have retained a role similar to that of the OFT: they can intervene to prevent cases of collusion and the abuse of monopoly power. The companies, however, do have the right of appeal to the Competition Commission.

Recap

- Regulation in the UK has involved setting up regulatory offices for the major privatised utilities. These generally operate informally, using negotiation and bargaining to persuade the industries to behave in the public interest.

- As far as prices are concerned, parts of the industries are required to abide by an 'CPI minus X' formula. This forces them to pass potential cost reductions on to the consumer. At the same time they are allowed to retain any additional profits gained from cost reductions greater than X. This provides them with an incentive to achieve even greater increases in efficiency.

- Many parts of the privatised industries are not natural monopolies. In these parts, competition may be a more effective means of pursuing the public interest.

- Various attempts have been made to make the privatised industries more competitive, often at the instigation of the regulator. Nevertheless, considerable market power remains in the hands of many privatised firms, and thus the need for regulation will continue.

QUESTIONS

1. Assume that a firm discharges waste into a river. As a result, the marginal social costs (*MSC*) are greater than the firm's marginal (private) costs (*MC*). The following table shows how *MC*, *MSC*, *AR* and *MR* vary with output.

Output	1	2	3	4	5	6	7	8
MC (£)	23	21	23	25	27	30	35	42
MSC (£)	35	34	38	42	46	52	60	72
TR (£)	60	102	138	168	195	219	238	252
AR (£)	60	51	46	42	39	36.5	34	31.5
MR (£)	60	42	36	30	27	24	19	14

(a) How much will the firm produce if it seeks to maximise profits?

(b) What is the socially efficient level of output (assuming no externalities on the demand side)?

(c) How much is the marginal external cost at this level of output?

(d) What size tax would be necessary for the firm to reduce its output to the socially efficient level?

(e) Why is the tax less than the marginal externality?

(f) Why might it be equitable to impose a lump-sum tax on this firm?

(g) Why will a lump-sum tax not affect the firm's output (assuming that in the long run the firm can still make at least normal profit)?

2. Distinguish between publicly provided goods, public goods and merit goods.

3. Some roads could be regarded as a public good, but some could be provided by the market. Which types of road could be provided by the market? Why? Would it be a good idea?

4. Make a list of pieces of information a firm might want to know and consider whether it could buy the information and how reliable that information might be.

5. Why might it be better to ban certain activities that cause environmental damage rather than to tax them?

6. How suitable are legal restrictions in the following cases?

(a) Ensuring adequate vehicle safety (e.g. that tyres have sufficient tread or that the vehicle is roadworthy).

(b) Reducing traffic congestion.

(c) Preventing the use of monopoly power.

(d) Ensuring that mergers are in the public interest.

(e) Ensuring that firms charge a price equal to marginal cost.

7. In what ways might business be socially responsible?

8. What economic costs and benefits might a business experience if it decided to adopt a more socially responsible position? How might such costs and benefits change over the longer term?

9. What problems are likely to arise in identifying which firms' practices are anti-competitive? Should the OFT take firms' assurances into account when deciding whether to grant an exemption?

10. If anti-monopoly legislation is effective enough, is there ever any need to prevent mergers from going ahead?

11. If two or more firms were charging similar prices, what types of evidence would you look for to prove that this was collusion rather than mere coincidence?

12. Should governments or regulators always attempt to eliminate the supernormal profits of monopolists/oligopolists?

13. Should regulators of utilities that have been privatised into several separate companies permit (a) horizontal mergers (within the industry); (b) vertical mergers; (c) mergers with firms in other related industries (e.g. gas and electricity suppliers)?

Additional Part C case studies on the Economic Environment of Business Website (www.booksites.net/sloman)

C.1 **B2B electronic marketplaces.** This case study examines the growth of firms trading with each other over the Internet (business to business or 'B2B') and considers the effects on competition.

C.2 **Measuring monopoly power.** This analyses how the degree of monopoly power possessed by a firm can be measured.

C.3 **Airline deregulation in the USA and Europe.** Whether the deregulation of various routes has led to more competition and lower prices.

C.4 **Bakeries: oligopoly or monopolistic competition.** A case study on the bread industry, showing that small-scale local bakeries can exist alongside giant national bakeries.

C.5 **Oligopoly in the brewing industry.** A case study showing how the UK brewing industry is becoming more concentrated.

C.6 **OPEC.** A case study examining OPEC's influence over oil prices from the early 1970s to the current day.

C.7 **Hybrid strategy.** Is it good for companies to use a mix of strategies?

C.8 **Stakeholder power.** An examination of the various stakeholders of a business and their influence on business behaviour.

C.9 **Merger activity in Europe.** An examination of merger trends in Europe.

C.10 **Logistics.** A case study of the use of the logistics industry by companies seeking to outsource their supply chain.

C.11 **Easy pricing.** An examination of the pricing strategy used by easyJet.

C.12 **Peak-load pricing.** An example of price discrimination: charging more when it costs more to produce.

C.13 **The rise and decline of the labour movement.** A brief history of trade unions in the UK.

C.14 **How useful is marginal productivity theory?** How accurately does the theory describe employment decisions by firms?

C.15 **Should health care provision be left to the market?** This identifies the market failures that would occur if health care provision were left to the free market.

C.16 **Corporate social responsibility.** An examination of social responsibility as a goal of firms and its effect on business performance.

C.17 **Technology and economic change.** How to get the benefits from technological advance.

C.18 **Green taxes.** Are they the perfect answer to the problem of pollution?

C.19 **Road pricing in Singapore.** A case study showing the methods Singapore has used to cut traffic congestion.

C.20 **Environmental auditing.** Are businesses becoming greener? A growing number of firms are subjecting themselves to an 'environmental audit' to judge just how 'green' they are.

C.21 **Cartels set in concrete, steel and cardboard.** This examines some of the best-known Europe-wide cartels of recent years.

C.22 **Taking your vitamins at a price.** A case study showing how vitamin-producing companies were fined for price fixing.

C.23 **Competition in the pipeline.** An examination of attempts to introduce competition into the gas industry in the UK.

C.24 **Selling power to the people.** Attempts to introduce competition into the UK electricity industry.

Websites relevant to Part C

Numbers and sections refer to websites listed in the Web Appendix and hotlinked from this book's website at www.booksites.net/sloman/

■ For news articles relevant to Part C, see the *Economics News Articles* link from the book's website.

■ For general news on the microeconomic environment of business see websites in section A of the Web Appendix, and particularly A1–5, 8, 9, 11, 12, 20–26, 35, 36. See also A38, 39 and 43 for links to newspapers worldwide; and A42 for links to economics news articles from newspapers worldwide.

■ For student resources relevant to Part C, see sites C1–7, 9, 10, 14, 19; D3.

■ For sites that looks at competition and market power, see B2; E4, 10, 18; G7, 8. See also links in I7, 11, 14 and 17. In particular see the following links in sites I7: *Microeconomics > Competition and Monopoly*.

■ For a site on game theory, see A40 including its home page. See also D4; C20; I17 and 4 (in the EconDirectory section).

■ For information on mergers, see sites E4, 10, 18, 20.

■ For information on stock markets, see sites F18 and A3.

■ Sites I7 and 11 contain links to *Financial Economics*.

■ For data on SMEs, see the SME database in B3 or E10.

■ For information on pricing, see site E10 and the sites of the regulators of the privatised industries: E16, 19, 21, 22, 25.

■ Sites I7 and 11 in the Business section contain links to *Business > Management > Organisational Management*.

■ For data on labour markets, see links in B1 or 2, especially to *Labour Market Trends* on the National Statistics site. Also see B9 and links in B19. Also see the labour topic in B33 and the *resources > statistics* links in H3.

■ For information on international labour standards and employment rights, see site H3.

■ Sites I7 and 11 contain links to *Labour economics, Labour force and markets* and *Labour unions* in the *Microeconomics* section and to *Distribution of income and wealth* in the *Macroeconomics* section. Site I4 has links in the *Directory* section to *Labor* and *Labor Economics*. Site I17 in the *Labor Economics* section has links to various topics, such as *Labor Unions, Minimum Wage, Poverty* and *Work*.

■ Links to the TUC and Confederation of British Industry sites can be found at E32 and 33.

■ Sites I7 and 11 contain links to *Competition and monopoly, Policy and regulation* and *Transport* in the *Microeconomics* section; they also have an *Industry and commerce* section. Site I4 has links to *Environmental* and *Environmental Economics* in the *EconDirectory* section. Site I17 has several sections of links in the *Issues in Society* section.

■ Sites I7 and 11 also contain links to sites related to corporate social responsibility: see *Industry and Commerce > Fair Trade > Corporate social Responsibility*.

■ For information on taxes and subsidies, see E30, 36; G13. For use of green taxes, see H5; G11; E2, 14, 30.

■ For information on health and the economics of health care (Web case H.2: see above), see E8; H9. See also links in I8 and 17.

■ For sites favouring the free market, see C17; D34. See also C18 for the development of ideas on the market and government intervention.

■ For the economics of the environment, see links in I4, 7, 11, 17. For policy on the environment and transport, see E2, 7, 11, 14, 29; G10, 11. See also H11.

■ UK and EU departments relevant to competition policy can be found at sites E10; G7, 8.

■ UK regulatory bodies can be found at sites E4, 11, 15, 16, 18, 19, 21, 22, 25, 29.

PART D

The macroeconomic environment of business

The success of an individual business depends not only on its own particular market and its own particular decisions. It also depends on the whole *macroeconomic* environment in which it operates.

If the economy is booming, then individual businesses are likely to be more profitable than if the economy is in recession. It is thus important for businesses to understand the forces that affect the whole business climate.

One of these forces is the level of confidence, both of consumers and business. If business confidence is high, then firms are likely to invest. Similarly, if consumer confidence is high, spending in the shops is likely to be high and this will increase business profitability. The result will be economic growth. If, however, people are predicting a recession, firms will hold off investing and consumer spending may well decline. This could tip the economy into recession.

Similarly, business confidence and business profitability are affected by the general level of prices and wages, and by the level of unemployment. It is thus important for managers to understand what causes inflation and what causes unemployment and how these are related to the overall level of business activity.

In Chapter 9 we look at the various forces affecting the performance of the economy.

Another key ingredient of the macroeconomic environment is government policy and the actions of the central bank (the Bank of England in the UK). If the government raises taxes or the Bank of England raises interest rates this could impact directly on business profitability and on business confidence. We examine macroeconomic policies in Chapter 10.

Business issues covered in this chapter

- What determines the level of activity in the economy and hence the overall business climate?

- If a stimulus is given to the economy, what will be the effect on business output?

- Why do economies experience periods of boom followed by periods of recession? What determines the length and magnitude of these 'phases' of the business cycle?

- How are interest rates determined and what is the role of the money supply in the process?

- What determines the supply of money in the economy?

- What are the causes of unemployment and how does unemployment relate to the level of business activity?

- What are the causes of inflation and how does inflation relate to the level of business activity?

CHAPTER 9

The economy and business activity

We start our examination of the macroeconomic environment by asking what determines the overall level of business activity. One of the most important determinants, at least in the short run, is the level of spending on firms' output. The more consumers spend, the more will firms want to produce in order to meet that consumer demand.

We use the term 'aggregate demand' (*AD*) to represent the total level of spending on the goods and services produced within the country over a given time period (normally a year). This spending consists of four elements: consumer spending on domestically produced goods and services (C_d), investment expenditure within the country by firms, whether on plant and equipment or on building up stocks (*I*), government spending on goods and services (such as health, education and transport) (*G*) and the expenditure by residents abroad on this country's exports (*X*). Thus:

$$AD = C_d + I + G + X$$

The total annual output of goods and services on which aggregate demand is spent is called GDP, or 'gross domestic product'. As long as there is spare capacity in the economy, a rise in aggregate demand will stimulate firms to produce more. GDP will rise.

A simple way of understanding this process is to use a 'circular flow of income diagram'. This is shown in Figure 9.1 overleaf.

In the diagram, the economy is divided into two major groups: *firms* and *households*. Each group has two roles. Firms are producers of goods and services; they are also the employers of labour. Households (which is the word we use for individuals) are the consumers of goods and services; they are also the suppliers of labour. In the diagram there is an inner flow and various outer flows of income between these two groups.

The inner flow, withdrawals and injections

The inner flow

Firms pay incomes to households in the form of wages and salaries. Some households also receive incomes from firms in the form of dividends on shares, or interest on loans or rent on property. Thus on the left-hand side of the diagram money flows directly from firms to households as household incomes.

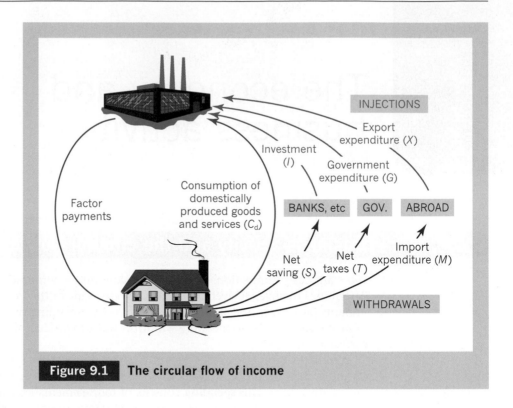

| Figure 9.1 | The circular flow of income |

Households, in turn, pay money to domestic firms when they **consume domestically produced goods and services (C_d)**. This is shown on the right-hand side of the inner flow. There is thus a circular flow of payments from firms to households to firms and so on.

If households spend *all* their incomes on buying domestic goods and services, and if firms pay out *all* this income they receive to domestic households, and if the speed at which money flows around the system does not change, the flow will continue at the same level indefinitely. The money just goes round and round at the same speed and incomes remain unchanged.

In the real world, of course, it is not as simple as this. Not all income gets passed on round the inner flow; some is *withdrawn*. At the same time, incomes are *injected* into the flow from outside. Let us examine these withdrawals and injections.

Withdrawals

There are three forms of **withdrawals (W)** (or 'leakages' as they are sometimes called).

Net saving (S). Saving is income that households choose not to spend but to put aside for the future. Savings are normally deposited in financial institutions such as banks and building societies. This is shown in the bottom right of the diagram. Money flows from households to 'banks, etc'. What we are seeking to measure here, however, is the net flow from households to the banking sector. We therefore have to subtract from saving any borrowing or drawing on past savings by households in order to get the *net* saving flow. Of course, if household borrowing exceeded saving, the net flow would be in the other direction: it would be negative.

Definition

The consumption of domestically produced goods and services (C_d)
The direct flow of money payments from households to firms.

Withdrawals (W) (or leakages)
Incomes of households or firms that are not passed on round the inner flow. Withdrawals equal net saving (S) plus net taxes (T) plus import expenditure (M): $W = S + T + M$.

Net taxes (T).   When people pay taxes (to either central or local government), this represents a withdrawal of money from the inner flow in much the same way as saving: only in this case people have no choice. Some taxes, such as income tax and employees' national insurance contributions, are paid out of household incomes. Others, such as VAT and excise duties, are paid out of consumer expenditure. Others, such as corporation tax, are paid out of firms' incomes before being received by households as dividends on shares. (For simplicity, however, we show taxes being withdrawn at just one point. It does not affect the argument.)

When, however, people receive *benefits* from the government, such as working tax credit, child benefit and pensions, the money flows the other way. Benefits are thus equivalent to a 'negative tax'. These benefits are known as **transfer payments**. They transfer money from one group of people (taxpayers) to others (the recipients).

In the model, 'net taxes' (*T*) represent the *net* flow to the government from households and firms. It consists of total taxes minus benefits.

Import expenditure (M).   Not all consumption is of home-produced goods. House-holds spend some of their incomes on imported goods and services. Although the money that consumers spend on such goods initially flows to domestic retailers, most of it will eventually find its way abroad when the retailers or wholesalers themselves import them. This expenditure on imports constitutes the third with-drawal from the inner flow. This money flows abroad.

Total withdrawals are simply the sum of net saving, net taxes and the expenditure on imports:

$$W = S + T + M$$

Injections

Only part of the demand for firms' output (aggregate demand) arises from consumers' expenditure. The remainder comes from other sources outside the inner flow. These additional components of spending are known as **injections** (*J*). There are three types of injection.

Investment (I).   This is the flow of money that firms spend which they obtain from various financial institutions – either past savings or loans, or through a new issue of shares. They may invest in plant and equipment or may simply spend the money on building up stocks of inputs, semi-finished or finished goods.

Government expenditure (G).   When the government spends money on goods and services produced by firms, this counts as an injection. Examples of such government expenditure are spending on roads, hospitals and schools. (Note that government expenditure in this model does not include state benefits. These transfer payments, as we saw above, are the equivalent of negative taxes and have the effect of reducing the *T* component of withdrawals.)

Export expenditure (X).   Money flows into the circular flow from abroad when residents abroad buy our exports of goods and services.

Total injections are thus the sum of investment, government expenditure and exports:

$$J = I + G + X$$

Aggregate demand, which is the total spending on output, is thus $C_d + J$.

Definition

Transfer payments
Moneys transferred from one person or group to another (e.g. from the government to individuals) without production taking place.

Injections (J)
Expenditure on the production of domestic firms coming from outside the inner flow of the circular flow of income. Injections equal investment (*I*) plus government expenditure (*G*) plus expenditure on exports (*X*).

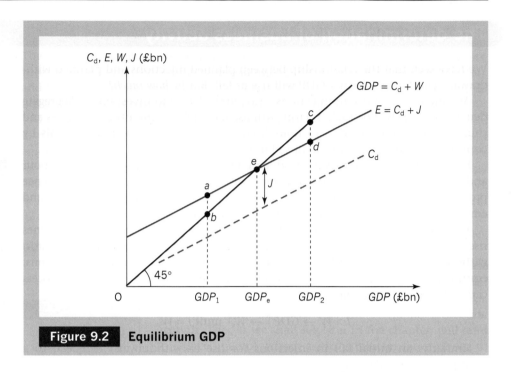

Figure 9.2 Equilibrium GDP

axis ($C_d + W$), the line will be at 45° (assuming that the axes are drawn to the same scale).

The other continuous line plots aggregate demand. In this diagram it is known as the *aggregate expenditure line* (E). It consists of $C_d + J$: i.e. the total spending on domestic firms.

To show how this line is constructed, consider the dashed line. This shows C_d. It is flatter than the 45° line. The reason is that for any given rise in GDP and hence people's incomes, only *part* will be spent on domestic product, while the remainder will be withdrawn: i.e. C_d rises less quickly than GDP. The E line consists of $C_d + J$. But we have assumed that J is constant with respect to changes in GDP. Thus the E line is simply the C_d line shifted upward by the amount of J.

If aggregate expenditure exceeded GDP, at say GDP_1, there would be excess demand in the economy (of $a - b$). In other words, people would be buying more than was currently being produced. Firms would thus find their stocks dwindling and would therefore increase their level of production. In doing so, they would employ more labour and other inputs. GDP would thus rise. As it did so, C_d and hence E would rise. There would be a movement up along the E line. But because not all the extra incomes earned from the rise in GDP would be consumed (i.e. some would be withdrawn), expenditure would rise less quickly than income: the E line is flatter than the GDP line. As income rises towards GDP_e, the gap between the GDP and E lines gets smaller. Once point e is reached, GDP = E. There is then no further tendency for GDP to rise.

Pause for thought

Why is India likely to have a steeper E curve than Luxembourg?

If GDP exceeded aggregate expenditure, at say GDP_2, there would be insufficient demand for the goods and services currently being produced ($c - d$). Firms would find their stocks of unsold goods building up. They would thus respond by producing less and employing fewer factors of production. GDP would thus fall and go on falling until GDP_e was reached.

The multiplier

As we have seen, when aggregate expenditure rises, this will cause a multiplied rise in GDP. The size of the **multiplier** is given by the letter k, where:

$$k = \Delta GDP/\Delta E$$

Thus, if aggregate expenditure rose by £10 million (ΔE) and as a result GDP rose by £30 million (ΔGDP), the multiplier would be 3. Figure 9.3 is drawn on the assumption that the multiplier is 3.

Assume in Figure 9.3 that aggregate expenditure rises by £20 billion, from E_1 to E_2. This could be caused by a rise in injections, or by a fall in withdrawals (and hence a rise in consumption of domestically produced goods) or by some combination of the two. Equilibrium GDP rises by £60 billion, from £100 billion to £160 billion (where the E_2 line crosses the GDP line).

Box 9.1 (overleaf) shows how the size of the multiplier can be calculated in advance.

Definition

The multiplier
The number of times a rise in GDP (ΔGDP) is bigger than the initial rise in aggregate expenditure (ΔE) that caused it. Using the letter k to stand for the multiplier, the multiplier is defined as $k = \Delta GDP/\Delta E$.

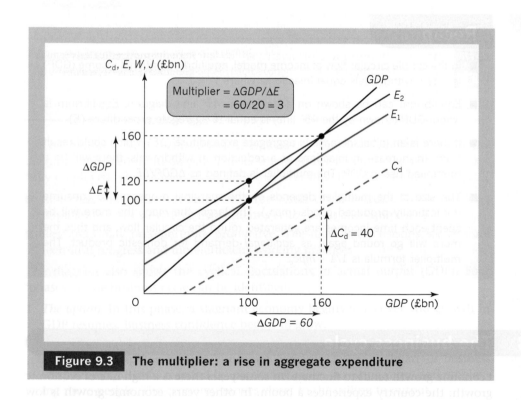

Figure 9.3 **The multiplier: a rise in aggregate expenditure**

4. *The slowdown, recession or slump*. During this phase, there is little or no growth or even a decline in output. Increasing slack develops in the economy as many businesses produce less and hold off from investing.

Pause for thought

Will the ceiling to output be in any way affected by the short-run rate of growth of GDP? If so, how?

The third (dashed) line shows the trend of GDP over time (i.e. ignoring the cyclical fluctuations around the trend). If the average level of capacity that is unutilised stays constant from one cycle to another, then the trend line will have the same slope as the output ceiling line.

The business cycle in practice

The business cycle illustrated in Figure 9.4 is a 'stylised' cycle. It is nice and smooth and regular. Drawing it this way allows us to make a clear distinction between each of the four phases. In practice, however, business cycles are highly irregular. They are irregular in two ways.

The length of the phases. Some booms are short lived, lasting only a few months or so. Others are much longer, lasting perhaps three or four years. Likewise some recessions are short, while others are long.

The magnitude of the phases. Sometimes in phase 2 there is a very high rate of economic growth, perhaps 5 per cent per annum or more. On other occasions in phase 2 growth is much gentler. Sometimes in phase 4 there is a recession, with an actual decline in output (e.g. in the early 1980s and early 1990s). On other occasions, phase 4 is merely a 'pause', with growth simply slowing down (e.g. in the early 2000s).

Nevertheless, despite the irregularity of the fluctuations, cycles are still clearly discernible, especially if we plot *growth* on the vertical axis rather than the *level* of output. This is done in Figure 9.5, which shows the business cycles in selected industrial countries from 1970 to 2005.

Causes of cyclical fluctuations

Why does the business cycle occur and what determines the length and magnitude of the phases of the cycle? To understand this we need to know why aggregate demand fluctuates. As we have seen, it is changes in aggregate demand that determine short-run economic growth. There are three questions we need to answer.

■ What causes aggregate demand to change in the first place?

■ Why do the effects of changes in aggregate demand persist? In other words, why do booms and recessions last for a period of time?

■ Why do booms and recessions come to an end? What determines the turning points?

What causes aggregate demand to change in the first place?

Anything that affects one of more of the four components of aggregate demand (C_d, I, G, or X) could be the reason for a change in GDP. For example, an increase in business confidence could increase investment; an increase in consumer confidence could increase consumption. A cut in interest rates may encourage increased business and consumer borrowing, and hence an increase in investment and consumption. A cut in taxes will increase consumption, as consumers have more 'disposable'

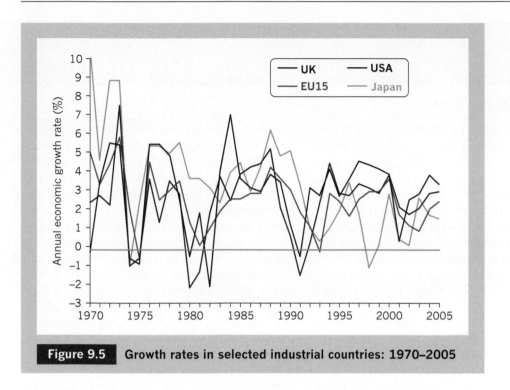

Figure 9.5   Growth rates in selected industrial countries: 1970–2005

income. A rise in government expenditure will directly increase aggregate demand. A change in conditions abroad, or a change in the exchange rate, will affect imports and exports (we examine these external factors in Part E).

Some of these factors, such as taxes and government expenditure, can be directly controlled by the government. In other words, government policy can be directed at controlling aggregate demand and hence the course of the business cycle. We call this 'demand management policy' – we will look at this in the next chapter.

Why do booms and recessions persist for a period of time?

Time lags.   It takes time for changes in aggregate demand to be fully reflected in changes in GDP and employment. The multiplier process takes time. Moreover, consumers, firms and government may not all respond immediately to new situations. Their responses are spread out over a period of time.

'Bandwagon' effects.   Once the economy starts expanding, expectations become buoyant. People think ahead and adjust their expenditure behaviour: they consume and invest more *now*. Likewise in a recession, a mood of pessimism may set in. The effect is cumulative.

One crucial effect here is called the **accelerator**. A rise in injections will cause a multiplied rise in GDP. But this rise in GDP will in turn cause a rise in investment, as firms seek to expand capacity to meet the extra demand. This compounds the increase in demand, as investment is itself an injection into the circular flow. This is the accelerator. The increased investment then causes a further multiplied rise in income. This then causes a further accelerator effect, a further multiplier effect, and so on.

Definition

The accelerator
The *level* of investment depends on the *rate of increase* in consumer demand, and as a result is subject to substantial fluctuations. Increases in investment via the accelerator can compound the multiplier effect.

Pause for thought

Under what circumstances would you expect a rise in national income to cause a large accelerator effect?

Box 9.2

Business expectations and their effect on investment

Recent European experience

Investment is highly volatile. It is subject to far more violent swings than GDP. This can be seen in Figure (a) which shows EU growth in GDP and growth in investment from 1985 to 2003. The maximum annual growth in GDP was 4.2 per cent and the maximum fall was 0.4 per cent. By contrast, the maximum annual growth in investment was 9.5 per cent and the maximum fall was 8.8 per cent. The differences were even greater for individual EU countries.

These figures are consistent with the accelerator theory, which argues that the level of investment depends on the rate of change of GDP and hence consumer demand. A relatively small percentage change in GDP can give a much bigger percentage change in investment.

Another factor affecting investment is the degree of business optimism. While this is partly determined by current rates of economic growth, there are many other factors that can affect the business climate. These include world political events (such as a war or a US election), national and international macroeconomic policies and shocks to the world economy (such as oil price changes). Of course, to the extent that these other factors affect confidence, which in turn affects investment, so they will affect economic growth.

In the boom years of the late 1980s, business optimism was widespread throughout Europe. Investment was correspondingly high, and with it there was a high rate of economic growth.

Surveys of European business expectations in the early 1990s, however, told a very different story. Pessimism was rife. Europe was in the grip of a recession. Growth slowed right down and output actually fell in 1993. Along with this decline in growth and deteriorating levels of business and consumer confidence, there was a significant fall in investment.

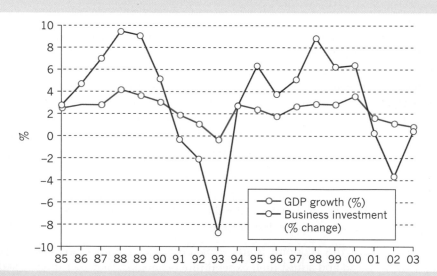

(a) EU-15 Growth in GDP and business investment
Source: *European Economy, Statistical Annex* (European Commission, 2003)

Why do booms and recessions come to an end? What determines the turning points?

Ceilings and floors.   Actual output can go on growing more rapidly than potential output only as long as there is slack in the economy. As full employment is approached and as more and more firms reach full capacity, so a ceiling to output is reached.

The industrial confidence indicator for the EU as a whole is plotted in Figure (b). The indicator shows the percentage excess of confident over pessimistic replies to business questionnaires: a negative figure means that there was a higher percentage of pessimistic responses. You can see that the indicator was strongly negative in 1993. After 1993, pessimism began to decrease, and by the last quarter of 1994 the EU industrial confidence indicator became positive.

Between 1995 and 2000, the industrial confidence indicator swung between positive and negative values. These swings were similar in direction to those in the rate of economic growth. For example, both the rate of growth and the confidence indicator rose in 1997/98 and 2000 and fell in 1996.

Then, in 2001, with the world economy slowing down and the September 11 attack on the World Trade Centre in New York, industrial confidence plummeted, and so did investment. As global uncertainties persisted and with impending and then actual war against Iraq, the confidence indicator remained low through 2002 and into 2003.

Questions

1. How is the existence of surveys of business confidence likely to affect firms' expectations and actions?
2. Why, if the growth in output slows down (but is still positive), is investment likely to fall (i.e. the growth in investment be negative)? If you look at Figure (a) you will see that this happened in 1991 and 1992, and in 2001 and 2002. (See section on the accelerator on page 223.)

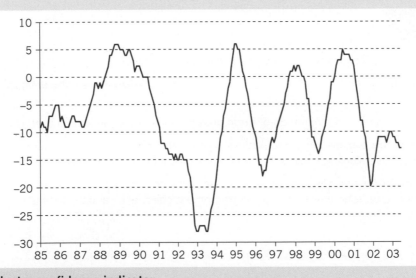

(b) EU-15 Industry confidence indicator
Source: *Business and Consumer Surveys* (European Commission, 2003)

At the other extreme, there is a basic minimum level of consumption that people tend to maintain. During a recession, people may not buy much in the way of luxury and durable goods, but they will continue to buy food and other basic goods. There is thus a floor to consumption.

The industries supplying these basic goods will need to maintain their level of replacement investment. Also there will always be some minimum investment demand as firms, in order to survive competition, need to install the latest equipment (such as computer hardware). There is thus a floor to investment too.

Echo effects. Durable consumer goods and capital equipment may last several years, but eventually they will need replacing. The replacement of goods and capital purchased in a previous boom may help to bring a recession to an end.

The accelerator. For investment to continue rising, consumer demand must rise at a *faster and faster* rate. After all, firms invest to meet *extra* demand. They will therefore only invest more than last period if the extra demand is more than last period: i.e. if the growth rate is *increasing*. If this does not happen, investment will fall back and the boom will break.

Random shocks. National or international political, social or natural events can affect the mood and attitudes of firms, governments and consumers, and thus affect aggregate demand.

Changes in government policy. In a boom, a government may become most worried by unsustainably high growth and inflation and thus pursue contractionary policies. In a recession, it may become most worried by unemployment and lack of growth and thus pursue expansionary policies. These government policies, if successful, will bring about a turning point in the cycle.

> **Pause for thought**
>
> *Why is it difficult to predict precisely when a recession will come to an end and the economy will start growing rapidly?*

Recap

- Economic growth fluctuates with the course of the business cycle.

- The cycle can be broken down into four phases: the upturn, the expansion, the peaking-out, and the slowdown or recession.

- In practice, the length and magnitude of these phases varies: the cycle is thus irregular.

- A major part of this explanation of the business cycle is the instability of investment. The accelerator theory explains this instability. It relates the level of investment to *changes* in GDP and consumer demand.

- Other reasons for fluctuations in aggregate demand include time lags, 'bandwagon' effects, ceilings and floors to output, echo effects, swings in government policy and random shocks.

9.4 Money, interest rates and business activity

Business and interest rates

One important determinant of business activity is the rate of interest. If interest rates rise, it will be more expensive for businesses to borrow; this will curtail investment. Higher interest rates are a particular problem for businesses that have a high ratio of borrowing at variable interest rates to their total turnover. In such cases, not only will a rise in interest rates discourage investment, it may also make it difficult for the business to find the money to pay the interest – to 'service' its debt.

Higher interest rates will also make it more expensive for the general public to borrow. If interest rates rise, whether on personal loans, on credit cards or on mortgages, consumers may well cut back on their borrowing and spending. Aggregate demand will fall.

Interest rates are also seen as a 'barometer' of the future course of the economy. If the Bank of England raises interest rates, this may be taken as a sign that the economy will slow down, especially if it is expected that rates are likely to be raised again in the near future. Business confidence may fall and so too, therefore, may investment. However, it all depends on how the rise in interest rates is interpreted. If it is seen as a means of preventing excessive expansion of the economy and therefore allowing expansion to be sustained, albeit at a more moderate rate, this may actually encourage investment.

But what determines interest rates? In a free market, interest rates are determined by the demand for and supply of money. In practice the free-market interest rate may not be the rate that the Bank of England wants, in which case it will alter it. This process of altering interest rates by the country's central bank (i.e. the Bank of England in the UK) is known as 'monetary policy'. We examine monetary policy in the next chapter. Here we look at the determination of interest rates in a free market.

The meaning of money

Before going any further we must define precisely what we mean by 'money'. Money is more than just notes and coins. In fact the main component of a country's money supply is not cash, but deposits in banks and other financial institutions. The bulk of the deposits appear merely as bookkeeping entries in the banks' accounts. People can access and use this money in their accounts through cheques, debit cards, standing orders, direct debits, etc. without the need for cash. Only a very small proportion of these deposits, therefore, needs to be kept by the banks in their safes or tills in the form of cash.

In UK official statistics, two main measures of money are used: a narrow measure M0 and a broad measure M4. **M0** consists mainly of cash, but also includes banks' own deposits in the Bank of England (a relatively small amount of money that banks can draw on if necessary). **M4** includes cash outside the banks plus *all* deposits in banks and building societies, whether in the form of cash or merely as bookkeeping entries. In January 2004, M0 was £40 billion. M4 was £1070 billion. When the term 'money supply' is used in the UK, it normally refers to M4.

> **Definition**
>
> **M0**
> Cash plus banks' balances with the Bank of England.
>
> **M4**
> Cash outside the banks plus all bank and building society deposits (including cash).

> **Pause for thought**
>
> *Why are debit and credit cards not counted as money?*

The supply of money

Banks and the creation of credit

By far the largest element of money supply (M4) is bank deposits. It is not surprising then that banks play an absolutely crucial role in the monetary system.

Banks are able to create additional money by increasing the amount of bank deposits. They do this by lending to people: granting people overdrafts or loans. When these loans are spent, the shops deposit the money in their bank accounts, or have it directly transferred when debit cards are swiped across their tills. Thus the

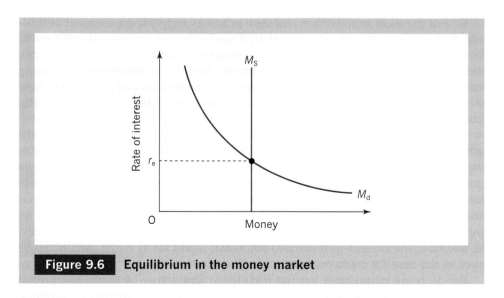

| Figure 9.6 | **Equilibrium in the money market** |

Pause for thought

Which way is the demand-for-money curve likely to shift in each of the following cases? (a) Prices rise, but real incomes stay the same. (b) Interest rates abroad rise relative to domestic interest rates. (c) People anticipate that share prices are likely to fall in the near future.

opportunity cost is the interest forgone by not holding higher interest-bearing assets, such as bonds or shares. Generally, if rates of interest rise, they will rise more on bonds and other securities than on bank accounts. The demand for money will thus fall as people switch to these alternative securities. The demand for money is thus inversely related to the rate of interest. This is illustrated in Figure 9.6.

The equilibrium rate of interest

Equilibrium in the money market occurs when the demand for money (M_d) is equal to the supply of money (M_s). Figure 9.6 shows the demand for and supply of money plotted against the rate of interest. For simplicity, it is assumed that the supply of money is independent of interest rates, and is therefore drawn as a vertical straight line.[1]

The equilibrium rate of interest is r_e. But why? If the rate of interest were above r_e, people would have money balances surplus to their needs. They would use these to buy shares, bonds and other assets. This would drive up the price of these assets. But the price of assets is inversely related to interest rates. The higher the price of an asset (such as a government bond), the less will any given interest payment be as a percentage of its price (e.g. £10 as a percentage of £100 is 10 per cent, but as a percentage of £200 is only 5 per cent). Thus a higher price of assets will correspond to lower interest rates.

As the rate of interest fell, so there would be a movement down along the M_s and M_d curves. The interest rate would go on falling until it reached r_e. Equilibrium would then be achieved.

---

[1] In practice, the supply-of-money curve is likely to be upward sloping. The reason is that a rise in aggregate demand will lead to an increased demand for money and hence a rise in interest rates. At the same time, banks are likely to respond to the rise in demand for money by creating more credit, thereby increasing the money supply. In other words, the higher interest rates correspond to an increased supply of money.

Similarly, if the rate of interest were below r_e, people would have insufficient money balances. They would sell securities, thus lowering their prices and raising the rate of interest until it reached r_e.

Causes of changes in interest rates

We saw above what would cause an increase in the supply of money. If money supply does increase, the M_s line will shift to the right in Figure 9.6. This will cause a fall in the rate of interest to the point where the new M_s line intersects with the M_d curve.

A change in interest rates will also occur if the demand for money changes (i.e. the M_d curve shifts). For example, a rise in incomes would lead to people wanting to hold larger money balances. This would shift the M_d curve to the right and drive up the rate of interest.

In practice, the Bank of England seeks to *control* the rate of interest. We see how it achieves this in the next chapter.

Effects of changes in interest rates

A reduction in interest rates (e.g. from a rise in money supply) will lead to a rise in investment and consumer spending as firms and consumers borrow more. This rise in aggregate demand will then lead to a multiplied rise in GDP. How much aggregate demand increases depends on (a) the elasticity of the demand-for-money curve – the steeper the M_d curve, the more will interest rates fall for any given rise in money supply; (b) the responsiveness of businesses and consumers to a change in interest rates – the more responsive they are, the bigger will be the rise in aggregate demand and hence the bigger the multiplied rise in GDP.

> **Pause for thought**
>
> *Assume that interest rates fall. Under what circumstances will this lead to (a) a large rise in business investment; (b) little or no change in business investment?*

Recap

- Interest rates are an important determinant of business activity. They are determined by the interaction of the demand and supply of money.

- Money in its narrow sense includes just cash and banks' balances in the central bank. In the UK this is called M0. Money is normally defined more broadly, however, to include all bank deposits, not just those in the form of cash. M4 is the name given in the UK to this broader measure of the money supply.

- Bank deposits expand through a process of credit creation. If banks' liquid assets increase, they can be used as a base for increasing loans. When the loans are redeposited in banks, they form the base for yet more loans, and thus takes place a process of multiple credit expansion. The ratio of the increase of deposits to an expansion of banks' liquidity base is called the 'bank multiplier'. It is the inverse of the liquidity ratio.

- Money supply will rise if (a) banks respond to an increased demand for money by increasing credit without an increase in liquidity; (b) there is an inflow of money from abroad; (c) the government has a PSNCR and finances it by borrowing from the banking sector.

- The demand for money is determined mainly by people's incomes, the risk attached to alternatives to money and the rate of interest (the opportunity cost of holding money). The higher the rate of interest, the lower the demand for money.

- The equilibrium rate of interest is where the supply of money is equal to the demand. A rise in the rate of interest can be caused by an increased demand for money or a reduced supply.

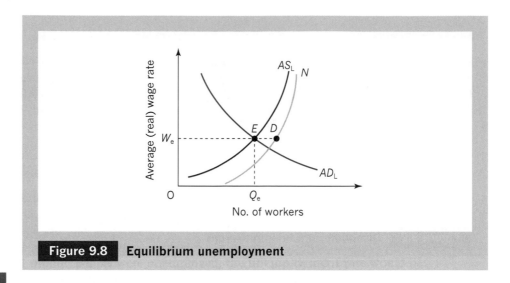

| Figure 9.8 | **Equilibrium unemployment** |

Definition

Real-wage unemployment
Disequilibrium unemployment caused by real wages being driven up above the market-clearing level.

Real-wage unemployment

Real-wage unemployment is where trade unions use their monopoly power to drive wages above the market-clearing level. In Figure 9.7, the wage rate is driven up above W_e. Excessive real wage rates were blamed by the Thatcher and Major governments for the high unemployment of the 1980s and early 1990s. The possibility of higher real-wage unemployment was also one of the reasons for their rejection of a national minimum wage.

The solution to real-wage unemployment would seem to be a reduction in real wage rates. However, it may be very difficult to prevent unions pushing up wages. Even if the government did succeed in reducing the average real wage rate, there would then be a problem of reduced consumer expenditure and hence a reduced demand for labour, with the result that unemployment might not fall at all.

Pause for thought

If this analysis is correct, namely that a reduction in wages will reduce the aggregate demand for goods, what assumption must we make about the relative proportions of wages and profits that are spent (given that a reduction in real wage rates will lead to a corresponding increase in rates of profit)? Is this a realistic assumption?

Demand-deficient unemployment

Demand-deficient unemployment is associated with economic recessions. As the economy moves into recession, consumer demand falls. Firms find that they are unable to sell their current level of output. For a time they may be prepared to build up stocks of unsold goods, but sooner or later they will start to cut back on production and cut back on the amount of labour they employ. In Figure 9.7 the AD_L curve shifts to the left. The deeper the recession becomes and the longer it lasts, the higher will demand-deficient unemployment become.

As the economy recovers and begins to grow again, so demand-deficient unemployment will start to fall. Because demand-deficient unemployment fluctuates with the business cycle, it is sometimes referred to as 'cyclical unemployment'. Figure 9.9 shows the fluctuations in unemployment in various industrial countries. If you compare this figure with Figure 9.5, you can see how unemployment tends to rise in recessions and fall in booms.

Definition

Demand-deficient or cyclical unemployment
Disequilibrium unemployment caused by a fall in aggregate demand with no corresponding fall in the real wage rate.

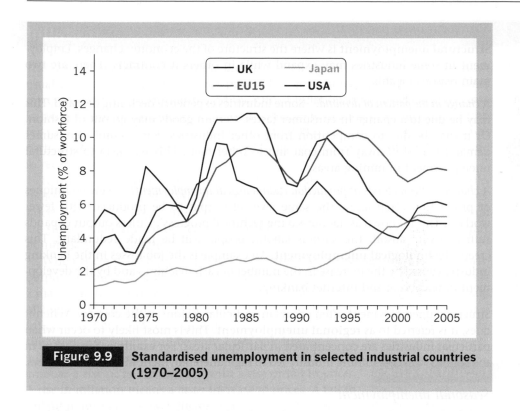

Figure 9.9 **Standardised unemployment in selected industrial countries (1970–2005)**

Equilibrium unemployment

If you look at Figure 9.9, you can see how unemployment was higher in the 1980s and 1990s than in the 1970s. Part of the reason for this was the growth in equilibrium unemployment.

Although there may be overall *macro*economic equilibrium, with the *aggregate* demand for labour equal to the *aggregate* supply, and thus no disequilibrium unemployment, at a *micro*economic level supply and demand may not match. In other words, there may be vacancies in some parts of the economy, but an excess of labour (unemployment) in others. This is equilibrium unemployment. There are various types of equilibrium unemployment.

Frictional (search) unemployment

Frictional unemployment occurs when people leave their jobs, either voluntarily or because they are sacked or made redundant, and are then unemployed for a period of time while they are looking for a new job. They may not get the first job they apply for, despite a vacancy existing. The employer may continue searching, hoping to find a better-qualified person. Likewise, unemployed people may choose not to take the first job they are offered. Instead they may continue searching, hoping that a better one will turn up.

The problem is that information is imperfect. Employers are not fully informed about what labour is available; workers are not fully informed about what jobs are available and what they entail. Both employers and workers, therefore, have to search: employers search for the right labour and workers search for the right jobs.

Definition

Frictional (search) unemployment
Unemployment that occurs as a result of imperfect information in the labour market. It often takes time for workers to find jobs (even though there are vacancies) and in the meantime they are unemployed.

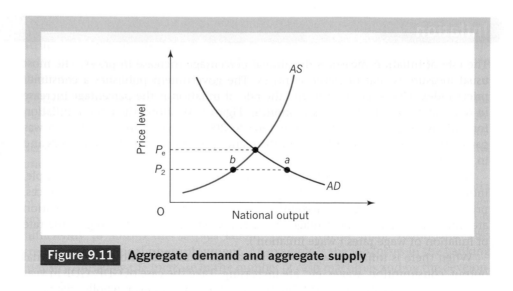

Figure 9.11 **Aggregate demand and aggregate supply**

Aggregate demand and supply and the level of prices

The level of prices in the economy is determined by the interaction of aggregate demand and aggregate supply. The analysis is similar to that of demand and supply in individual markets (see Chapter 2), but there are some crucial differences. Figure 9.11 shows aggregate demand and supply curves. Let us examine each in turn.

Aggregate demand curve

Remember what we said about aggregate demand earlier in the chapter. It is the total level of spending on the country's products: that is, by consumers, by the government, by firms on investment, and by people residing abroad. The aggregate demand curve shows how much national output (GDP) will be demanded at each level of prices. But why does the *AD* curve slope downwards: why do people demand fewer products as prices rise? There are three main reasons:

■ If prices rise, people will be encouraged to buy fewer of the country's products and more imports instead (which are now relatively cheaper); also the country will sell fewer exports. Thus aggregate demand will be lower.

■ As prices rise, people will need more money in their accounts to pay for their purchases. With a given supply of money in the economy, this will have the effect of driving up interest rates (the M_d curve shifts to the right in Figure 9.6). The effect of higher interest rates will be to discourage borrowing and encourage saving. Both will have the effect of reducing spending and hence reducing aggregate demand.

■ If prices rise, the value of people's savings will be eroded. They may thus save more (and spend less) to compensate.

Aggregate supply curve

The aggregate supply curve slopes upwards – at least in the short run. In other words, the higher the level of prices, the more will be produced. The reason is simple: provided that input prices (and, in particular, wage rates) do not rise as rapidly as product prices, firms' profitability at each level of output will be higher than before. This will encourage them to produce more.

Equilibrium

The equilibrium price level will be where aggregate demand equals aggregate supply. To demonstrate this, consider what would happen if aggregate demand exceeded aggregate supply: e.g. at P_2 in Figure 9.11. The resulting shortages throughout the economy would drive up prices. This would cause a movement up along both the AD and AS curves until $AD = AS$ (at P_e).

Shifts in the AD or AS curves

If there is a change in the price level there will be a movement *along* the AD and AS curves. If any other determinant of AD or AS changes, the respective curve will shift. The analysis here is very similar to shifts and movements along demand and supply curves in individual markets (see pages 36 and 40).

The aggregate demand curve will shift if there is a change in any of its components – consumption, investment, government expenditure or exports minus imports. Thus if the government decides to spend more, or if consumers spend more as a result of lower taxes, or if business confidence increases so that firms decide to invest more, the AD curve will shift to the right.

Similarly, the aggregate supply curve will shift to the right if there is a rise in labour productivity or in the stock of capital: i.e. if there is a rise in potential output.

Causes of inflation

Demand-pull inflation

Demand-pull inflation is caused by continuing rises in aggregate demand. In Figure 9.12, the AD curve shifts to the right, and continues doing so. Firms will

Definition

Demand-pull inflation
Inflation caused by persistent rises in aggregate demand.

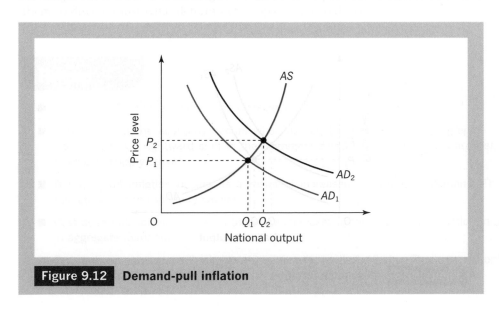

Figure 9.12   **Demand-pull inflation**

Box 9.3

Deflation danger

Running out of steam?

Inflation no longer seems a serious worry in many developed economies. Instead, 'deflation' (i.e. falling prices) has become a source of concern. The Japanese economy has been in deflation for the past ten years, but more recently the US Federal Reserve (America's central bank) and the European Central Bank have sounded warnings that deflation is a real and present danger to us all, set to engulf the global economic system. The following extract, taken from an article appearing in *The Sunday Times* of 11 May 2003, assesses the extent of the deflationary threat.

Consumers have had a good run in America. Twenty years ago a Burger King Whopper cost $1.40. Today the same burger costs 99c. Ten years ago Delta Airlines charged $388 for a flight from New York to San Francisco; this weekend flights are available for $302. Five years ago the average new car cost $25 000; now it is $24 500.

The same is true for clothes, computers, holidays and television sets. As wages have risen, prices seem to have fallen across the board. But can you have too much of a good thing?

Last week, America's central bankers warned that falling prices could harm the US economy. The Federal Reserve even went as far as to raise the spectre of deflation – an economic malaise that has paralysed the Japanese economy for a decade and was last seen in America during the Great Depression of the 1930s.

Not all prices are falling – house prices remain high, insurance costs are rising and so are medical bills. But the Fed's move signalled a profound change in attitude.

The European Central bank (ECB) followed suit with a subtle yet significant shift in policy. The ECB now says its aim is to keep inflation 'close to 2%'; in the past its aim was for inflation to hover between 0% and 2%.

Consumers normally welcome falling prices, but in a deflating economy such falls can create a damaging downward spiral. Profits fall as companies are unable to offset costs by raising prices. Companies then cut staff to save money. Job losses lead to falling sales.

Declining sales also make it harder for companies and people to meet their debts, leading to further declines in sales and a rise in bankruptcies. Falling prices also lead people to defer purchases in the belief that prices will come down further.

Such a spiral of decline had held back the Japanese economy sine the 1990s. Most economists see the threat of deflation as a remote possibility in America, but it is a possibility that they are starting to take seriously. . . .

Stephen Roach, Morgan Stanley's chief economist, has consistently warned of the dangers of deflation. 'The hope is that is that if we take this threat dead seriously, it won't happen,' he says.

Roach says there are three factors pushing America towards deflation.

The business cycle. Recessions by their very nature are deflationary. A weak recovery like the one we are experiencing does not favour price increases.

The bubble. the economy is still struggling to find its feet after over-indulging during the boom of the late 1990s. 'Too much supply was put into the market. The legacy is still there,' says Roach.

Globalisation. 'It's not a bad thing but it is deflationary. Low-cost countries are brought into the equation, and not just in goods but in services too.' The increasing transfer of call centres to countries like India is an example of this.

'The net result is that the unthinkable has become possible. I believe it is perfectly appropriate for policymakers to view deflation as the single greatest risk in shaping their economies,' he says.

Questions

1. Describe the impact of deflation on the practice of business.
2. What long-term economic benefits might deflation generate for business and the economy in general?

QUESTIONS

1. The following table shows index numbers for real GDP (national output) for various countries (1995 = 100).

	1995	1996	1997	1998	1999	2000	2001	2002	2003
USA	100.0	103.6	108.1	112.8	117.1	121.6	121.9	124.9	126.9
Japan	100.0	103.5	105.4	104.2	104.4	107.3	107.8	108.1	108.3
Germany	100.0	100.8	102.2	104.3	106.3	109.6	110.3	110.6	110.7
France	100.0	101.1	103.0	106.6	110.0	114.6	116.7	118.1	119.2
UK	100.0	102.6	106.1	109.3	111.9	115.4	117.7	119.6	121.0

Sources: *Various*

Using the formula $G = (Y_t - Y_{t-1})/Y_{t-1} \times 100$ (where G is the rate of growth, Y is the index number of output, t is any given year and $t - 1$ is the previous year):

(a) Work out the growth rate for each country for each year from 1996 to 2003.

(b) Plot the figures on a graph. Describe the pattern that emerges.

2. In terms of the UK circular flow of income, are the following net injections, net withdrawals or neither? If there is uncertainty, explain your assumptions.

(a) Firms are forced to take a cut in profits in order to give a pay rise.

(b) Firms spend money on research.

(c) The government increases personal tax allowances.

(d) The general public invests more money in building societies.

(e) UK investors earn higher dividends on overseas investments.

(f) The government purchases US military aircraft.

(g) People draw on their savings to finance holidays abroad.

(h) People draw on their savings to finance holidays in the UK.

(i) The government runs a budget deficit (spends more than it receives in tax revenues).

3. Assume that the multiplier has a value of 3. Now assume that the government decides to increase aggregate demand in an attempt to reduce unemployment. It raises government expenditure by £100 million with no increase in taxes. Firms, anticipating a rise in their sales, increase investment by £200 million, of which £50 million consists of purchases of foreign machinery. How much will GDP rise? (Assume that nothing else changes.)

Business issues covered in this chapter

- What sorts of government macroeconomic policy are likely to impact on business and in what way?

- What will be the impact on the economy and business of various fiscal policy measures?

- What determines the effectiveness of fiscal policy in smoothing out fluctuations in the economy?

- What fiscal rules are adopted by the government and is following them a good idea?

- How does monetary policy work in the UK and what is the role of the Bank of England?

- How does targeting inflation influence interest rates and hence business activity?

- Are there better rules for determining interest rates other than sticking to a simple inflation target?

- How can supply-side policy influence business and the economy?

- What types of supply-side policies can be pursued and what is their effectiveness?

CHAPTER 10

Government macroeconomic policy

A key influence on the macroeconomic environment of business is the government. Governments like to achieve economic success, including sustained and stable economic growth, low unemployment and low inflation. To achieve these objectives, various types of policy are used. This chapter looks at the three main categories of macroeconomic policy.

The first is **fiscal policy**. This is where the government uses the balance of taxation (a withdrawal from the circular flow of income) and government expenditure (an injection) to influence the level of aggregate demand. If the economy is in recession, the government could increase government expenditure and/or cut taxes. The effect would be a higher level of aggregate demand and hence a multiplied rise in GDP and lower unemployment. If the economy was expanding too rapidly in a way that was unsustainable and hence with rising inflation, the government could do the reverse: it could cut government expenditure and/or raise taxes. This would help to slow the economy down and dampen inflation.

The second type of policy is **monetary policy**. Here the government sets the framework of policy, which in many countries, including the UK, means setting a target for the rate of inflation. In the UK the rate is 2 per cent, as it is also in the eurozone. The central bank is then charged with adjusting interest rates to keep inflation on target.

These first two types of policy are referred to as **demand-side** or **demand management policies** as they seek to control the level of aggregate demand. The third category of policy is **supply-side policy**. This seeks to control aggregate supply directly. For example, the government might seek ways of encouraging greater productivity through increased research and development or better training programmes. Or it might seek to improve the country's transport and communications infrastructure, for example by investing in the railways or building more roads.

The difference between demand-side and supply-side policies is illustrated in Figure 10.1 (overleaf), which shows an aggregate demand and an aggregate supply curve.

Demand-side policy seeks to shift the *AD* curve. An expansionary fiscal or monetary policy would shift the *AD* curve to the right, helping to increase GDP and employment, but resulting in higher prices. A contractionary fiscal or monetary policy would help to curb rightward shifts in the *AD* curve or even cause the curve to shift to the left. The policy could be used to tackle inflation, but would run the risk of a reduction in the rate of growth of GDP, or even a recession, and higher unemployment.

Supply-side policy seeks to shift the *AS* curve to the right. If successful, it will lead to both higher GDP and employment and lower prices (or at least lower inflation).

Definition

Fiscal policy
Policy to affect aggregate demand by altering government expenditure and/or taxation.

Monetary policy
Policy to affect aggregate demand by central bank action to alter interest rates or money supply.

Demand-side (or demand management) policy
Policy to affect aggregate demand (i.e. fiscal or monetary policy).

Supply-side policy
Policy to affect aggregate supply directly.

taxes. In other words, not all the tax cuts will be passed on round the circular flow of income as extra expenditure. Thus if one-fifth of a cut in taxes is withdrawn and only four-fifths is spent, the tax multiplier will only be four-fifths as big as the government expenditure multiplier.

Box 10.1

Fiscal policy and business

Indirect and direct effects

When the government adopts an expansionary fiscal policy there are indirect effects on virtually all firms from the expansion of the economy. Higher GDP means higher consumer demand. The greater the income elasticity of demand for a firm's products, the more it will benefit from increased sales as GDP expands.

Higher GDP, via the accelerator, also means higher investment. This will benefit the construction industry as new factories and offices are built. It will also benefit businesses producing machinery and other capital equipment.

In addition to these indirect effects there are also *direct* effects on business from increased government expenditure. If new roads, hospitals or schools are built, the construction industry will directly benefit. If the government spends money

on refurbishing existing premises, then the building industry will directly benefit, as will the furnishing industry and businesses supplying computers and other equipment.

Similarly, there will be direct benefits from tax cuts. If corporation tax (the tax on business profits) is cut, after-tax profits will immediately increase. There will be a similar effect if employers' national insurance contributions are reduced.

? Question

Apart from the industries mentioned above, what other industries are likely to benefit directly from an expansionary fiscal policy?

The effectiveness of fiscal policy

How successful will fiscal policy be? Will it be able to 'fine-tune' demand? Will it be able to achieve the level of GDP that the government would like it to achieve? Before changing government expenditure or taxation, the government will need to calculate the effect of any such change on GDP, employment and inflation. Predicting these effects, however, is often very unreliable.

Difficulty in predicting effects of changes in government expenditure. A rise in government expenditure of £x may lead to a rise in total injections (relative to withdrawals) that is smaller than £x. A major reason for this is a phenomenon known as **crowding out**. If the government relies on **pure fiscal policy** – that is, if it does not finance an increase in the budget deficit by increasing the money supply – it will have to borrow the money from individuals and firms. It will thus be competing with the private sector for finance and will have to offer higher interest rates. This will force the private sector also to offer higher interest rates, which may discourage firms from investing and individuals from buying on credit. Thus government borrowing *crowds out* private borrowing. In the extreme case, the fall in consumption and investment may completely offset the rise in government expenditure, with the result that aggregate demand does not rise at all.

Difficulty in predicting effects of changes in taxes. A rise in taxes, by reducing people's real disposable income, will reduce not only the amount they spend, but also the amount they save. The problem is that it is not easy to predict just how much people

Definition

Crowding out
Where increased public expenditure diverts money or resources away from the private sector.

Pure fiscal policy
Fiscal policy which does not involve any change in money supply.

will cut down on their spending and how much on their saving. In part it will depend on whether people feel that the rise in tax is only temporary, in which case they may well cut savings in order to maintain their level of consumption, or permanent, in which case they may well reduce their consumption.

Difficulty in predicting the resulting multiplied effect on GDP.   The size of the multiplier and accelerator (see pages 219–23) is difficult to predict, mainly because the effects depend largely on people's confidence. For example, if the business community believe that a cut in taxes will be successful in pulling the economy out of recession, firms will invest. This will help to bring about the very recovery that firms predicted. There will be a big multiplier effect. If, however, businesses are pessimistic about the likely success of the policy, they are unlikely to invest. The economy may not recover.

Random shocks.   Forecasts cannot take into account the unpredictable. For that you would have to consult astrologers or fortune tellers! Unfortunately, unpredictable events, such as a war or a major industrial dispute, do occur and may seriously undermine the government's fiscal policy.

> **Pause for thought**
>
> *Give some other examples of 'random shocks' that could undermine the government's fiscal policy.*

Problems of timing.   Fiscal policy can involve considerable time lags. It may take time to recognise the nature of the problem; tax or government expenditure changes take time to plan and implement; the effects of such changes take time to work their way through the economy via the multiplier and accelerator.

If time lags are long enough, fiscal policy could even be destabilising. Expansionary policies taken to cure a recession may not take effect until the economy has already recovered and is experiencing a boom. Under these circumstances, expansionary policies are quite inappropriate: they simply worsen the problems of overheating. Similarly, deflationary policies taken to prevent excessive expansion may not take effect until the economy has already peaked and is plunging into recession. The deflationary policies only deepen the recession.

This problem is illustrated in Figure 10.2. Path (a) shows the course of the business cycle without government intervention. Ideally, with no time lags, the economy should be dampened in stage 2 and stimulated in stage 4. This would make the resulting course of the business cycle more like path (b), or even, if the policy were

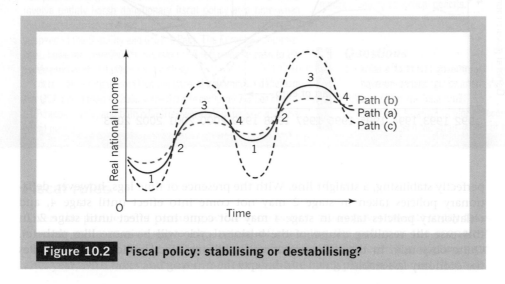

Figure 10.2   **Fiscal policy: stabilising or destabilising?**

For example, a target could be set for the PSNCR, with government expenditure and taxes being adjusted to keep the PSNCR at or within its target level. Box 10.2 looks at some examples of fiscal targets.

The approach to fiscal policy in the UK

Since 1998, the government has set targets for government expenditure, not for just one year, but for a three-year period. Does this mean, therefore, that fiscal policy as a means of adjusting aggregate demand had been abandoned? In one sense, this is the case. The government is now committed to following its 'golden rule', whereby public-sector receipts should cover all current spending, averaged over the course of the business cycle (see Box 10.2).

But despite this apparent rejection of short-term discretionary fiscal adjustments, there is still a role for *automatic* fiscal stabilisers: with deficits rising in a recession and falling in a boom. There is also still the possibility, within the golden rule, of financing additional *investment* by borrowing, thereby providing a stimulus to a sluggish economy.

The golden rule also permits increased government expenditure (or tax cuts) if there is a budget surplus. Thus in the 2001 Budget the Chancellor announced spending increases of 3.7 per cent per year for three years. The effect was to provide a stimulus to the economy just at a time when the world economy was slowing down. This helped to make the slowdown in UK economic growth in the period 2001–3 much less severe than in many other countries.

Recap

■ The government's fiscal policy will determine the size of the budget deficit or surplus and the size of the PSNCR.

■ Automatic fiscal stabilisers are tax revenues that rise and benefits that fall as GDP rises. They have the effect of reducing the size of the multiplier and thus reducing cyclical upswings and downswings.

■ Discretionary fiscal policy is where the government deliberately changes taxes or government expenditure in order to alter the level of aggregate demand. Changes in government expenditure on goods and services will have a full multiplier effect. Changes in taxes and benefits will have a smaller multiplier effect as some of the tax/benefit changes will merely affect other withdrawals and thus have a smaller net effect on consumption of domestic product.

■ There are problems in predicting the magnitude of the effects of discretionary fiscal policy. Expansionary fiscal policy can act as a pump primer and stimulate increased private expenditure, or it can crowd out private expenditure. The extent to which it acts as a pump primer depends crucially on business confidence – something that is very difficult to predict beyond a few weeks or months. The extent of crowding out depends on monetary conditions and the government's monetary policy.

■ There are various time lags involved with fiscal policy. If these are very long, the policy could be destabilising rather than stabilising.

■ Today many governments prefer a more passive approach towards fiscal policy. Targets are set for one or more measures of the public-sector finances, and then taxes and government expenditure are adjusted so as to keep to the target.

Monetary policy   10.2

Each month the Bank of England's Monetary Policy Committee meets to set interest rates. The event gets considerable media coverage. Pundits, for two or three days before the meeting, try to predict what the MPC will do and economists give their 'considered' opinions about what the MPC *ought* to do. Business leaders look at the potential impact on consumer spending, business confidence and investment.

The fact is that changes in interest rates have gained a central significance in macroeconomic policy. And it is not just in the UK. Whether it is the European Central Bank setting interest rates for the eurozone countries, or the Federal Reserve Bank setting US interest rates, or any other central bank around the world choosing what the level of interest rates should be, monetary policy is seen as having a major influence on a whole range of macroeconomic indicators.

But is monetary policy simply the setting of interest rates? In reality, it involves the central bank intervening in the money market to ensure that the interest rate that has been announced is also the *equilibrium* interest rate.

The policy setting

In framing its monetary policy, the government must decide on what the goals of the policy are. Is the aim simply to control inflation, or does the government wish also to affect output and employment, or does it want to control the exchange rate?

A decision also has to be made about who is to carry out the policy. There are three possible approaches here.

In the first, the government both sets the policy and decides the measures necessary to achieve it. Here the government would set the interest rate, with the central bank simply influencing money markets to achieve this rate. This first approach was used in the UK before 1997.

The second approach is for the government to set the policy *targets*, but for the central bank to be given independence in deciding interest rates. This is the approach adopted in the UK today. The government has set a target rate of inflation of 2 per cent, but then the MPC is free to choose the rate of interest.

The third approach is for the central bank to be given independence not only in carrying out policy, but in setting the policy targets themselves. The ECB, within the statutory objective of maintaining price stability over the medium term, decides on (a) the target rate of inflation – currently that inflation for the eurozone should be kept near to 2 per cent, and (b) the target rate of growth in money supply. It then sets interest rates to meet these targets.

Implementing monetary policy

Monetary policy may be off target. Alternatively, the government (or central bank) may wish to alter its monetary policy. What can it do? There are two main approaches. The first is to alter the money supply; the second is to alter interest rates. These are illustrated in Figure 10.3 (overleaf), which shows the demand for and supply of money (this is similar to Figure 9.6 on page 230). With an initial supply of money of M_S the equilibrium interest rate is r_1.

Assume that the central bank wants to tighten monetary policy in order to reduce inflation. It could (a) seek to shift the supply of money curve to the left,

money will rise. Similarly, if people think exchange rates will rise, they will demand sterling while it is still relatively cheap. The demand for money will rise.

It is very difficult for the authorities to predict what people's expectations will be. Speculation depends so much on world political events, rumour and 'random shocks'.

If the demand curve shifts very much, and if it is inelastic, then monetary control will be very difficult. Furthermore, the authorities will have to make frequent and sizeable adjustments to interest rates. These fluctuations can be very damaging to business confidence and may discourage long-term investment.

The net result of an inelastic and unstable demand for money is that substantial interest rate changes may be necessary to bring about the required change in aggregate demand. An example occurred in 2001, when the US Federal Reserve, seeing the economy moving rapidly into recession, had to cut interest rates several times. At the beginning of 2001, the US 'federal funds rate' was 6 per cent. By the end of the year it had been reduced to 1.75 per cent.

> **Pause for thought**
>
> *Assume that the central bank announces a rise in interest rates and backs this up with open-market operations. What determines the size of the resulting fall in aggregate demand?*

Difficulties with choice of target

Assume that the government or central bank sets an inflation target. Should it then stick to that rate, come what may? Might not an extended period of relatively low inflation warrant a lower inflation target? The government must at least have the discretion to change the rules, even if only occasionally.

Then there is the question of whether success in achieving the target will bring success in achieving other macroeconomic objectives, such as low unemployment and stable economic growth. The problem is that something called **Goodhart's Law** is likely to apply. The law, named after Charles Goodhart, formerly of the Bank of England, states that attempts to control an indicator of a problem may, as a result, make it cease to be a good indicator of the problem.

Targeting inflation may make it become a poor indicator of the state of the economy. If people believe that the central bank will be successful in achieving its inflation target, then those expectations will feed into their inflationary expectations, and not surprisingly the target will be met. But that target rate of inflation may now be consistent with both a buoyant and a depressed economy. Achieving the inflation target has not tackled the much more serious problem of creating stable economic growth and an environment which will therefore encourage long-term investment.

Use of a Taylor rule. For this reason, many economists have advocated the use of a **Taylor rule**,[1] rather than a simple inflation target. A Taylor rule takes two objectives into account – (1) inflation and (2) either real GDP or unemployment – and seeks to get the optimum degree of stability of the two. The degree of importance attached to each of the two objectives can be decided by the government or central bank. The central bank adjusts interest rates when either the rate of inflation diverges from its target or the level of real GDP (or unemployment) diverges from its sustainable (or equilibrium) level.

> **Definition**
>
> **Goodhart's Law**
> Controlling a symptom or indicator of a problem is unlikely to cure the problem; it will simply mean that what is being controlled now becomes a poor indicator of the problem.
>
> **Taylor rule**
> A rule adopted by a central bank for setting the rate of interest. It will raise the interest rate if (a) inflation is above target or (b) growth is above the sustainable level (or unemployment below the equilibrium rate). The rule states how much interest rates will be changed in each case. In other words a relative weighting is attached to each of these two objectives.

---

[1] Named after John Taylor, from Stanford University, who proposed that for every 1 per cent that GDP rises above sustainable GDP, real interest rates should be raised by 0.5 percentage points and for every 1 per cent that inflation rises above its target level, real interest rates should be raised by 0.5 percentage points (i.e. nominal rates should be raised by 1.5 percentage points).

Take the case where inflation is above its target level. The central bank following a Taylor rule will raise the rate of interest. It knows, however, that this will reduce real GDP. This, therefore, limits the amount that the central bank is prepared to raise the rate of interest. The more weight it attaches to stabilising inflation, the more it will raise the rate of interest. The more weight it attaches to stabilising real GDP, the less it will raise the rate of interest.

Thus the central bank has to trade off inflation stability against real GDP stability.

Using monetary policy

It is impossible to use monetary policy as a precise means of controlling aggregate demand. It is especially weak when it is pulling against the expectations of firms and consumers and when it is implemented too late. However, if the authorities operate a tight monetary policy firmly enough and long enough, they should eventually be able to reduce lending and aggregate demand. But there will inevitably be time lags and imprecision in the process.

An expansionary monetary policy is even less reliable. If the economy is in recession, no matter how low interest rates are driven, people cannot be forced to borrow if they do not wish to. Firms will not borrow to invest if they predict a continuing recession.

Despite these problems, changing interest rates can be quite effective. After all, they can be changed very rapidly. There are not the time lags of implementation that there are with fiscal policy. Indeed, since the early 1990s most governments or central banks in OECD countries have used interest rate changes as the major means of keeping aggregate demand and inflation under control.

Recap

- The government or central bank can use monetary policy to restrict the growth in aggregate demand by reducing money supply directly or by reducing the demand for money by raising interest rates.

- The money supply can be reduced directly by using open-market operations. This involves selling more government securities and thereby reducing banks' reserves when their customers pay for them from their bank accounts.

- The current method of control involves the Bank of England's Monetary Policy Committee announcing the interest rate and then the Bank of England bringing this rate about by its operations in the repo market. It keeps banks short of liquidity, and then supplies them with liquidity through gilt repos at the chosen interest rate (gilt repo rate). This then has a knock-on effect on interest rates throughout the economy.

- Higher interest rates, by reducing the demand for money, effectively also reduce the supply. However, with an inelastic demand for loans, interest rates may have to rise to very high levels in order to bring the required reduction in monetary growth.

- Controlling aggregate demand through interest rates is made even more difficult by *fluctuations* in the demand for money. These fluctuations are made more severe by speculation against changes in interest rates, exchange rates, the rate of inflation, etc.

- Nevertheless, controlling interest rates is a way of responding rapidly to changing forecasts, and can be an important signal to markets that inflation will be kept under control, especially when, as in the UK and the eurozone, there is a firm target for the rate of inflation.

- Achieving inflation targets is becoming increasingly easy, but unrelated to other key objectives, such as economic growth or unemployment. Some economists advocate using a Taylor rule, which involves targeting a weighted average of inflation and economic growth.

Table 10.2 General government outlays as a percentage of GDP

	1961–70	1971–80	1981–85	1986–90	1991–95	1996–2000	2001–03
Belgium	33.7	50.6	61.5	55.3	54.1	50.9	49.7
Germany	37.0	45.3	48.2	46.0	48.2	48.6	48.6
France	38.3	42.4	51.5	50.2	53.0	54.1	53.4
Japan	–	26.8	33.2	10.5	33.2	39.1	39.9
Netherlands	39.9	49.3	59.5	55.0	53.0	47.5	47.0
Sweden	–	52.8	65.0	58.5	65.6	61.4	58.2
UK	36.5	41.2	44.6	39.8	42.3	40.0	40.8
USA	29.1	33.1	36.5	34.9	35.9	33.1	34.6

Source: Adapted from *European Economy Statistical Annex*, Spring 2004 (European Commission)

Tax cuts

Income tax cuts. Cutting the marginal rate of income tax was a major objective of the Thatcher and Major governments (1979–97). In 1979 the standard rate of income tax in the UK was 33 per cent and the top rate was 83 per cent. By 1997 the standard rate was only 23 per cent (with a starting rate of just 20 per cent), and the top rate was only 40 per cent. The Blair government continued with this policy. In 2004, the standard rate was 22 per cent and the starting rate was only 10 per cent. Cuts in the marginal rate of income tax are claimed to have many beneficial effects: e.g. people work longer hours; more people wish to work; people work more enthusiastically; unemployment falls; employment rises. The evidence regarding the truth of these claims, however, is less than certain.

For example, will people will be prepared to work longer hours? On the one hand, each hour worked will be more valuable in terms of take-home pay, and thus people may be encouraged to work more and have less leisure time. This is a substitution effect (see page 33): people substitute work for leisure. On the other hand, a cut in income tax will make people better off, and therefore they may feel less need to do overtime than before. This is an income effect (see page 33): they can afford to work less. The evidence on these two effects suggests that they just about cancel each other out. Anyway, for many people there is no such choice in the short run. There is no chance of doing overtime or working a shorter week. In the long run, there may be some flexibility in that people can change jobs.

Tax cuts for business and other investment incentives. A number of financial incentives can be given to encourage investment. Market-orientated policies seek to reduce the general level of taxation on profits, or to give greater tax relief to investment.

A cut in corporation tax (the tax on business profits) will increase after-tax profits. This will create more money for ploughing back into investment, and the higher after-tax return on investment will encourage more investment to take place. In 1983 the main rate of corporation tax in the UK stood at 52 per cent. A series of reductions have taken place since then, and by 2004 the rate was 30 per cent for large companies and 19 per cent for small ones, with a starting rate of only 10 per cent.

Reducing the power of labour

The argument here is that if labour costs to employers are reduced, their profits will probably rise. This could encourage and enable more investment and hence economic growth. If the monopoly power of labour is reduced, then cost-push inflation will also be reduced.

The Thatcher government took a number of measures to weaken the power of labour. These included restrictions on union closed shops (where employees in a given business have to be members of the specified union) and enforced secret ballots on strike proposals. It set a lead in resisting strikes in the public sector. Unlike previous Labour governments, it did not consult with union leaders over questions of economic policy. It was publicly very critical of trade union militancy and blamed the unions for many of the UK's economic ills. As a result, unions lost a lot of political standing and influence.

As labour markets have become more flexible, with increased part-time working and short-term contracts, so this has further eroded the power of labour in many sectors of the economy (see section 7.5).

Policies to encourage competition

If the government can encourage more competition, this should have the effect of increasing national output and reducing inflation. Four major types of policy have been pursued under this heading.

Privatisation. If privatisation simply involves the transfer of a natural monopoly to private hands (e.g. the water companies), the scope for increased competition is limited. However, where there is genuine scope for increased competition (e.g. in the supply of gas and electricity), privatisation can lead to increased efficiency, more consumer choice and lower prices. Alternatively, privatisation can involve the introduction of private services into the public sector (e.g. private contractors providing cleaning services in hospitals, or refuse collection for local authorities). Private contractors may compete against each other for the franchise, thus driving down costs.

Introducing market relationships into the public sector. This is where the government tries to get different departments or elements within a particular part of the public sector to 'trade' with each other, so as to encourage competition and efficiency. The most well-known examples are within education and health.

The process often involves 'devolved budgeting'. For example, under the local management of schools scheme (LMS), schools have become self-financing. Rather than the local authority meeting the bill for teachers' salaries, the schools have to manage their own budgets. The objective is to encourage them to cut costs, thereby reducing the burden on council tax payers. However, one result is that schools have tended to appoint inexperienced (and hence cheaper) teachers rather than those who can bring the benefits of their years of teaching.

In 2003, the Labour government introduced foundation hospitals. Foundation status would be given to hospitals which meet various quality targets. While still part of the public sector, foundation hospitals would have greater financial freedom, greater local accountability and greater ability to make their own decisions.

The Private Finance Initiative. In 1993 the government introduced its Private Finance Initiative (PFI). This became the new way in which public projects were to

Recap

- Supply-side policies, if successful, will shift the aggregate supply curve to the right, and help to achieve faster economic growth without higher inflation.

- Market-orientated supply-side policies aim to increase the rate of growth of aggregate supply and reduce the rate of unemployment by encouraging private enterprise and the freer play of market forces.

- Reducing government expenditure as a proportion of GDP is a major element of such policies.

- Tax cuts can be used to encourage more people to take up jobs, and people to work longer hours and more enthusiastically. The effects of tax cuts will depend on how people respond to incentives.

- Various policies can be introduced to increase competition. These include privatisation, introducing market relationships into the public sector, and freer international trade and capital movements.

- The UK has had a lower rate of investment than most other industrialised countries. This has contributed to a historically low rate of economic growth and imports of manufacture growing faster than exports. In response many argue for a more interventionist approach to supply-side policy.

- Intervention can take the form of grants, supporting research and development, advice and persuasion, investing in training and the direct provision of infrastructure.

QUESTIONS

1. 'The existence of a budget deficit or a budget surplus tells us very little about the stance of fiscal policy.' Explain and discuss.

2. Adam Smith, the founder of modern economics, remarked in *The Wealth of Nations* (1776) concerning the balancing of budgets, 'What is prudence in the conduct of every private family can scarce be folly in that of a great kingdom.' What problems might there be if the government decided to follow a balanced budget approach to its spending?

3. Imagine you were called in by the government to advise on whether it should attempt to prevent cyclical fluctuations by the use of fiscal policy. What advice would you give and how would you justify the advice?

4. Why is it difficult to use fiscal policy to 'fine-tune' the economy?

5. When the Bank of England announces that it is putting up interest rates, how will it achieve this, given that interest rates are determined by demand and supply?

6. How does the Bank of England attempt to achieve the target rate of inflation of 2 per cent? What determines its likelihood of success in meeting the target?

7. What is meant by a Taylor rule? In what way is it a better rule for central banks to follow than one of adhering to a simple inflation target?

8. Under what circumstances would adherence to an inflation target lead to (a) more stable interest rates, (b) less stable interest rates, than pursuing discretionary demand management policy?

9. Define *demand-side* and *supply-side* policies. Are there any ways in which such policies are incompatible?

10. What types of tax cuts are likely to create the greatest (a) incentives, (b) disincentives to effort?

11. Imagine that you are asked to advise the government on ways of increasing investment in the economy. What advice would you give and why?

12. In what ways can interventionist industrial policy work *with* the market, rather than against it? What are the arguments for and against such policy?

Additional Part D case studies on the Economic Environment of Business Website (www.booksites.net/sloman)

D.1   **Output gaps.** A way of measuring how far actual output falls short of long-term trend output.

D.2   **The costs of economic growth.** Why economic growth may not be an unmixed blessing.

D.3   **Comparing national income statistics.** The importance of taking the purchasing power of local currencies into account.

D.4   **John Maynard Keynes (1883–1946).** A profile of the great economist.

D.5   **Has there been an accelerator effect since 1978?** An examination of the evidence for an accelerator effect in the UK.

D.6   **The attributes of money.** What makes something, such as metal, paper or electronic records, suitable as money?

D.7   **UK monetary aggregates.** This examines the various measures of money supply in the UK using both UK and eurozone monetary aggregates.

D.8   **Changes in the banking industry.** This case study looks at mergers and diversification in the banking industry.

D.9   **Technology and unemployment.** Does technological progress destroy jobs?

D.10   **The national debt.** This explores the question of whether it matters if a country has a high national debt.

D.11 **Trends in public expenditure.** This case examines attempts to control public expenditure in the UK and relates them to the crowding out debate.

D.12 **The crowding-out effect.** The circumstances in which an increase in public expenditure can replace private expenditure.

D.13 **Managing the US economy.** The use of active fiscal and monetary policy in 2001 and 2002 to stimulate the US economy.

D.14 **The daily operation of monetary policy.** What practical steps does the Bank of England take to ensure that the market rate of interest is its own chosen rate?

D.15 **Monetary policy in the eurozone.** This looks at how interest rates are set in the eurozone and what rules govern the behaviour of the European Central Bank.

D.16 **Central banking and monetary policy in the USA.** This case examines how the Fed conducts monetary policy.

D.17 **Productivity and economic growth.** This discusses the determinants of productivity growth and how productivity can be measured.

D.18 **A new approach to industrial policy.** This looks at changes in the approach to industrial policy around the world.

D.19 **Welfare to work.** An examination of the policy of the UK Labour government whereby welfare payments are designed to encourage people into employment.

Websites relevant to Part D

Numbers and sections refer to websites listed in the Web Appendix and hotlinked from this book's website at www.booksites.net/sloman/

■ For news articles relevant to Part D, see the *Economics News Articles* link from the book's website.

■ For general news on macroeconomic issues, both national and international, see websites in section A, and particularly A1–5, 7–9. For general news on money, banking and interest rates, see again A1–5, 7–9 and also 20–22, 25, 26, 31, 35, 36. For all of Part D, see also links to macroeconomic and financial news in A42. See also links to newspapers worldwide in A38, 39 and 43, and the news search feature in Google at A41. See also links to economics news in A42.

■ For macroeconomic data, see links in B1 or 2; also see B4 and 12. For UK data, see B3 and 34. For EU data, see G1 > *The Statistical Annex*. For US data, see *Current economic indicators* in B5 and the *Data* section of B17. For international data, see B15, 21, 24, 31, 33. For links to data sets, see B28; I14.

■ For national income statistics for the UK (Appendix), see B1, *1. National Statistics* > the fourth link > *Economy* > *United Kingdom Economic Accounts* and *United Kingdom National Accounts – The Blue Book.*

■ For data on UK unemployment, see B1, *1. National Statistics* > the fourth link > *Labour Market* > *Labour Market Trends.* For International data on unemployment, see G1; H3 and 5.

■ For monetary and financial data (including data for money supply and interest rates), see section F and particularly F2. Note that you can link to central banks worldwide from site F17. See also the links in B1 or 2.

■ For information on UK fiscal policy and government borrowing, see sites E30, 36; F2. See also sites A1–8 at Budget time. For fiscal policy in the eurozone, see *Public Finances in EMU* in H1.

■ Sites I7 and 11 contain links to fiscal policy: go to *Macroeconomics* > *Macroeconomic Policy* > *Taxes and Taxation.*

■ For links to sites on money and monetary policy, see the *Financial Economics* sections in I4, 7, 11, 17.

■ For demand-side policy in the UK, see the latest Budget Report (e.g. section on maintaining macroeconomic stability) at site E30.

■ For inflation targeting in the UK and eurozone see sites F1 and 6.

■ For the current approach to UK supply-side policy, see the latest Budget Report (e.g. sections on productivity and training) at site E30. See also sites E5 and 9.

■ For information on training in the UK and Europe, see sites D7; E5; G5, 14.

■ For support for a market-orientated approach to supply-side policy see C17 and E34.

■ For student resources relevant to Part D, see sites C1–7, 9, 10, 12, 13, 19. See also '2nd floor – economic policy' in site D1. See also the *Labour market reforms* simulation in D3.

PART E

The global business environment

Businesses around the world are locked into the world economy through trade, investment, production and finance. They are also influenced by global institutions, such as the United Nations, the World Trade Organisation (WTO) and non-governmental organisations such as Greenpeace. Business is also influenced by, and seeks to influence, global culture. People around the world are subject to fashion trends, to advertising and branding; there are companies known the world over – companies such as Coca-Cola, Nike, Sony and Microsoft. Increasingly the world communicates via the Internet and e-mail and increasingly firms outsource and supply through the Internet.

Globalisation is the process of developing these links. There has always been a degree of economic, political and cultural interdependence. What makes globalisation an issue today is the speed at which interdependence is growing. This is partly the result of unprecedented technological change, particularly in respect to transport and communication, and partly the result of a political drive to remove barriers between countries and embrace foreign influences.

Business, caught within this process of globalisation, will invariably seek to take advantage of what it has to offer, which is essentially a borderless world or one that is increasingly so. A global economy enables a business to locate the different dimensions of its value chain wherever it is likely to get the best deal, whether this is lower costs or better quality or both. Globalisation encourages this process of relocation and the framing of business strategy within a global context.

In Chapter 11 we look at the global environment in which businesses operate and at the role of governments and international institutions in affecting that environment. We look at what firms can gain from trading internationally and at how exchange rates affect trade and financial flows.

In the final chapter we look at the types of strategy a firm can adopt in order to benefit from the global economy. We look at the activities of multinational companies and at their relationship with host states.

Business issues covered in this chapter

- What are the benefits to countries and firms of international trade?

- Why do countries sometimes try to restrict trade and protect their domestic industries?

- What is the role of the World Trade Organisation (WTO) in international trade?

- What is meant by 'the balance of payments' and how do trade and financial movements affect it?

- How are exchange rates determined and what are the implications for business of changes in the exchange rate?

- How do governments and/or central banks seek to influence the exchange rate and what are the implications for other macroeconomic policies and for business?

- How do the major economies of the world seek to coordinate their policies and what difficulties arise in the process?

- What are the advantages and disadvantages of the euro for members of the eurozone and for businesses inside and outside the eurozone?

CHAPTER 11

The global context of business

11.1 International trade

Without international trade we would all be much poorer. There would be some items like pineapples, coffee, cotton clothes, foreign holidays and uranium that we would simply have to go without. Then there would be other items like wine and spacecraft that we could produce only very inefficiently.

International trade has the potential to benefit *all* participating countries. Totally free trade, however, may bring problems to countries or to groups of people or businesses within those countries. Many people argue strongly for restrictions on trade. Textile workers see their jobs threatened by cheap imported cloth. Car manufacturers in the USA and Europe worry about falling sales as customers switch to Japanese models or other east Asian ones. This section, therefore, also examines the arguments for restricting trade. Are people justified in fearing international competition, or are they merely trying to protect some vested interest at the expense of everyone else?

The growth of world trade

Since 1947, world trade has consistently grown faster than world GDP. This is illustrated in Figure 11.1 (overleaf). In 2003, world merchandise exports were worth over $6 trillion, some 26 per cent of world GDP.

The major industrial economies dominate world trade (see Figure 11.2 – overleaf). Some 70 per cent of all merchandise trade is conducted by the developed economies and the top eight nations account for over 50 per cent of all world trade. The most important individual country in respect to trade is the USA, followed by Germany and Japan. The USA sells some 12 per cent of world exports and consumes approximately 18 per cent of world imports.

The advantages of trade

Specialisation as the basis for trade

Why do countries trade with each other and what do they gain out of it? The reasons for international trade are really only an extension of the reasons for trade *within* a nation. Rather than people trying to be self-sufficient and doing everything for themselves, it makes sense to specialise.

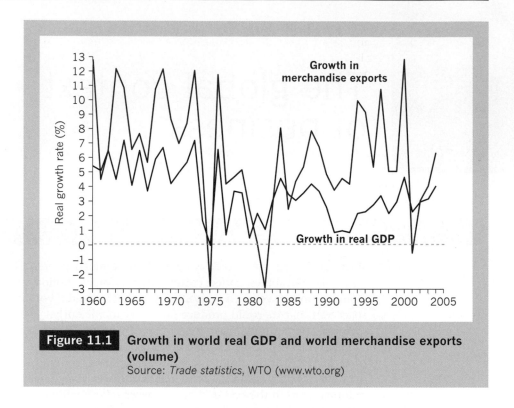

Figure 11.1 **Growth in world real GDP and world merchandise exports (volume)**
Source: *Trade statistics*, WTO (www.wto.org)

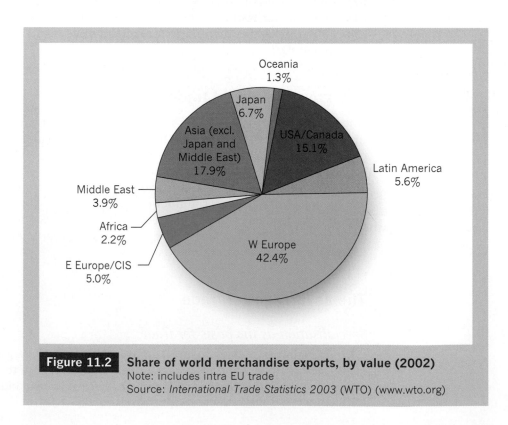

Figure 11.2 **Share of world merchandise exports, by value (2002)**
Note: includes intra EU trade
Source: *International Trade Statistics 2003* (WTO) (www.wto.org)

Firms specialise in producing certain types of goods. This allows them to gain economies of scale and to exploit their entrepreneurial and management skills and the skills of their labour force. It also allows them to benefit from their particular location and from the ownership of any particular capital equipment or other assets they might possess. With the revenues that firms earn, they buy in the inputs they need from other firms and the labour they require. Firms thus trade with each other.

Countries also specialise. They produce more than they need of certain goods. What is not consumed domestically is exported. The revenues earned from the exports are used to import goods which are not produced in sufficient amounts at home.

But which goods should a country specialise in? What should it export and what should it import? The answer is that it should specialise in those goods in which it has a *comparative advantage*. Let us examine what this means.

The law of comparative advantage

Countries have different resources. They differ in population density, labour skills, climate, raw materials, capital equipment, etc. Thus the ability to supply goods differs between countries.

What this means is that the relative costs of producing goods will vary from country to country. For example, one country may be able to produce 1 fridge for the same cost as 6 tonnes of wheat or 3 CD players, whereas another country may be able to produce 1 fridge for the same cost as only 3 tonnes of wheat but 4 CD players. It is these differences in relative costs that form the basis of trade.

At this stage we need to distinguish between *absolute advantage* and *comparative advantage*.

Absolute advantage.   When one country can produce a good with fewer resources than another country, it is said to have an **absolute advantage** in that good. If France can produce wine with fewer resources than the UK, and the UK can produce gin with fewer resources than France, then France has an absolute advantage in wine and the UK an absolute advantage in gin. Production of both wine and gin will be maximised by each country specialising and then trading with the other country. Both will gain.

Comparative advantage.   The above seems obvious, but trade between two countries can still be beneficial even if one country could produce *all* goods with fewer resources than the other, providing the *relative* efficiency with which goods can be produced differs between the two countries.

Take the case of an advanced country that is absolutely more efficient than a developing country at producing both wheat and cloth. Assume that with a given amount of resources (labour, land and capital) the alternatives shown in Table 11.1 (overleaf) can be produced in each country.

Despite the advanced country having an absolute advantage in both wheat and cloth, the developing country has a ***comparative* advantage** in wheat, and the advanced country has a *comparative* advantage in cloth. This is because wheat is relatively cheaper in the developing country: only 1 metre of cloth has to be sacrificed to produce 2 kilos of wheat, whereas 8 metres of cloth would have to be sacrificed in the advanced country to produce 4 kilos of wheat. In other words, the opportunity cost of wheat is 4 times higher in the advanced country (8/4 compared with 1/2).

Definition

Absolute advantage
A country has an absolute advantage over another in the production of a good if it can produce it with fewer resources than the other country.

Comparative advantage
A country has a comparative advantage over another in the production of a good if it can produce it at a lower opportunity cost: i.e. if it has to forgo less of other goods in order to produce it.

To prevent the establishment of a foreign-based monopoly. Competition from abroad could drive domestic producers out of business. The foreign company, now having a monopoly of the market, could charge high prices with a resulting misallocation of resources. The problem could be tackled either by restricting imports or by subsidising the domestic producer(s).

All the above arguments suggest that governments should adopt a 'strategic' approach to trade. **Strategic trade theory** argues that protecting certain industries allows a net gain in the *long* run from increased competition in the market (see Box 11.1).

To spread the risks of fluctuating markets. A highly specialised economy – Zambia with copper, Cuba with sugar – will be highly susceptible to world market fluctuations. Greater diversity and greater self-sufficiency, although maybe leading to less efficiency, can reduce these risks.

To reduce the influence of trade on consumer tastes. The assumption of fixed consumer tastes dictating the pattern of production through trade is false. Multinational companies through their advertising and other forms of sales promotion may influence consumer tastes. Many developing countries object to the insidious influence of western consumerist values expounded by companies such as Coca-Cola and McDonald's.

To take account of externalities. Free trade will tend to reflect private costs. Both imports and exports, however, can involve externalities. The mining of many minerals for export may adversely affect the health of miners; the production of chemicals for export may involve pollution; the importation of juggernaut lorries may lead to structural damage to houses.

The arguments considered so far are of general validity: restricting trade for such reasons could be of net benefit to the world. There are two other arguments, however, that are used by individual governments for restricting trade, where their country will gain, but at the *expense* of other countries, such that there will be a net loss to the world.

The first argument concerns taking advantage of market power in world trade. If a country, or a group of countries, has monopsony power in the purchase of imports (i.e. they are individually or collectively a very large economy, such as the USA or the EU), then they could gain by restricting imports so as to drive down their price. Similarly, if countries have monopoly power in the sale of some export (e.g. OPEC countries with oil), then they could gain by forcing up the price.

The second argument concerns giving protection to declining industries. The human costs of sudden industrial closures can be very high. In such circumstances, temporary protection may be justified to allow the industry to decline more slowly, thus avoiding excessive structural unemployment. Such policies will be at the expense of the consumer, however, who will be denied access to cheaper foreign imports.

Problems with protection

Protection will tend to push up prices and restrict the choice of goods available. But apart from these direct costs to the consumer, there are several other problems. Some are a direct effect of the protection, others follow from the reactions of other nations.

Protection as 'second-best'. Many of the arguments for protection amount merely to arguments for some type of government intervention in the economy. Protection,

---

Definition

Strategic trade theory
The theory that protecting/supporting certain industries can enable them to compete more effectively with large monopolistic rivals abroad. The effect of the protection is to increase long-run competition and may enable the protected firms to exploit a comparative advantage that they could not have done otherwise.

Box 11.1

Strategic trade theory

The case of Airbus

Supporters of *strategic trade theory* hold that comparative advantage need not be the result of luck or circumstance, but may in fact be created by government. By diverting resources into selective industries, usually high tech and high skilled, a comparative advantage can be created through intervention.

An example of such intervention was the European aircraft industry, and in particular the creation of the European Airbus Consortium.

The European Airbus Consortium was established in the late 1960s, its four members being Aérospatiale (France), British Aerospace (now BAE Systems) (UK), CASA (Spain) and DASA (Germany). The setting up of this consortium was seen as essential for the future of the European aircraft industry for three reasons:

■ To share high R&D costs.

■ To generate economies of scale.

■ To compete successfully with the market's major players in the USA – Boeing and McDonnell Douglas (which have since merged).

The consortium, although privately owned, was sponsored by government and received state aid, especially in its early years when the company failed to make a profit. Then, in 2000, an Airbus Integrated Company was created as a single entity to replace the looser Airbus Consortium. Shortly afterwards, it was announced that enough orders had been secured for the planned new 550+ seater A3XX for production to go ahead. This new jumbo will be a serious competitor to the long-established Boeing 747.

In recent years Airbus has become very successful, capturing a larger and larger share of the world commercial aircraft market. In 2003, for the first time, Airbus sold more passenger aircraft than Boeing (305 compared with 281 for Boeing).

So does the experience of Airbus support the arguments of the strategic trade theorists? Essentially two key benefits are claimed to flow from Airbus and its presence in the aircraft market: lower prices and economic spillovers.

■ Without Airbus the civil aircraft market would have been dominated by two American firms, Boeing and McDonnell Douglas (and possibly one, if the 1997 merger had still gone ahead). Therefore the presence of Airbus would be expected to promote competition and thereby keep prices down. Studies in the 1980s and 1990s tended to support this view, suggesting that consumers have made significant gains from lower prices. One survey estimated that without Airbus commercial aircraft prices would have been 3.5 per cent higher than they currently are, and without both Airbus *and* McDonnell Douglas they would have been 15 per cent higher.

■ Economic spillovers from the Airbus Consortium, such as skills and technology developments, might be expected to benefit other industries. Findings are inconclusive on this point. It is clear, however, that although aggregate R&D in the whole aircraft industry has risen, so has the level of R&D duplication.

On balance it appears that Airbus has had many positive effects and that the strategic trade theory that has underpinned state aid, in this instance, has led to a successful outcome. A competitive advantage has been created, and it looks as though it will be maintained into the future, and probably without state aid!

Questions

1. In what other industries could the setting up of a consortium, backed by government aid, be justified as a means of exploiting a potential comparative advantage?
2. Is it only in industries that could be characterised as world oligopolies that strategic trade theory is relevant?

however, may not be the best way of dealing with the problem, since protection may have undesirable side-effects. There may be a more direct form of intervention that has no side-effects. In such a case, protection will be no more than a *second-best* solution.

For example, using tariffs to protect old inefficient industries from foreign competition may help prevent unemployment in those parts of the economy, but the consumer will suffer from higher prices. A better solution would be to subsidise

■ Often, however, the arguments for restricting trade are in the context of one country benefiting even though other countries may lose more. Countries may intervene in trade in order to exploit their monopoly/monopsony power or to protect declining industries.

■ Even if government intervention to protect certain parts of the economy is desirable, restricting trade is unlikely to be a first-best solution to the problem, since it involves side-effect costs.

■ Most countries of the world are members of the WTO and in theory are in favour of moves towards freer trade. The WTO can impose sanctions on countries not abiding by WTO rules.

Box 11.2

EU trade and the Single Market

Benefiting from comparative advantage and competition?

In recognition of the benefits of free trade within the EU, the member countries signed the Single European Act of 1986. This sought to dismantle all barriers to internal trade within the EU by 1993, and create a genuine 'single market'. Although tariffs between member states had long been abolished, there were all sorts of non-tariff barriers, such as high taxes on wine by non-wine-producing countries, special regulations designed to favour domestic producers, governments giving contracts to domestic producers (e.g. for defence equipment), and so on.

Most of the barriers were indeed removed by 1993, and by the mid-1990s it was becoming clear from the evidence that the single market was bringing substantial benefits.

■ The elimination of border controls for goods had reduced costs and shortened delivery times and resulted in a larger choice of suppliers.

■ The simplification of VAT arrangements had reduced costs.

■ A substantial expansion of trade between member states had taken place.

■ Increased competition between firms had led to lower costs, lower prices and a wider range of products available to consumers. This was particularly so in newly liberalised service sectors such as transport, financial services, telecommunications and broadcasting.

■ Mergers and other forms of industrial restructuring had resulted in economies of scale and lower prices.

The economic evidence was backed up by the perceptions of business. Firms from across the range of industries felt that the single market project had removed a series of obstacles to trade within the EU and had increased market opportunities.

Nevertheless, the internal market was still not 'complete'. In other words, various barriers to trade between member states still remained. Thus, in June 1997, an Action Plan was adopted by the European Council. Its aim was to ensure that all barriers were dismantled by the launch of the euro in January 1999.

The Action Plan was largely, but not totally successful. In 1997, individual member countries had on average failed to transpose into their national law 35 per cent of over 1300 measures identified as being necessary to complete the internal market. By 1999, this 'transposition deficit' was less than 10 per cent. By May 2002, despite additional measures to implement, the figure was just 1.8 per cent, although it had risen to 2.3 per cent by November 2003.

In January 2004, the *Implementation Report on the Internal Market Strategy* claimed that, 'Since the abolition of EU internal frontiers ten years ago, the Internal Market has boosted EU economic growth by at least 1.8%, adding nearly 900 billion euro to the EU's collective prosperity and helping create 2.5 million extra jobs.'

Despite this success, national governments have continued to introduce *new* technical standards, several of which have had the effect of erecting new barriers to trade. Also, infringements of single market rules by governments have not always been dealt with. The net result is that, although trade is much freer today than in the early 1990s, especially given the transparency of pricing with the euro, there still do exist various barriers, especially to the free movement of goods.

? **Question**

If there have been clear benefits from the single market programme, why do individual member governments still try to erect barriers, such as new technical standards?

International finance   11.2

When companies trade internationally, whether as importers or exporters, this will have a macroeconomic impact. Similarly, when companies invest abroad or foreign companies invest in this country, this too will affect the economy. One major effect is on exchange rates. Any changes in exchange rates will then, in turn, affect trade by altering the relative prices of imports, exports and domestic goods sold within the country.

In this section we look at the financial flows associated with international trade and international investment. This will involve considering both the balance of payments and the exchange rate. We first explain what is meant by the balance of payments. In doing so, we will see just how the various monetary transactions between the domestic economy and the rest of the world are recorded.

Then we will examine how rates of exchange are determined, and how they are related to the balance of payments. Finally, we will see what causes exchange rate fluctuations, and what will happen if the government intervenes in the foreign exchange market to prevent these fluctuations.

The balance of payments

A country's balance of payments account records all the flows of money between residents of that country and the rest of the world. *Receipts* of money from abroad are regarded as *credits* and are entered in the accounts with a positive sign. *Outflows* of money from the country are regarded as *debits* and are entered with a negative sign.

There are three main parts of the balance of payments account: the *current account*, the *capital account* and the *financial account*. We shall look at each part in turn, and take the UK as an example. Table 11.2 gives a summary of the UK balance of payments for 2003.

Table 11.2 UK balance of payments, 2003 (£m)

Current account	
Balance on trade in goods and services (exports minus imports)	–21 023
Net income flows (wages and investment income)	+20 426
Net current transfers (government and private)	–9 247
Balance on current account	**–9 624**
Capital account (net capital transfers, etc.)	**+1 096**
Financial account	
Investment (direct and portfolio) and short-term flows	+6729
Reserves	+459
Balance on financial account	**+7188**
(Net errors and omissions)	**+1340**
Total	**0**

Source: *Financial Statistics* (ONS)

Definition

Exchange rate index
A weighted average exchange rate expressed as an index, where the value of the index is 100 in a given base year. The weights of the different currencies in the index add up to 1.

Pause for thought

How did the pound 'fare' compared with the dollar, the (former) lira and the yen from 1980 to 2001? What conclusions can be drawn about the relative movements of these three currencies?

Likewise, if Americans want to come on holiday to the UK or to buy UK assets, or American firms want to import UK goods or to invest in the UK, they will require sterling. They will be quoted an exchange rate for the pound in the USA: say, £1 = $1.64. This means that they will have to pay $1.64 to obtain £1 worth of UK goods or assets.

Exchange rates are quoted between each of the major currencies of the world. These exchange rates are constantly changing. Minute by minute, dealers in the foreign exchange dealing rooms of the banks are adjusting the rates of exchange.

One of the problems, however, in assessing what is happening to a particular currency is that its rate of exchange may rise against some currencies (weak currencies) and fall against others (strong currencies). In order to gain an overall picture of its fluctuations, it is best to look at a weighted average exchange rate against all other currencies. This is known as the **exchange rate index**. The weight given to each currency in the index depends on the proportion of transactions done with that country.

Table 11.3 shows exchange rates between the pound and various currencies and the sterling exchange rate index from 1980 to 2004.

The determination of the rate of exchange in a free market

In a free foreign exchange market, the rate of exchange is determined by demand and supply. Thus the sterling exchange rate is determined by the demand and supply of pounds. This is illustrated in Figure 11.4.

For simplicity, assume that there are just two countries: the UK and the USA. When UK importers wish to buy goods from the USA, or when UK residents wish to invest in the USA, they will *supply* pounds on the foreign exchange market in order to obtain dollars. In other words, they will go to banks or other foreign exchange dealers to buy dollars in exchange for pounds. The higher the exchange rate, the more dollars they will obtain for their pounds. This will effectively make American goods cheaper to buy, and investment more profitable. Thus the *higher* the exchange rate, the *more* pounds will be supplied. The supply curve of pounds therefore typically slopes upwards.

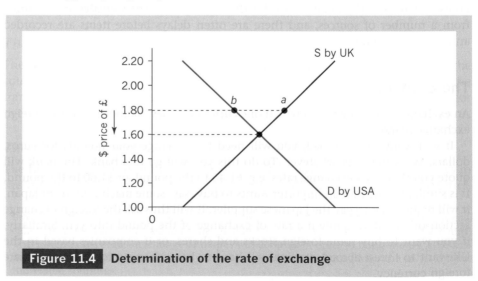

Figure 11.4 Determination of the rate of exchange

Table 11.3 Sterling exchange rates: 1980–2004

	US dollar	Japanese yen	French franc	German mark	Italian lira	Euro	Sterling exchange rate index (1990 = 100)
1980	2.33	526	9.83	4.23	1992		124.4
1981	2.03	445	10.94	4.56	2287		127.9
1982	1.75	435	11.48	4.24	2364		123.2
1983	1.52	360	11.55	3.87	2302		115.6
1984	1.34	317	11.63	3.79	2339		111.4
1985	1.30	307	11.55	3.78	2453		111.3
1986	1.47	247	10.16	3.18	2186		101.4
1987	1.64	236	9.84	2.94	2123		99.4
1988	1.78	228	10.60	3.12	2315		105.4
1989	1.64	226	10.45	3.08	2247	(1.45)	102.3
1990	1.79	258	9.69	2.88	2133	(1.40)	100.0
1991	1.77	238	9.95	2.92	2187	(1.43)	100.7
1992	1.77	224	9.32	2.75	2163	(1.36)	96.9
1993	1.50	167	8.51	2.48	2360	(1.28)	89.0
1994	1.53	156	8.49	2.48	2467	(1.29)	89.2
1995	1.58	148	7.87	2.26	2571	(1.22)	84.8
1996	1.56	170	7.99	2.35	2408	(1.25)	86.3
1997	1.64	198	9.56	2.84	2789	(1.45)	100.5
1998	1.66	217	9.77	2.91	2876	(1.48)	103.9
1999	1.62	184	(9.96)	(2.97)	(2941)	1.52	103.8
2000	1.52	163	(10.77)	(3.21)	(3180)	1.64	107.5
2001	1.44	175	(10.55)	(3.15)	(3115)	1.61	105.8
2002	1.50	188	–	–	–	1.59	106.0
2003	1.64	189	–	–	–	1.45	100.2
2004, Q2	1.81	198	–	–	–	1.50	105.2

Source: data without brackets are from the Bank of England Interactive Database (www.bankofengland.co.uk). Data in brackets are the author's own calculation

Note: Prior to 1999, a 'synthetic' euro has been used, based on the exchange rates with the countries which have adopted the euro. From 1999 to 2001, exchange rates into the French franc, German mark and Italian lira are based on the fixed exchange rates of these 'residual' currencies with the euro.

When US residents wish to purchase UK goods or to invest in the UK, they will require pounds. They *demand* pounds by selling dollars on the foreign exchange market. In other words, they will go to banks or other foreign exchange dealers to buy pounds in exchange for dollars. The lower the dollar price of the pound (the exchange rate), the cheaper it will be for them to obtain UK goods and assets, and hence the more pounds they are likely to demand. The demand curve for pounds, therefore, typically slopes downwards.

The equilibrium exchange rate is where the demand for pounds equals the supply. In Figure 11.4 this is at an exchange rate of £1 = $1.60. But what is the mechanism that equates demand and supply?

Managing the exchange rate

The government may be unwilling to let the country's currency float freely. Frequent shifts in the demand and supply curves would cause frequent changes in the exchange rate. This, in turn, might cause uncertainty for businesses, which might curtail their trade and investment.

Assume, for example, that the government believes that an exchange rate of €1.60 to the pound is approximately the long-term equilibrium rate. Short-term leftward shifts in the demand for sterling and rightward shifts in the supply, however, are causing the exchange rate to fall below this level (see Figure 11.5). What can be done? The central bank, on behalf of the government, can do one or more of three things.

Using reserves. The Bank of England can sell gold and foreign currencies from the reserves to buy pounds. This will shift the demand for sterling back to the right. The problem here is that countries' reserves are limited. If people are convinced that the sterling exchange rate will fall, there will be massive selling of pounds. It is unlikely that using the reserves to buy pounds will be adequate to stem the fall.

Borrowing from abroad. The government can negotiate a foreign currency loan from other countries or from an international agency such as the International Monetary Fund. The Bank of England can then use these monies to buy pounds on the foreign exchange market, thus again shifting the demand for sterling back to the right.

Raising interest rates. If the government raises interest rates, it will encourage people to deposit money in the UK and encourage UK residents to keep their money in the country. The demand for sterling will increase and the supply of sterling will decrease.

This is likely to be more effective than the other two measures, but using interest rates to control the exchange rate may conflict with using interest rates to target inflation. You cannot use one instrument (the rate of interest) to control two separate targets (the exchange rate and the rate of inflation) if the two objectives require a different rate of interest.

Advantages of managed exchange rates

Surveys reveal that most businesspeople prefer relatively stable exchange rates: if not totally fixed, then with minimum fluctuations. The following arguments are used to justify this preference.

Certainty. With stable exchange rates, international trade and investment become much less risky, since profits are not affected by violent movements in the exchange rate.

Assume a firm correctly forecasts that its product will sell in the USA for $1.50. It costs 80p to produce. If the rate of exchange is stable at £1 = $1.50, each unit will earn £1 and hence make a 20p profit. If, however, the rate of exchange fluctuated these profits could be wiped out. If, say, the rate appreciated to £1 = $2, and if units continued to sell for $1.50, they would now earn only 75p each, and hence make a 5p loss.

The less elastic are the demand and supply curves for the currency in Figure 11.5, the greater the change in exchange rate that will be necessary to restore equilibrium following a shift in either demand or supply. In the long run, in a competitive world with domestic substitutes for imports and foreign substitutes for exports, demand and supply curves are relatively elastic. Nevertheless, in the short run, given that many firms have contracts with specific overseas suppliers or distributors, the demands for imports and exports are less elastic and, without intervention, exchange rate fluctuations can be large.

Little or no speculation. If people believe that the exchange rate will remain constant – there is nothing to be gained from speculating. For example, between 1999 and 2001, when the old currencies of the eurozone countries were still used, but were totally fixed to the euro, there was no speculation that the German mark, say, would change in value against the French franc or the Dutch guilder.

With a totally free floating exchange rate, by contrast, given that large amounts of short-term deposits are internationally 'footloose', speculation can be highly destabilising in the short run. If people think that the exchange rate will fall, then they will sell the currency, and this will cause the exchange rate to fall even further.

Disadvantages of managed exchange rates

Exchange rate policy may conflict with the interests of domestic business and the economy as a whole. Managing the exchange rate will almost inevitably involve using interest rates for that purpose. But this may conflict with other macroeconomic objectives. For example, a depreciating exchange rate may force the central bank to raise interest rates to arrest the fall. But this may discourage business investment. If the economy is already in a recession, the higher interest rates could deepen the recession. In other words, the rate of interest that is suitable for the exchange rate may be unsuitable for the rest of the economy.

Under a free-floating rate, by contrast, the central bank can choose whatever rate of interest is necessary to meet domestic objectives, such as achieving a target rate of inflation. The exchange rate will simply adjust to the new rate of interest – a rise in interest rates causing an appreciation, a fall causing a depreciation.

Inability to adjust to shocks. Sometimes, it will prove impossible to maintain the exchange rate at the desired level. For example, a sudden increase in oil prices can have a large effect on the balance of payments. Oil-importing countries may find that the downward pressure on their exchange rate is too strong to contain.

Speculation. If speculators believe that the central bank cannot prevent the exchange rate falling (or rising), speculation is likely to be massive. The speculation will bring about the very fall (or rise) in the exchange rate that the speculators anticipated and may well cause the exchange rate to overshoot its longer-run equilibrium rate.

> **Pause for thought**
>
> *If speculators on average gain from their speculation, who loses?*

Exchange rates in practice

Most countries today have a relatively free exchange rate. Nevertheless, the problems of instability that this can bring are well recognised, and thus many countries seek to regulate or manage their exchange rate.

There have been many attempts to regulate exchange rates since 1945. By far the most successful was the Bretton Woods system, which was adopted worldwide from the end of World War II until 1971. This was a form of **adjustable peg** exchange

> **Definition**
>
> **Adjustable peg**
> A system whereby exchange rates are fixed for a period of time, but may be devalued (or revalued) if a deficit (or surplus) becomes substantial.

Box 11.4

The euro/dollar seesaw

Ups and downs in the currency market

On 1 January 1999, the euro was launched and exchanged for $1.16. By October 2000 the euro had fallen to $0.85. What was the cause of this 27 per cent depreciation? The main cause was the growing fear that inflationary pressures were increasing in the USA and that, therefore, the Federal Reserve Bank would have to raise interest rates. At the same time, the eurozone economy was growing only slowly and inflation was well below the 2 per cent ceiling set by the ECB. There was thus pressure on the ECB to cut interest rates.

The speculators were not wrong. As the diagram shows, US interest rates rose, and ECB interest rates initially fell, and when eventually they did rise (in October 1999), the gap between US and ECB interest rates soon widened again.

In addition to the differences in interest rates, a lack of confidence in the recovery of the eurozone economy and a continuing confidence in the US economy encouraged investment to flow to the US. This inflow of finance (and lack of inflow to the eurozone) further pushed up the dollar relative to the euro.

The low value of the euro meant a high value of the pound relative to the euro. This made it very difficult for UK companies exporting to eurozone countries and also for those competing with imports from the eurozone (which had been made cheaper by the fall in the euro).

In October 2000, with the euro trading at around 85¢, the ECB plus the US Federal Reserve Bank (America's central bank), the Bank of England and the Japanese central bank all intervened on the foreign exchange market to buy euros. This arrested the fall, and helped to restore confidence in the currency. People were more willing to hold euros, knowing that central banks would support it.

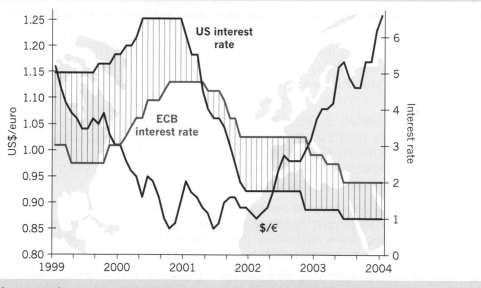

Fluctuations between the euro and the dollar

The position completely changed in 2001. With the US economy slowing rapidly and fears of an impending recession, the Federal Reserve Bank reduced interest rates 11 times during the year: from 6 per cent at the beginning of the year to 1.25 per cent at the end. Although the ECB also cut interest rates, the cuts were relatively modest: from 4.75 at the beginning of the year to 3.25 at the end. With eurozone interest rates now considerably above US rates, the euro began to rise.

In addition, massive debts on the US current account, and a budget deficit nearing 4 per cent of GDP, made foreign investors reluctant to invest in the American economy. In fact, investors were pulling out of the USA. One estimate suggests that European investors alone sold $70 billion of US assets during 2002. The result of all this was a massive depreciation of the dollar and appreciation of the euro, so that by January 2004 the exchange rate had risen to $1.28: a 50 per cent appreciation since June 2001! By 2004, the US budget deficit had risen to over 5 per cent of GDP – well above the budget deficits in France and Germany (see Box 10.2).

The effects on business in the eurozone

So is a strong euro bad for European business? With over 20 per cent of the eurozone's GDP determined by export sales, and a large part of those exports going to America, the dollar/euro exchange rate will invariably be significant. The question is how significant? The concern was that, with slow growth in the eurozone, the rise in the euro and the resulting fall in exports would slow growth rates even further. With the German economy on the brink of recession, the euro's rise might be simply too much for the German economy to bear. The investment bank Morgan Stanley estimated that for every 10 per cent rise in the value of the euro against the dollar, European corporate profits fall by 3 per cent.

And it was not just the fact that the euro was strong. What also worried European business was the *speed* at which the euro strengthened against the dollar. The question was whether they could adjust quickly enough to accommodate the rise.

However, the impact of the euro's rise on eurozone business was tempered by a number of other factors:

- Companies are increasingly using sophisticated management and operational systems, in which value creation is spread throughout a global value chain. Often procurement systems are priced in dollars.

- Firms hedge their currency risks. BMW, for example, uses forward exchange markets to agree to buy or sell currencies in the future at a price quoted today (this, of course, costs it a premium).

- Many European companies (again BMW is an example) have located some of their production facilities in the USA and use them to help meet demand in the American market. This helps to insulate them from the effects of the rise in the value of the euro.

Businesses in the eurozone seem initially to have accommodated the euro's rapid rise. However, if the value of the euro continues to strengthen on world markets, the achievement of even slow eurozone growth might prove increasingly difficult to maintain.

Question

Find out what has happened to the euro/dollar exchange rate over the past 12 months. (You can find the data from the Bank of England's Statistical Interactive Database at www.bankofengland.co.uk/statistics.htm). Explain why the exchange rate has moved the way it has.

(e) Assuming that price equals marginal cost, which of the following would represent possible exchange ratios?

(i) 1 computer for 40 tonnes of coal; (ii) 2 computers for 140 tonnes of coal; (iii) 1 computer for 100 tonnes of coal; (iv) 1 computer for 60 tonnes of coal; (v) 4 computers for 360 tonnes of coal.

(f) Assume that trade now takes place and that 1 computer exchanges for 65 tonnes of coal. Both countries specialise completely in the product in which they have a comparative advantage. How much does each country produce of its respective product?

(g) The country producing computers sells 6 million domestically. How many does it export to the other country?

(h) How much coal does the other country consume?

2. To what extent are the arguments for countries specialising and then trading with each other the same as those for individuals specialising in doing the jobs to which they are relatively well suited?

3. If countries are so keen to reduce the barriers to trade, why do many countries frequently attempt to erect barriers?

4. If rich countries stand to gain substantially from freer trade, why have they been so reluctant to reduce the levels of protection of agriculture?

5. The following are the items in the UK's 2001 balance of payments:

	£ billions
Exports of goods	191.2
Imports of goods	224.3
Exports of services	77.1
Imports of services	65.4
Net income flows	+11.2
Net current transfers	−7.2
Net capital transfers	+1.4
Net investment in UK from abroad (direct and portfolio)	75.5
Net UK investment abroad (direct and portfolio)	116.7
Other financial inflows	219.1
Other financial outflows	161.1
Reserves	+3.1

Calculate the following: (a) the balance of trade in goods and services; (b) the balance of payments on current account; (c) the financial account balance; (d) the total current plus capital plus financial account balance; (e) net errors and omissions.

6. Assume that there is a free-floating exchange rate. Will the following cause the exchange rate to appreciate or depreciate? In each case you should consider whether there is a shift in the demand or supply curves of sterling (or both) and which way the curve(s) shift(s).

   (a) More video recorders are imported from Japan.
   Demand curve *shifts left/shifts right/does not shift*
   Supply curve *shifts left/shifts right/does not shift*
   Exchange rate *appreciates/depreciates*

   (b) UK interest rates rise relative to those abroad.
   Demand curve *shifts left/shifts right/does not shift*
   Supply curve *shifts left/shifts right/does not shift*
   Exchange rate *appreciates/depreciates*

   (c) The UK experiences a higher rate of inflation than other countries.
   Demand curve *shifts left/shifts right/does not shift*
   Supply curve *shifts left/shifts right/does not shift*
   Exchange rate *appreciates/depreciates*

   (d) Speculators believe that the rate of exchange will appreciate.
   Demand curve *shifts left/shifts right/does not shift*
   Supply curve *shifts left/shifts right/does not shift*
   Exchange rate *appreciates/depreciates*

7. What is the relationship between the balance of payments and the rate of exchange?

8. Consider the argument that in the modern world of large-scale short-term international financial movements, the ability of individual countries to affect their exchange rate is very limited.

9. What adverse effects on the domestic economy may follow from (a) a depreciation of the exchange rate and (b) an appreciation of the exchange rate?

10. What are the economic (as opposed to political) difficulties in achieving an international harmonisation of economic policies so as to avoid damaging currency fluctuations?

11. What are the causes of exchange-rate volatility? Have these problems become greater or lesser in the past ten years? Explain why.

12. By what means would a depressed country in an economic union with a single currency be able to recover? Would the market provide a satisfactory solution or would (union) government intervention be necessary, and if so, what form would the intervention take?

13. Assume that just some of the members of a common market like the EU adopt full economic and monetary union, including a common currency. What are the advantages and disadvantages to those members joining the full EMU and to those not joining?

Business issues covered in this chapter

- What is the magnitude and pattern of global foreign direct investment?

- What forms do multinational corporations take?

- For what reasons do companies become multinational ones?

- In what ways do multinationals have a cost advantage over companies based in a single country?

- What competitive advantages do multinationals have over companies based in a single country?

- What disadvantages are companies likely to face from having their operations spread over a number of countries?

- What are the advantages and disadvantages of multinational investment for the host state and how can the multinational use its position to gain the best deal from the host state?

- To what extent does the world gain or lose from the process of the globalisation of business?

CHAPTER 12

Multinational corporations and business strategy in a global economy

In the previous chapter we saw how international trade has consistently grown faster than world GDP. In this chapter we see why companies benefit not only from trading internationally but also from becoming multinational companies: companies producing and selling in many different countries.

12.1 Multinational corporations

Definition

Multinational corporations
Businesses that either own or control foreign subsidiaries in more than one country.

There are some 65 000 **multinational corporations** (MNCs) worldwide. Between them they control a total of 85 000 foreign subsidiaries. In 2003, the global stock of foreign direct investment (FDI) was $7.5 trillion. Foreign affiliates accounted for nearly 11 per cent of world GDP, up from 7 per cent in 1990 and their sales, at around $19 trillion, were more than double the level of world exports.

But just what is an MNC? At the most basic level it is a business that either owns or controls subsidiaries in more than one country. It is this ownership or control of productive assets in other countries that makes the MNC distinct from an enterprise that does business overseas by simply exporting goods or services. However, merely to define an MNC as a company with overseas subsidiaries fails to reflect the immense diversity of multinationals.

Diversity among MNCs

Size. Many, if not most, of the world's largest firms – IBM, Shell, General Motors, etc. – are multinationals. Indeed, the turnover of some of them exceeds the national income of many smaller countries (see Table 12.1 – overleaf).

And yet there are also thousands of very small, often specialist multinationals, which are a mere fraction of the size of the giants. What is more, since the mid-1980s many large multinational businesses have been downsizing. They have been shrinking the size of their headquarters, removing layers of bureaucracy, and re-organising their global operations into smaller autonomous profit centres. Gone is the philosophy that big companies will inevitably do better than small ones.

In fact, it now appears that multinationals are seeking to create a hybrid form of business organisation, which combines the advantages of size (i.e. economies of scale) with the responsiveness and market knowledge of smaller firms. The key for the modern multinational is flexibility, and to be at one and the same time both global and local.

Numerical flexibility   Where employers can change the size of their workforce as their labour requirements change.

Observations of market behaviour   Information gathered about consumers from the day-to-day activities of the business within the market.

Oligopoly   A market structure where there are few enough firms to enable barriers to be erected against the entry of new firms.

Oligopsony   A market with just a few buyers or employers.

Open-market operations   The sale (or purchase) by the authorities of government securities in the open market in order to reduce (or increase) money supply.

Opportunity cost   The cost of any activity measured in terms of the best alternative forgone.

Organisational slack   When managers allow spare capacity to exist, thereby enabling them to respond more easily to changed circumstances

Overheads   Costs arising from the general running of an organisation, and only indirectly related to the level of output.

Perfectly competitive market (preliminary definition)   A market in which all producers and consumers of the product are price takers.

PEST analysis   Where the political, economic, social and technological factors shaping a business environment are assessed by a business so as to devise future business strategy.

Picketing   Where people on strike gather at the entrance to the firm and attempt to dissuade workers or delivery vehicles from entering.

Plant economies of scale   Economies of scale that arise because of the large size of the factory.

Price-cap regulation   Where the regulator puts a ceiling on the amount by which a firm can raise its price.

Price discrimination   Where a firm sells the same product at different prices in different markets for reasons unrelated to costs.

Price elasticity of demand   A measure of the responsiveness of quantity demanded to a change in price.

Price elasticity of supply   The responsiveness of quantity supplied to a change in price: the proportionate change in quantity supplied divided by the proportionate change in price.

Price leadership   When firms (the followers) choose the same price as that set by a one of the firms in the industry (the leader). The leader will normally be the largest firm.

Price mechanism   The system in a market economy whereby changes in price in response to changes in demand and supply have the effect of making demand equal to supply.

Price taker   A person or firm with no power to be able to influence the market price.

Primary labour market   The market for permanent full-time core workers.

Primary market in capital   Where shares are sold by the issuer of the shares (i.e. the firm) and where, therefore, finance is channelled directly from the purchasers (i.e. the shareholders) to the firm.

Primary production   The production and extraction of natural resources, plus agriculture.

Principal–agent problem   One where people (principals), as a result of lack of knowledge, cannot ensure that their best interests are served by their agents.

Prisoners' dilemma   Where two or more firms (or people), by attempting independently to choose the best strategy for whatever the other(s) are likely to do, end up in a worse position than if they had cooperated in the first place.

Privatisation   Selling nationalised industries to the private sector. This may be through the public issue of shares, by a mangement buyout or by selling it to a private comapny.

Product differentiation   Where a firm's product is in some way distinct from its rivals' products.

Production   The transformation of inputs into outputs by firms in order to earn profit (or meet some other objective).

Productivity deal   Where, in return for a wage increase, a union agrees to changes in working practices that will increase output per worker.

Profit-maximising rule   Profit is maximised where marginal revenue equals marginal cost.

Profit satisficing   Where decision makers in a firm aim for a target level of profit rather than the absolute maximum level.

Public good   A good or service which has the features of non-rivalry and non-excludability and as a result would not be provided by the free market.

Public-sector net cash requirement (PSNCR)   The (annual) deficit of the public sector (central government, local government and public corporations), and thus the amount that the public sector must borrow.

Pure fiscal policy   Fiscal policy which does not involve any change in money supply.

Quantity demanded   The amount of a good that a consumer is willing and able to buy at a given price over a given period of time.

Quota (set by a cartel)   The output that a given member of a cartel is allowed to produce (production quota) or sell (sales quota).

Random walk   Where fluctuations in the value of a share away from its 'correct' value are random. When charted over time, these share price movements would appear like a 'random walk' – like the path of someone staggering along drunk.

Rate of inflation   The percentage increase in prices over a 12-month period.

Rational choices   Choices that involve weighing up the benefit of any activity against its opportunity cost.

Rationalisation   The reorganising of production (often after a merger) so as to cut out waste and duplication and generally to reduce costs.

Real growth values   Values of the rate of growth in GDP or any other variable after taking inflation into account. The real value of the growth in a variable equals its growth in money (or 'nominal') value minus the rate of inflation.

Real-wage unemployment   Disequilibrium unemployment caused by real wages being driven up above the market-clearing level.

Recession   A period of falling GDP: i.e. of negative economic growth. Officially, a recession is where this occurs for two quarters or more.

Regional unemployment   Structural unemployment occurring in specific regions of the country.

Replacement costs   What the firm would have to pay to replace inputs it currently owns.

Resale price maintenance   Where the manufacturer of a product (legally) insists that the product should be sold at a specified retail price.

Revaluation   Where the government or central bank re-pegs the exchange rate at a higher level.

Risk   This is when an outcome may or may not occur, but where the probability of its occurring is known.

Sale and repurchase agreement (repo)   An agreement between two financial institutions whereby one in effect borrows from another by selling some of its assets, agreeing to buy them back (repurchase them) at a fixed price and on a fixed date.

Sales revenue maximisation   An alternative theory of the firm which assumes that managers aim to maximise the firm's short-run total revenue.

Scarcity   The excess of human wants over what can actually be produced to fulfil these wants.

Seasonal unemployment   Unemployment associated with industries or regions where the demand for labour is lower at certain times of the year.

Secondary labour market   The market for peripheral workers, usually employed on a temporary or part-time basis, or a less secure 'permanent' basis.

Secondary market in capital   Where shareholders sell shares to others. This is thus a market in 'second-hand' shares.

Secondary production   The production from manufacturing and construction sectors of the economy.

Self-fulfilling speculation   The actions of speculators tend to cause the very effect that they had anticipated.

Short run   The period of time over which at least one input is fixed.

Short run under perfect competition   The period during which there is too little time for new firms to enter the industry.

Short-run shut-down point   Where the AR curve is tangential to the AVC curve. The firm can only just cover its variable costs. Any fall in revenue below this level will cause a profit-maximising firm to shut down immediately.

Short-termism   Where firms and investors take decisions based on the likely short-term performance of a company, rather than on its long-term prospects. Firms may thus sacrifice long-term profits and growth for the sake of quick return.

Social benefit   Private benefit plus externalities in consumption.

Social cost   Private cost plus externalities in production.

Social efficiency   Production and consumption at the point where $MSB = MSC$.

Specialisation and division of labour   Where production is broken down into a number of simpler, more specialised tasks, thus allowing workers to acquire a high degree of efficiency.

Speculation   This is where people make buying or selling decisions based on their anticipations of future prices.

Spreading risks (for an insurance company)   The more policies an insurance company issues and the more independent the risks of claims from these policies are, the more predictable will be the number of claims.

Stakeholder   An individual affected by the operations of a business.

Stakeholders (in a company)   People who are affected by a company's activities and/or performance (customers, employees, owners, creditors, people living in the neighbourhood, etc.). They may or may not be in a position to take decisions, or influence decision taking, in the firm.

Standard Industrial Classification (SIC)   The name given to the formal classification of firms into industries used by the government in order to collect data on business and industry trends.

Standardised unemployment rate   The measure of the unemployment rate used by the ILO and OECD. The unemployed are defined as people of working age who are without work, available for work and actively seeking employment.

Strategic alliance   Where two firms work together, formally or informally, to achieve a mutually desirable goal.

Strategic management   The management of the strategic long-term decisions and activities of the business.

Strategic trade theory   The theory that protecting/supporting certain industries can enable them to compete more effectively with large monopolistic rivals abroad. The effect of the protection is to increase long-run competition and may enable the protected firms to exploit a comparative advantage that they could not have done otherwise.

Structural unemployment   Unemployment that arises from changes in the pattern of demand or supply in the economy. People made redundant in one part of the economy cannot immediately take up jobs in other parts (even though there are vacancies).

Subcontracting   Where a firm employs another firm to produce part of its output or some of its input(s).

Substitute goods   A pair of goods which are considered by consumers to be alternatives to each other. As the price of one goes up, the demand for the other rises.

Substitutes in supply   These are two goods where an increased production of one means diverting resources away from producing the other.

Substitution effect   The effect of a change in price on quantity demanded arising from the consumer switching to or from alternative (substitute) products.

Supernormal profit   The excess of total profit above normal profit.

Supply curve   A graph showing the relationship between the price of a good and the quantity of the good supplied over a given period of time.

Supply schedule   A table showing the different quantities of a good that producers are willing and able to supply at various prices over a given time period. A supply schedule can be for an individual producer or group of producers, or for all producers (the market supply schedule).

Supply-side policy   Policy to affect aggregate supply directly

Tacit collusion   When oligopolists take care not to engage in price cutting, excessive advertising or other forms of competition. There may be unwritten 'rules' of collusive behaviour such as price leadership.

Takeover   Where one business acquires another. A takeover may not necessarily involve mutual agreement between the two parties. In such cases, the takeover might be viewed as 'hostile'.

Takeover constraint   The effect that the fear of being taken over has on a firm's willingness to undertake projects that reduce distributed profits.

Tapered vertical integration   Where a firm is partially integrated with an earlier stage of production: where it produces *some* of an input itself and buys some from another firm.

Taylor rule   A rule adopted by a central bank for setting the rate of interest. It will raise the interest rate if (a) inflation is above target or (b) growth is above the sustainable level (or unemployment below the equilibrium rate). The rule states how much interest rates will be changed in each case. In other words a relative weighting is attached to each of these two objectives.

Technological unemployment   Structural unemployment that occurs as a result of the introduction of labour-saving technology.

Technology transfer   Where a host state benefits from the new technology that an MNC brings with its investment.

Tertiary production   The production from the service sector of the economy.

Total consumer expenditure (*TE*) (per period) The price of the product multiplied by the quantity purchased. $TE = P \times Q$.

Total cost (*TC*) (per period) The sum of total fixed costs (*TFC*) and total variable costs (*TVC*): $TC = TFC + TVC$.

Total revenue (*TR*) (per period) The total amount received by firms from the sale of a product, before the deduction of taxes or any other costs. The price multiplied by the quantity sold. $TR = P \times Q$.

Tradable permits Each firm is given a permit to produce a given level of pollution. If less than the permitted amount is produced, the firm is given a credit. This can then be sold to another firm, allowing it to exceed its original limit.

Transfer payments Moneys transferred from one person or group to another (e.g. from the government to individuals) without production taking place.

Transfer pricing The pricing system used within a business to transfer intermediate products between its various divisions, often in different countries.

U-form business organisation One in which the central organisation of the firm (the chief executive or a managerial team) is responsible both for the firm's day-to-day administration and for formulating its business strategy.

Uncertainty This is when an outcome may or may not occur and where its probability of occurring is not known.

Unemployment rate The number unemployed expressed as a percentage of the labour force.

Unit elasticity When the price elasticity of demand is unity, this is where quantity demanded changes by the same proportion as the price. Price elasticity is equal to –1.

Value chain The stages or activities that help to create product value

Variable costs Total costs that do vary with the amount of output produced.

Variable input An input that *can* be increased in supply within a given time period.

Vertical integration A business growth strategy that involves expanding within an existing market, but at a different stage of production. Vertical integration can be 'forward', such as moving into distribution or retail, or 'backward', such as expanding into extracting raw materials or producing components.

Vertical merger Where two firms in the same industry at different stages in the production process merge.

Vertically integrated multinational A multinational that undertakes the various stages of production for a given product in different countries.

Wage taker The wage rate is determined by market forces.

Withdrawals (*W*) (or leakages) Incomes of households or firms that are not passed on round the inner flow. Withdrawals equal net saving (*S*) plus net taxes (*T*) plus import expenditure (*M*): $W = S + T + M$.

Working to rule Workers do no more than they are supposed to, as set out in their job descriptions.

Index